AUTO-BIOGRAPH

C000068354

This page enables you to compile a list of useful data on your car, so that whether you're ordering spares or just checking the tyre pressures, all the key information - the information that is 'personal' to your car - is easily within reach.

Registration number: ....

Model: ....

Body colour: ....

Paint code number: ....

Date of first registration:..

Date of manufacture (if different): ....

VIN (or 'chassis') number: ....

Engine number:..

Ignition key number: ....

Door lock key/s number/s: ....

Fuel locking cap key number (if fitted): ....

Alarm remote code (if fitted):..

Alarm remote battery type:..

Radio/cassette security code (if fitted): ....

Tyre size

Front:..................................Rear: ....

Tyre pressure (normally laden)

Front:..................................Rear: ....

Tyre pressure (fully laden)

Front:..................................Rear: ....

Insurance

    Name and address of insurer:...

    ....

    Policy number:...

Modifications

    Information that might be useful when you need to purchase parts:...

    ....

Suppliers

    Address and telephone number of your garage and parts suppliers:

    ....

    ....

First published in 1996 by Porter Publishing Ltd.

Porter Publishing Ltd.
The Storehouse
Little Hereford Street
Bromyard
Hereford HR7 4DE
England

© Copyright Lindsay Porter and Porter
Publishing Ltd, 1996.

British Library Cataloguing in Publication Data.

A catalogue record for this book is available from the British Library.

ISBN 1-899238-16-6

Series Editor: Lindsay Porter
Design: Martin Driscoll, Lindsay Porter and Lyndsay Berryman
Layout and Typesetting: Pineapple Publishing, Worcester
Cover photography: Jeremy Gale
Printed in England by The Trinity Press, Worcester.

Every care has been taken to ensure that the material contained in this
Service Guide is correct. However, no liability can be accepted by the
authors or publishers for damage, loss, accidents, or injury resulting
from any omissions or errors in the information given.

Titles in this Series:
Absolute Beginners' Service Guide
Auto Electrics - DIY Service Manual
Caravan Owner's Manual & Service Guide
Classic 'Bike Service Guide
Diesel Car Engines Service Guide
Ford Escort (Front Wheel Drive) & Orion Service Guide
Ford Fiesta (All models to 1995) Service Guide
Ford Sierra (All models) Service Guide
Land Rover Series I, II, III Service Guide
Land Rover Discovery and Range Rover Service Guide
Land Rover Defender, 90 & 110 Service Guide
Metro (1980-1990) Service Guide
MG Midget & Austin-Healey Sprite Service Guide
Mini (all models 1959-1994) Service Guide
MGB (including MGC, MGB GT V8 and MG RV8) Service Guide
Peugeot 205 Service Guide
Vauxhall Astra & Belmont (All models-1995) Service Guide
Vauxhall Cavalier Service Guide
Vauxhall Nova Service Guide
VW Beetle Service Guide

- With more titles in production -

Vauxhall Nova
(including Opel Corsa)
Service Guide & Owner's Manual
by
Andy MacQuillan
& Lindsay Porter

OIL AND WATER DON'T MIX

It is important to remember that even a small quantity of oil is harmful to water and wildlife. And tipping oil down the drain is as good as tipping it into a river. Many drains are connected directly to a river or stream and pollution will occur.

Each year the National Rivers Authority deals with over 6,000 oil related water pollution incidents. Many of these are caused by the careless disposal of used oil.

The used oil from the sump of just one car can cover an area of water the size of two football pitches, cutting off the oxygen supply and harming swans, ducks, fish and other river life.

OIL POLLUTES WATER
USE YOUR BRAIN-
NOT THE DRAIN!

Follow the Oil Care Code

- ◆ *When you drain your engine oil - don't oil the drain!* Pouring oil down the drain will cause pollution. It is also an offence.

- ◆ Don't mix used oil with other materials, such as paint or solvents, because this makes recycling very difficult.

- ◆ Take used oil to an oil recycling bank. Telephone FREE on 0800 663366 to find the location of your nearest oil bank, or contact your local authority recycling officer.

OIL CARE
FOLLOW THE CODE

CONTENTS

	Auto-Biography	*1*
	Introduction and Acknowledgements	*6*
CHAPTER 1:	*Safety First!*	*7*
	PART I: Important Points	*7*
	PART II: Hazards	*8*
	PART III: General Workshop Safety	*10*
CHAPTER 2:	*Buying Guide*	*11*
	PART I: Buying a Second-Hand Car	*11*
	PART II: What Wears, and When	*13*
	PART III: Buying Spares	*13*
CHAPTER 3:	*Servicing Your Car*	
	Using the Service Schedules	*15*
	Raising the Car	*16*
	Every 500 miles, Weekly or Before a Long Journey	*21*
	Every 1,500 miles - or Every Month	*29*
	Every 3,000 miles - or Every Three Months	*31*
	Every 6,000 miles - or Every Six Months	*39*
	Every 12,000 miles - or Every Twelve Months	*61*
	Spark Plug Conditions	*65*
	Every 24,000 miles - or Every Twenty Four Months	*74*
	Every 36,000 miles - or Every Thirty Six Months	*74*
	Every 48,000 miles - or Every Forty Eight Months	*76*
	Every 72,000 miles - or Every Six Years	*76*
CHAPTER 4:	*Vauxhall Nova Bodywork*	*77*
	PART I: The Body Beautiful	*77*
	PART II: Repairing Bodywork Blemishes	*79*
CHAPTER 5:	*Rustproofing*	*81*
CHAPTER 6:	*Fault Finding*	*87*
CHAPTER 7:	*Getting Through the MoT*	*91*
	PART I: The Background	*91*
	PART II: The Checklist	*93*
CHAPTER 8:	*Facts and Figures*	*101*
	PART I: Major Milestones	*101*
	PART II: Capacities and Settings	*102*
CHAPTER 9:	*Tools and Equipment*	*105*
APPENDIX 1:	*Recommended Castrol Lubricants*	*109*
APPENDIX 2:	*Specialists and Suppliers*	*110*
APPENDIX 3:	*Service History*	*111*
	INDEX	*127*

Introduction

Over the years, I have run any number of cars, from superb classic cars and modern cars, to those with one foot in the breakers yard. And I know only too well that any car is only enjoyable to own if it's safe, reliable and basically sound - and the only way of ensuring that it stays that way is to service it regularly. That's why we have set about creating this book, which aims to show the owner interested in DIY car servicing that there's nothing to fear; you really can do it yourself!

Making It Easy! Porter Publishing Service Guides are the first books to give you all the service information you might need, with step-by-step instructions, along with a complete Service History section for you to complete and fill in as you carry out regular maintenance on your car over the months ahead. Using the information contained in this book, you will be able to:

◆ see for yourself how to carry out every Service Job, from weekly and monthly checks, right up to longer-term maintenance items.
◆ carry out regular body maintenance and rustproofing, saving a fortune in body repairs over the years to come.
◆ enhance the value of your car by completing a full Service History of every maintenance job you carry out on your car.

I hope you enjoy keeping your car in trim while saving lots of money by servicing your car yourself, with the help of this book. Happy motoring!

Lindsay Porter
Porter Publishing Ltd

Lindsay Porter

Andy MacQuillan

Acknowledgements

The fact that the Nova had a production life of ten years with few major changes testifies to its good initial design. It's a relatively easy car to work on too, with excellent access to all the major components in the spacious engine bay. Reliability is always a plus-point with Vauxhall models and the Nova is no different. The engines used in this model are tough, long-lived and economical, and have shown no particular weak-spots throughout production - a record many other manufacturers would be envious of, and which Vauxhall can be proud.

There's been help from many people and companies in preparing this book, ranging from the huge multinational concern General Motors, that we know as Vauxhall, through to the lady neighbour - Bernadette - who so generously (and trustingly!) lent her car for the many photo sessions and mechanical jobs featured in Chapter Three.

Although writing books such as this can be hard work at times, the task could never be described as onerous; 'fixing' cars runs in my family and is almost second nature, while being able to write about them too is a bonus. In fact, if my father was alive today he'd probably describe it as a privilege - and as usual, he'd be right, so this one's for him. Cheers Pop!

Andy MacQuillan

SPECIAL THANKS
The Publisher would like to thank: Vauxhall Motors for their advice and use of illustrative material, A E Clegg, Vauxhall dealer, Hallow, for allowing their cars to be photographed for the cover, Gunsons for equipment, line drawings and advice and Dinitrol for their kind assistance with Chapter 5.

CHAPTER 1 - SAFETY FIRST!

You must always ensure that safety is the first consideration in any job you carry out. A slight lack of concentration, or a rush to finish the job quickly can easily result in an accident, as can failure to follow the precautions outlined in this Chapter. Whereas skilled motor mechanics are trained in safe working practices you, the home mechanic, must find them out for yourself and act upon them.

Remember, accidents don't just happen, they are caused, and some of those causes are contained in the following list. Above all, ensure that whenever you work on your car you adopt a safety-minded approach at all times, and remain aware of the dangers that might be encountered.

Be sure to consult the suppliers of any materials and equipment you may use, and to obtain and read carefully any operating and health and safety instructions that may be available on packaging or from manufacturers and suppliers.

PART I: IMPORTANT POINTS

Vehicle Off Ground

ALWAYS ensure that the vehicle is properly supported when raised off the ground. Don't work on, around, or underneath a raised vehicle unless axle stands are positioned under secure, load bearing underbody areas, or the vehicle is driven onto ramps, with the wheels remaining on the ground securely chocked to prevent movement.

ALWAYS ensure that the safe working load rating of any jacks, hoists or lifting gear used is sufficient for the job, and that lifting gear is used only as recommended by the manufacturer.

NEVER attempt to loosen or tighten nuts that require a lot of force to turn (e.g. a tight oil drain plug) with the vehicle raised, unless it is safely supported. Take care not to pull the vehicle off its supports when applying force to a spanner. Wherever possible, initially slacken tight fastenings before raising the car off the ground.

ALWAYS wear eye protection when working under the vehicle and when using power tools.

Working On The Vehicle

ALWAYS seek specialist advice unless you are justifiably confident about carrying out each job. The safety of your vehicle affects you, your passengers and other road users.

DON'T lean over, or work on, a running engine unless it is strictly necessary, and keep long hair and loose clothing well out of the way of moving mechanical parts. Note that it is theoretically possible for fluorescent striplighting to make an engine fan appear to be stationary - double check whether it is spinning or not! This is the sort of error that happens when you're really tired and not thinking straight. So...

...DON'T work on your car when you're over tired.

ALWAYS work in a well ventilated area and don't inhale dust - it may contain asbestos or other harmful substances.

REMOVE your wrist watch, rings and all other jewellery before doing any work on the vehicle - and especially when working on the electrical system.

DON'T remove the radiator or expansion tank filler cap when the cooling system is hot, or you may get scalded by escaping coolant or steam. Let the system cool down first and even then, if the engine is not completely cold, cover the cap with a cloth and gradually release the pressure.

NEVER drain oil, coolant or automatic transmission fluid when the engine is hot. Allow time for it to cool sufficiently to avoid scalding you.

ALWAYS keep antifreeze, brake and clutch fluid away from vehicle paintwork. Wash off any spills immediately.

TAKE CARE to avoid touching any engine or exhaust system component unless it is cool enough not to burn you.

Running The Vehicle

NEVER start the engine unless the gearbox is in neutral (or 'Park' in the case of automatic transmission) and the hand brake is fully applied.

NEVER run catalytic converter equipped vehicles without the exhaust system heat shields in place.

TAKE CARE when parking vehicles fitted with catalytic

converters. The 'cat' reaches extremely high temperatures and any combustible materials under the car, such as long dry grass, could be ignited.

Personal Safety

NEVER siphon fuel, antifreeze, brake fluid or other such toxic liquids by mouth, or allow contact with your skin. There is an increasing awareness that they can damage your health. Best of all, use a suitable hand pump and wear gloves.

BEFORE undertaking dirty jobs, use a barrier cream on your hands as a protection against infection. Preferably, wear thin gloves, available from DIY outlets.

WEAR GLOVES for sure when there is a risk of used engine oil coming into contact with your skin. It can cause cancer.

WIPE UP any spilt oil, grease or water off the floor immediately, before there is an accident.

MAKE SURE that spanners and all other tools are the right size for the job and are not likely to slip. Never try to 'double-up' spanners to gain more leverage.

SEEK HELP if you need to lift something heavy which may be beyond your capability. Don't forget that when lifting a heavy weight, you should keep your back straight and bend your knees to avoid injuring your back.

NEVER take risky short-cuts or rush to finish a job. Plan ahead and allow plenty of time.

BE METICULOUS and keep the work area tidy - you'll avoid frustration, work better and lose less.

KEEP children and animals right-away from the work area and from unattended vehicles.

ALWAYS tell someone what you're doing and have them regularly check that all is well, especially when working alone on, or under, the vehicle.

PART II: HAZARDS

Fire!

Petrol (gasoline) is a dangerous and highly flammable liquid requiring special precautions. When working on the fuel system, disconnect the vehicle battery earth (ground) terminal whenever possible and always work outside, or in a very well ventilated area. Any form of spark, such as that caused by an electrical fault, by two metal surfaces striking against each other, by a central heating boiler in the garage 'firing up', or even by static electricity built up in your clothing can, in a confined space, ignite petrol vapour causing an explosion. Take great care not to spill petrol on to the engine or exhaust system, never allow any naked flame anywhere near the work area and, above all, don't smoke.

Invest in a workshop-sized fire extinguisher. Choose the carbon dioxide type or preferably, dry powder but never a water type extinguisher for workshop use. Water conducts electricity and can make worse an oil or petrol-based fire, in certain circumstances.

DON'T disconnect any fuel pipes on a fuel injected engine while the ignition is switched on. The fuel in the line is under very high pressure - sufficient to cause serious injury. Remember that many injection systems have residual pressure in the pipes for days after switching off. Consult the workshop manual or seek specialist advice before carrying out any work.

Fumes

In addition to the fire dangers described previously, petrol (gasoline) vapour and the types of vapour given off by many solvents, thinners, and adhesives are highly toxic and under certain conditions can lead to unconsciousness or even death, if inhaled. The

risks are increased if such fluids are used in a confined space so always ensure adequate ventilation when handling materials of this nature. Treat all such substances with care, always read the instructions and follow them with care.

Always ensure that the car is out of doors and not in an enclosed space when the engine is running. Exhaust fumes contain poisonous carbon monoxide, even when the car is fitted with a catalytic converter, since 'cats' sometimes fail and don't function when the engine is cold.

Never drain petrol (gasoline) or use solvents, thinners adhesives or other toxic substances in an inspection pit as the extremely confined space allows the highly toxic fumes to concentrate. Running the engine with the vehicle over the pit can have the same results. It is also dangerous to park a vehicle for any length of time over an inspection pit. The fumes from even a slight fuel leak can cause an explosion when the engine is started. Petrol fumes are heavier than air and will accumulate in the pit.

Mains Electricity

Best of all, avoid the use of mains electricity when working on the vehicle, whenever possible. For instance, you could use rechargeable

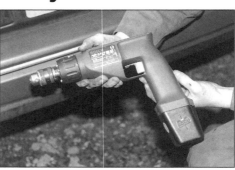

tools and a DC inspection lamp, powered from a remote 12V battery - both are much safer. However, if you do use mains-powered equipment, ensure that the appliance is wired correctly to its plug, that where necessary it is properly earthed (grounded), and that the fuse is of the correct rating for the appliance is fitted. For instance, a 13 amp fuse in lead lamp's plug will not provide adequate protection. Do not use any mains powered equipment in damp conditions or in the vicinity of fuel, fuel vapour or the vehicle battery.

Also, before using any mains powered electrical equipment, take one more simple precaution - use an RCD (Residual Current Device) circuit breaker. Then, if there is a short, the RCD circuit breaker minimises the risk of electrocution by instantly cutting the power supply. Buy one from any electrical store or DIY centre. RCDs fit simply into your electrical socket before plugging in your electrical equipment.

The Ignition System

You should never work on the ignition system with the ignition switched on, or with the engine being turned over on the starter, or running.

Touching certain parts of the ignition system, such as the HT leads, distributor cap, ignition coil etc, can result in a severe electric shock. This is especially likely where the insulation on any of these components is weak, or if the components are dirty or damp. Note also that voltages produced by electronic ignition systems are much higher than those produced by conventional systems and could prove fatal, particularly to people with cardiac pacemaker implants. Consult your handbook or main dealer if in any doubt.

An additional risk of injury can arise while working on running engines, if the operator touches a high voltage lead and pulls his or her hand away on to a sharp, conductive or revolving part.

The Battery

Never cause a spark, smoke, or allow a naked light near the vehicle's battery, even in a well ventilated area. Highly explosive hydrogen gas will be given off as part of the charging process.

Battery terminals on the car should be shielded, since a battery contains energy and a spark can be caused by any metal object which touches the battery's terminals or connecting straps.

Before working on the fuel or electrical systems, always disconnect the battery earth (ground) terminal. (But before doing so, read the relevant **FACT FILE** in *Chapter 3* regarding saving computer and radio settings.)

When using a battery charger, care should be taken to avoid causing a spark by switching off the power supply before the battery charger leads are connected or disconnected. Before charging the battery from an external source, disconnect both battery leads before connecting the charger. If the battery is not of the 'sealed-for-life' type, loosen the filler plugs or remove the cover before charging. For best results the battery should be given a low rate trickle charge overnight. Do not charge at an excessive rate or the battery may burst.

Always wear gloves and goggles when carrying or when topping up the battery. Even in diluted form (as it is in the battery) the acid electrolyte is extremely corrosive and must not be allowed to contact the eyes, skin or clothes.

Brakes and Asbestos

Obviously, a car's brakes are among its most important safety related items. ONLY work on your vehicle's braking system if you are trained and competent to do so. If you have not been trained in this work, but wish to carry out the jobs described in this book, we strongly recommend that you have a garage or qualified mechanic check your work before using the car.

Whenever you work on the braking system's mechanical components, or remove front or rear brake pads or shoes: i) wear an efficient particle mask; ii) wipe off all brake dust from the brakes after spraying on a proprietary brand of brake cleaner (never blow dust off with compressed air); iii) dispose of brake dust and discarded shoes or pads in a sealed plastic bag; iv) wash your hands thoroughly after you have finished working on the brakes and certainly before you eat or smoke; v) replace shoes and pads only with asbestos-free shoes or pads. Note that asbestos brake dust can cause cancer if inhaled.

Brake Fluid

Brake fluid absorbs moisture rapidly from the air and can become dangerous resulting in brake failure. Castrol (U.K.) Ltd. recommend that you should have your brake fluid tested at least once a year by a properly equipped garage with test equipment and you should change the fluid in accordance with your vehicle manufacturer's recommendations or as advised in this book if we recommend a shorter interval than the manufacturer. You should buy no more brake fluid than you need, in smaller rather than larger containers. Never store an opened container of brake fluid. Dispose of the remainder at your Local Authority Waste Disposal Site, in the designated disposal unit, not with general waste or with waste oil.

Engine Oils

Take care to observe the following precautions when working with used engine oil. Apart from the obvious risk of scalding when draining the oil from a hot engine, there is the danger from contamination contained in all used oil.

Always wear disposable plastic or rubber gloves when draining the oil from your engine. i) Note that the drain plug and the oil are often hotter than you expect. Wear gloves if the plug is too hot to touch and keep your hand to one side so that you are not scalded by the spurt of oil as the plug comes away; ii) There are very real health hazards associated with used engine oil. In the words of one manufacturer's handbook "Prolonged and repeated contact may cause serious skin disorders, including dermatitis and cancer." Use a barrier cream on your hands and try not to get oil on them. Always wear gloves and wash your hands with hand cleaner soon after carrying out the work. Keep oil out of the reach of children; iii) NEVER, EVER dispose of old engine oil into the ground or down a drain. In the UK, and in most EC countries, every local authority must provide a safe means of oil disposal. In the UK, try your local Environmental Health Department for advice on waste disposal facilities.

Plastic Materials

Work with plastic materials brings additional hazards into workshops. Many of the materials used (polymers, resins, adhesives and materials acting as catalysts and accelerators) contain dangers in the form of poisonous fumes, skin irritants, and the risk of fire and explosions. Do not allow resin or 2-pack adhesive hardener, or that supplied with filler or 2-pack stopper, to come into contact with skin or eyes. Read carefully the safety notes supplied on the can, tube or packaging and always wear impervious gloves and goggles when working with them.

Jacks and Axle Stands

Throughout this book you will see many references to the correct use of jacks, axle stands and similar equipment - and we make no apologies for being repetitive. This is one area where safety cannot be overstressed - your life could be at stake!

Special care must be taken when any type of lifting equipment is used. Jacks are made for lifting the vehicle only, not for supporting it while it is being worked on. Never work under the car using only a jack to support the weight. Jacks must be supplemented by adequate additional means of support, positioned under secure load-bearing parts of the frame or underbody. Axle stands are available from most auto. parts stores. Drive-on ramps are limiting because of their design and size but they are simple to use, reliable and offer the most stable type of support. We strongly recommend their use.

Full details on jacking and supporting the vehicle will be found near the beginning of *Chapter 3.*

Fluoroelastomers
MOST IMPORTANT! PLEASE READ THIS SECTION!

If you service your car in the normal way, none of the following may be relevant to you. Unless, for example, you encounter a car which has been on fire (even in a localised area), subject to heat in, say, a crash-damage repairer's workshop or a vehicle breaker's yard, or if any second-hand parts have been heated in any way.

Many synthetic, rubber-like materials used in motor cars contain a substance called fluorine. These materials are known as fluoro-elastomers and are commonly used for oil seals, wiring and cabling, bearing surfaces, gaskets, diaphragms, hoses and 'O' rings. If they are subjected to temperatures greater than 315 degrees C, they will decompose and can be potentially hazardous. Fluoroelastomer materials will show physical signs of decomposition under such conditions in the form of charring of black sticky masses. Some decomposition may occur at temperatures above 200 degrees C, and it is obvious that when a car has been in a fire or has been dismantled with the assistance of a cutting torch or blow torch, the fluoroelastomers can decompose in the manner indicated above.

In the presence of any water or humidity, including atmospheric moisture, the by-products caused by the fluoroelastomers being heated can be extremely dangerous. According to the Health and Safety Executive, "Skin contact with this liquid or decomposition residues can cause painful and penetrating burns. Permanent irreversible skin and tissue damage can occur". Damage can also be caused to eyes or by the inhalation of fumes created as fluoroelastomers are burned or heated.

After a vehicle has been exposed to fire or high temperatures:

1. Do not touch blackened or charred seals or equipment.

2. Allow all burnt or decomposed fluoroelastomer materials to cool before inspection, investigations, tear-down or removal.

3. Preferably, don't handle parts containing decomposed fluoroelastomers, but if you must, wear goggles and PVC (polyvinyl chloride) or neoprene protective gloves whilst doing so. Never handle such parts unless they are completely cool.

4. Contaminated parts, residues, materials and clothing, including protective clothing and gloves, should be disposed of by an approved contractor to landfill or by incineration according to national or local regulations. Oil seals, gaskets and 'O' rings, along with contaminated material, must not be burned.

PART III: GENERAL WORKSHOP SAFETY

1. Always have a fire extinguisher of the correct type at arm's length when working on the fuel system.

If you do have a fire, DON'T PANIC. Use the extinguisher effectively by directing it at the base of the fire.

2. NEVER use a naked flame anywhere in the workplace.

3. KEEP your inspection lamp well away from any source of petrol (gasoline) such as when disconnecting a carburettor float bowl or fuel line.

4. NEVER use petrol (gasoline) to clean parts. Use paraffin (kerosene), white spirits, or a proprietary degreaser.

5. NO SMOKING. There's a risk of fire or of transferring dangerous substances to your mouth and, in any case, ash falling into mechanical components is to be avoided.

6. BE METHODICAL in everything you do, use common sense, and think of safety at all times.

CHAPTER 2 - BUYING GUIDE

In this Chapter, we show you how to go about buying a second hand car. We also look at which parts wear out, and we explain when they are likely to need replacement, so that whether you are giving your own car the once-over, or you're looking at a prospective purchase, you'll know what to expect; and we examine the best ways of buying parts for your pride and joy.

PART I: BUYING A SECOND-HAND CAR

In general, the safest - but also the most expensive - way of buying second hand is through a main dealer: NOT the same as a general second-hand dealer, whose standards are almost certain to be lower! We *strongly* recommend the use of HPI Autodata checks mentioned on page 110, because even main dealers can make 'mistakes', but once you've done that, and selected the main-dealer car you want, it's better to have an AA or

RAC inspection carried out rather than carry out your own checks. But for many people, it's a question of saving money and buying privately, and that's what this Chapter is mainly about. But don't find yourself with the *worst* of both worlds...

Spot The Rogue Trader

One of the biggest dangers with buying privately is that you might encounter a real cheat: a trader masquerading as a private seller. Cars offered by such people are likely to be among the worst on offer, they may have had their mileometers tampered with and deep seated faults may have been cleverly concealed. Here's how to spot them:

• take note of the way traders often word their advertisements. Key phrases include: "a very clean car", "very straight", "a beautiful motorcar" and other glib phrases.

• when you telephone in response to an ad., *always* say, "I'm calling about the car..." If the person on the other end asks, "Which car?", put the 'phone down before the spiel starts.

• if you get past the telephone stage, take careful note of the attitude of the seller. Part-time, 'black economy' dealers often seem blase, even bored by the whole thing, and slicker than most private sellers.

• insist on looking at the Registration Document. If the seller isn't the registered keeper, why not?

How To Inspect A Used Vehicle

STAGE ONE: Even if you know very little about cars, you can root out the obvious no-hopers before arranging for a local main agent, AA or RAC inspection. The text in italics explains the problems.

• catch the light along all sides of the car. Can you see any ripples? Check for overspray inside wheel arches, inside engine bay and on tyres and trim. Does all the paint match? *All indicate poorly carried out crash repairs.*

• look at the gaps between panels. Also, look very carefully inside the engine bay and inside the boot for evidence of rippling in the metal. Look low down, mainly in the vicinity of structural members. *Tell-tale signs of crash damage.*

STAGE TWO: If your car passes Stage One, look more closely at the bodywork - the most expensive part to repair.

• check the sills by lifting the carpets just inside the doors and also check the footwells, especially around the edges. *Rust!*

• look inside the engine bay especially at the tops of struts. *Check for corrosion.*

• check the bottoms of wings, the 'skirts' beneath front and rear bumpers and the tops of wing panels for corrosion. *Rust covered with filler will quickly burst through again.*

SPECIALIST SERVICE: It's hardly worth trying to check beneath a car without the use of a hoist. Leave it to the pro. inspection mentioned earlier, or see if you can persuade a local garage to lend or hire their hoist:

• check around spring mountings, the joints between floors and sills, all box-section 'chassis' members and anywhere that suspension components are fixed to the car's body structure.

• check all brake pipes and hoses. *Look for rubbing or corrosion.*

- look at the shock absorbers. *Fluid leakage means failure.*

- check the exhaust. *Look for rust, holes or patches.*

- examine each tyre carefully for bulges or splits. *Tyres worn more on one side than the other might mean that the car's tracking needs checking - easily adjustable - or it might indicate suspension damage, maybe from an accident.*

> *making it easy!* If you are buying an older car which needs work doing to it, try making the owner an offer 'subject to MoT test'. Then, you can have the car tested as an inexpensive (though not necessarily complete) condition check.

Mechanical Components

- before starting up, remove the oil filler cap. *Grey sludge around the cap is a certain indicator that the engine is on its last legs.*

- pull out the dipstick. Is the oil level very low? Is the oil a dirty black and does it feel gritty between finger and thumb? *Not a well maintained car! Does it have droplets of water on it? Big problems! Probably a blown head gasket.*

- check inside the radiator cap (ONLY if the engine is cold!). Do you see anti-freeze colour? *Good!* Do you see rust? *Bad!* Do you see droplets of oil? *Disastrous! See previous paragraph.*

- start the car and note whether the starter motor sounds lively or whether it is struggling to keep up. *Could be duff battery; or tired starter motor.*

- undo and remove the oil filler cap again. (N.B. Most engines spray oil around in *copious* quantities. Ensure that you don't get covered!) *If oil mist chugs out, the engine bores are badly worn. Also...*

- ...look at the exhaust. Steam (especially in colder weather) and even water dripping out is no problem, although it should go away after the car has been driven. 'Rev' the engine, hard and several times. *If you see puffs or even clouds of black smoke (not grey steam), the engine is probably on the slippery slope.*

- does the oil pressure warning light flicker with engine cold? *Low oil pressure equals an engine rebuild?*

- bonnet open. Does the 'top' of the engine rattle on start up? *Mechanical tappets: adjustment needed.* If the rattle continues after 30 seconds, *the engine may need an expensive replacement camshaft. Hydraulic tappets: noise is always expensive!*

- rev the engine. Does it rattle in a deep, growly way, low down in the engine? *The big end and/or main bearings are gone - replacement engine time!*

Static Checks

- are the carpets wet? *water is leaking in. Windscreen seal leaks can often be cured easily. But if the car is old the screen surround may have corroded, requiring expensive welding. Alternatively, water coming in from beneath suggests that the car's lower structure has as much future as an old car park ticket. If water is leaking from the heater, remember that it can be expensive and tricky to replace.*

- seat rips can be a pain and devalue the car. *It can be difficult to find the right colour match on second hand seats.* Do your knees come up as your backside goes down. *The seat springing has gone.*

- can you live with headlining rips or severe discolouration? *It's difficult to clean easily and replacement is usually expensive.*

- take a *close* look at seat belts and mountings. *Life saver - and quite expensive to replace.*

- check that the heater works properly. *Or you'll end up hating the car!*

- take time to check every switch, accessory and electrical fitting on the car. *Replacements can be expensive.* Check that the stereo works - *and check that it's included with the car!*

- don't accept lame excuses when things don't work! *If things are so easy to fix, why haven't they been done already?*

- check the spare wheel and the condition (existence?) of the jack and toolkit. *More expense!*

- open and close windows and sunroof. *(Also look for stains around sunroof aperture - they can leak!)*

Finally, but perhaps most important of all, make sure that the person who is selling the car actually owns it!

- ask to see the Registration Document. *If it's not available it could be: the 'owner' has a) lost it; b) has it but it doesn't show the 'owner's' name because he is a trader; c) the car doesn't belong to the seller. If you can't see the Registration Document, walk away!*

- ask to see the owner's original purchase receipt and check that the car is owned by the 'owner' and is not subject to a finance agreement. See below. *IMPORTANT NOTE: You may be amazed to learn that, if you pay for a car that is subsequently found to belong to someone else, you will lose the car and the money!*

- check that the VIN (Vehicle Identification Number) shown on the Registration document is the same as those on the VIN plate riveted to the car. See "Fact File" later in this chapter for the precise location of these numbers. *If any of the numbers in these three locations are different, missing, or have obviously been tampered with, then under no circumstances consider buying the car unless the seller can provide an explanation, in writing, satisfactory to a third party, such as an AA or RAC inspector, or the Police!*

Spot The Rogue Car

Before buying *any* used car, check it out with HPI Autodata. (See Page 110.) A postal or telephone enquiry (cheques or credit card payments accepted) will (i) confirm that the vehicle details shown (make, model, colour, engine size, fuel type) are all correct, (ii) tell you if the vehicle is reported as stolen, or subject to an outstanding finance agreement, (iii) tell you if the vehicle has been logged as having a major insurance claim (not foolproof; many don't show up), (iv) identify vehicles which have had a registration plate change.

PART II: WHAT WEARS, AND WHEN

The following list provides a great way of checking what is likely to be worn on your vehicle, and at what stage it is likely to need replacement - useful when checking your own car, or when buying another. Please bear in mind that the mileages shown are only intended as an approximation of the lifespan of each component. In real life, some will wear out faster and some slower, of course but the chart below provides a useful rough guide.

SAFETY FIRST!
Read and take note of *Chapter 1, Safety First!* and the Safety information in *Chapter 3* before carrying out any of these checks.

COMPONENT:	COULD NEED REPLACEMENT AT:	CHECKS OR SYMPTOMS:
Alternator	70,000 miles	Fails without warning.
Battery	4 to 7 years (original parts); 1 to who-knows (non-original parts)	Goes flat, even though disconnected, or can't be recharged.
Brake Pads - Front	15 to 20,000 miles	See Job 63
Brake Pads/Shoes - Rear	35 to 40,000 miles	See Job 65.
Cambelt	36,000 miles	Should be renewed - see Job 109.
Clutch	Up to 75,000 normally	Check for slipping when pulling away, or hill climbing.
Diesel Glowplugs	60,000 miles	Engine reluctant to start from cold and smokes (even though battery in good condition).
Diesel Injectors	75,000 miles	Excessive smoke; engine misfires.
Exhaust mountings	Rears can fracture after two or three years.	Examine visually; twist manually.
Exhaust pipe	(Vauxhall parts) Up to 4 years (non-original parts) 1 to 3 years	Examine visually - see Job 30; listen for blowing.
Shock absorbers Shock absorbers	(front) 40,000 miles (rear) 60,000 miles	Clean off and look for oil leaks. Grasp and twist, looking for wear in bushes top and bottom.
Starter motor	150,000 miles	Turns engine slowly or fails to engage when battery and connections are in good condition
Turbocharger	(diesel) 140,000 miles	Seal failure leads to engine oil being consumed - engine smokes through exhaust when turbo operates.
Tyres	(most models) 15 - 20,000 miles	Check visually, especially inside tyre walls and spare.

PART III - BUYING SPARES

One of the great advantages of DIY servicing is that you can choose which parts you buy, where you buy your parts, and how much you pay for them, whereas if the dealer services your car you buy their parts at their prices!

Of course, you must take care not to buy poor quality parts, but it's worth bearing in mind that many of the car makers' parts are the same as those available from 'independents'.

Buying The Right Parts

All manufacturers change the parts they use on the production line, often with startling frequency. The only way of ensuring that the parts you buy are the right ones for your car is to take your car's Vehicle Identification Number (VIN) and engine number with you when buying spares.

Main Dealers

Main dealers more than anyone else should be able to match your car's VIN number to the precise part you need, so have it to hand. This can also be the key to a more helpful approach by some Parts Department staff! Also, try to avoid calling on the parts department in the early mornings and other busy periods, and you may find that staff have more time to help you. Consumable items are almost certain to be too expensive from your main dealer. Try high street auto accessory stores or out-of-town Superstores for best prices.

Auto Accessory Stores

Local parts factors and big-name motor accessory shops can be extremely useful for obtaining servicing parts at short notice - many 'accessory' outlets open late in the evening, and on both days at weekends. You'll find that the high-street shops and Superstores will usually be open when you need them, their prices are usually the keenest of all, because they can buy-in in great quantities, and the quality of the parts is excellent from the best-known shops, since they use the same big-name manufacturers as many of the original car makers.

Buying Second-Hand

Purchasing any safety-related items second-hand - braking, steering or suspension parts - is something to avoid. That's not to decry buying second-hand altogether. Replacing a worn out distributor or carburettor, for instance, with a second-hand component that you know to be 'low mileage' can make a lot of sense. Equally, non-performance related items, such as wheel trims, interior trim and other interior parts can often be obtained at a fraction of the 'new' cost.

Reconditioned Parts

These are best obtained from reputable retail suppliers. When buying, always enquire about the terms of the guarantee. Don't buy if there isn't a good one! 'Exchange' alternators and starter motors are good value - but only buy from a reputable source.

Steering racks are invariably available as exchange items. Ensure that you rotate the operating shaft fully from lock to lock, feeling for any undue free play, roughness, stiffness, or 'notchiness' as you do so. Reject any units showing signs of any of these problems.

Tyres

We recommend buying only good quality radial ply tyres. Cheaper tyres rarely perform as well as top brands, even when they are the cheaper brand of a top manufacturer. Your car may steer more erratically, have less grip on cornering and braking and be noisier than if you pay the small extra amount required for top brand tyres - and they usually last longer, too. Remould tyres are available at lower initial cost, but life expectancy is not as long as with new tyres and we don't recommend them.

Shopping Around

If you want to buy good quality parts *and* save money, you must be prepared to shop around. Ring each of your chosen suppliers with a shopping list to hand, and your car's personal data, from the Auto-Biography at the front of this book, in front of you. Keep a written note of prices - including VAT, delivery etc - whether the parts are proper 'brand name' parts or not and - most importantly! - whether or not the parts you want are in stock. Parts expected 'soon' have been known never to materialise. A swivel pin in the hand is worth two in the bush. (Bad pun!)

FACT FILE: IDENTIFICATION NUMBERS

All manufacturers change the parts they use on the production line, often with startling frequency. The only way of ensuring that the parts you buy are the right ones for your car is to take your car's Vehicle Identification Number (VIN) and engine number with you when buying spares.

There are three main numbers you will need to know in order to buy parts and touch-up paint for your car. The VIN is your car's internationally unique number and tells your parts supplier exactly which model and year the car is. Quote the VIN whenever you buy spares for your car.

1. The Nova's VIN plate is positioned on the front or "slam"-panel of the engine bay (left of centre, viewed from front of car) and the number should be the same as that shown on your vehicle documents.

The engine number will usually be found on the engine block, on a small flat area beneath

the right hand-most spark plug (overhead camshaft engines), or to the left of the dipstick (overhead valve engines), but may be stamped into a small aluminium plate in the same position.

2. The VIN number is also stamped onto the floor-pan at manufacture and is found beneath a small flap in the carpet between the drivers' seat and the door sill. Make sure it is the same as that shown on the VIN plate! (Illustrations, courtesy Vauxhall Motors Limited)

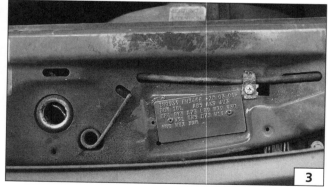

3. INSIDE INFORMATION: If you need an exact paint colour match, you'll need the car's paint code number. Although the VIN plate will carry the basic colour code, the paint/trim code plate will contain precise details of the shade and the type of trim fitted. It is situated also on the front "slam" panel, to the right of the VIN plate and is usually painted in the body colour. Most aerosol paints won't relate to this number, although at least one brand claims to be able to produce cans matched to your car's code colour, to special order. Alternatively, have your local paint factor mix a small quantity of matching paint for you.

Please read the whole of the Introduction to this Chapter before carrying out any work on your car.

SERVICING YOUR CAR

CHAPTER 3 - SERVICING YOUR CAR

Everyone wants to own a car that starts first time, runs reliably and lasts longer than the average. And there's no magic about how to put your car into that category, it's all a question of thorough maintenance! If you follow the Service Jobs listed here or even if you have a garage or mechanic do it for you - you can almost *guarantee* that your car will still be going strong when others have fallen by the wayside... or the hard shoulder.

If you want your car to be as well looked after as possible, you'll follow the Jobs shown here, but if you don't want to go all the way, you can pick and choose from the most essential items in the list. But do bear in mind that the Jobs we recommend are there for some very good reasons:

◆ *body maintenance* is rarely included in most service schedules. We believe it to be essential.

◆ *preventative maintenance* figures very high on our list of priorities. And that's why so many of our service jobs have the word "Check..." near the start!

 *We think it's very important to keep things as straight-forward as possible. And where you see this heading, you'll know there's an extra tip to help 'make it easy' for you!*

The 'Catch-up' Service

When you first buy a used car, you never know for sure just how well it's been looked after. Even one with a full service history is unlikely to have been serviced as thoroughly as one with a Porter Manual Service History! So, if you want to catch-up on all the servicing that may have been neglected on your car, just work through the entire list of Service Jobs listed for the longest term servicing jobs listed in this Manual, and your car will be bang up to date and serviced as well as you could hope for. Do allow several days for all of this work, not least because it will almost certainly throw up a number of extra jobs - potential faults that have been lurking beneath the surface - all of which will need putting right before you can 'sign off' your car as being in tip-top condition.

The Service History

Those people fortunate enough to own a new car, or one that has been well maintained from new will have the opportunity to keep a 'Service History' of their car, usually filled in by a main dealer. Now you can keep your own complete record, using the tick list in the Appendix at the back of this book.

Your car's Service History will then be more complete and detailed than any manufacturer's service record, with the extra bonus that there is space for you to keep a record of all those extras: New tyres; replacement exhaust; extra accessories, so if your battery goes down only 11 months after buying it, you'll be able to look up where and when you bought it.

SAFETY FIRST!
SAFETY FIRST! *information must always be read with care and always taken seriously. In addition, please read the whole of Chapter 1, Safety First! before carrying out any work on your car. There are many hazards associated with working on a car but all of them can be avoided by adhering strictly to the safety rules. Don't skimp on safety!*

RAISING THE CAR

Raising The Car Before Working On It

RAISING A CAR - SAFELY!
You will often need to raise your car off the ground in order to carry out the Service Jobs shown here. To start off with, here's what you must never do - never work beneath a car held on a jack, not even a trolley jack. Quite a number of deaths have been caused by a car slipping off a jack while someone has been working beneath. On the other hand, the safest way is by raising a car on a proprietary brand of ramps. Sometimes, there is no alternative but to use axle stands. Please read all of the following information and act upon it!

When using car ramps:

(I) Make absolutely certain that the ramps are parallel to the wheels of the car and that the wheels are exactly central on each ramp.

Always have an assistant watch both sides of the car as you drive up. Drive up to the end 'stops' on the ramps but never over them!

Apply the hand brake firmly, put the car in first or reverse gear, or 'Park', in the case of an automatic.

(II) Chock both wheels remaining on the ground, both in front and behind so that the car can't move in either direction.

INSIDE INFORMATION: wrap a strip of carpet into a loop around the first 'rung' of each of the ramps and drive over the doubled-up piece of carpet on the approach to the ramps. This prevents the ramps from skidding away, as they are inclined to do, as the car is driven on to them.

When using axle stands:

On other occasions, you might need to work on the car while it is supported on an axle stand or a pair of axle stands. These are inherently less stable than ramps and so you must take much greater care when working beneath them. In particular:

• ensure that the axle stand is on flat, stable ground, never on a surface where one side can sink in to the ground.

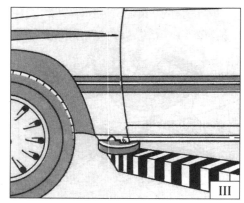

• ensure that the car is on level ground and that the hand brake is off and the transmission in neutral.

• raise the car with a trolley jack - invest in one if you don't already own one; the car's wheel changing jack is often too unstable. Place a piece of cloth over the head of the jack if your car is nicely finished on the underside. Ensure that the ground is sufficiently clear and smooth for the trolley jack wheels to roll as the car is raised and lowered, otherwise it could slip off the jack.

Raising the Front of the Car

(III) Position the jack immediately behind the front wheel arch, with the jack head bearing on the sill reinforced sill edge, as shown. (Illustration, courtesy Vauxhall Motors Limited)

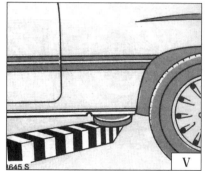

(IV) Place the axle stand beneath the chassis box-member as shown; NEVER put axle stands under the engine or gearbox.

Raising the Rear of the Car

(V) Position the jack immediately in front of the rear wheel arch, with the jack head bearing on the reinforced sill edge, as shown. (Illustration, courtesy Vauxhall Motors Limited)

(VI) Take care to locate the top of each axle stand on this short box-section situated just behind the sill and ahead of each rear wheel. You should never use a movable suspension part (because the part can move and allow the axle stand to slip) or the floor of the car (which is just too weak).

Just as when using ramps - only even more importantly! - apply the hand brake firmly once the car is supported on the axle stands, put the car in first or reverse gear (or 'Park', in the case of an automatic) and chock both wheels remaining on the ground, both in front and behind.

General Advice

Be especially careful when applying force to a spanner or when pulling hard on anything, when the car is supported off the ground. It is all too easy to move the car so far that it topples off the axle stands. And remember that if a car falls on you, YOU COULD BE KILLED!

Whenever working beneath a car, have someone primed to keep an eye on you! If someone pops out to see how you are getting on every quarter of an hour or so, it could be enough to save your life!

Do remember that, in general, a car will be more stable when only one wheel is removed and one axle stand used than if two wheels are removed in conjunction with two axle stands. You are strongly advised never to work on the car with all four wheels off the ground, on four axle stands. The car would then be very unstable and dangerous to work beneath.

Before lowering the car to the ground, remember to remove the chocks, release the hand brake and place the transmission in neutral.

Raising the Car in an Emergency

SAFETY FIRST!
Wheel changing jacks can be dreadfully unstable! Take great care not to get any part of your body under the car when supported by one of these jacks.

It happens too often - a roadside puncture, probably in the dark, probably in the rain, the spare is flat, you don't know where the car jack is, or the wheelbrace, and even if you did you don't know where the jack should go, and the wheel bolts are far too tight to be shifted by that bit of bent rod they call a wheelbrace! If you've never done it before, changing a wheel is a daunting prospect, so practise the wheel-change routine at home, before the worst happens to you.

(VII) START by finding where the jack and wheelbrace are normally stowed - on all Novas this is beneath the spare wheel which is found in the rear luggage area, beneath the floor covering. Make sure the securing nut doesn't become seized by oiling the threads occasionally.

(VIII) Jack and wheelbrace are kept in a tool-roll, but they are susceptible to damp and corrosion, so oil the jack's threaded parts and joints occasionally too.

CHECK that the spare hasn't gone flat, by checking it every week, along with the other wheels/tyres.

PREPARE by ensuring that in the boot and/or glovebox you have an old waterproof, something to kneel on, a rag to clean your hands if necessary, and also protective gloves, and a torch.

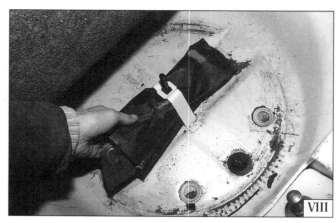

(IX) Wheel bolts should be done up to a specified degree of tightness, but all too often they're done up by a chap behaving like a gorilla with a toothache! Give yourself a better chance by buying one of these extendible wrenches, complete with the right-sized socket to fit your wheel bolts. Its superior strength and leverage will shift wheel bolts that the car-kit brace wouldn't even look at - it's an absolute 'must', not just for those who haven't got the strength of a raging gorilla but to replace that feeble wheel brace in the boot.

(X) In many instances, you will first have to lever off a wheeltrim - or plastic caps over the bolts that look like the real thing but are not! The car-kit wheelbrace might have a flattened end made for the job, otherwise find yourself perhaps a suitable screwdriver (keep it in the car) and lever carefully around the circumference of the trim: note where the tyre valve protrudes through, making a pencil mark if necessary. Once the wheeltrim is partly unclipped - it often needs vigorous levering, so watch that bodywork! - you may be better off donning your gloves and pulling.

(XI) With the wheel still on the ground, loosen (don't remove!), the wheel bolts. For your physical wellbeing you should always bear down on the wheelbrace, rather than pull it upwards - if you're stuck with that bent-rod car-kit brace, you'll probably need a length of pipe to slip over it to extend its leverage but it will probably be a struggle to keep it on the bolt. If you try slackening the bolts after you've raised the wheel, all you'll do is rotate the wheel, not the bolt! (Illustration, courtesy Vauxhall Motors Limited)

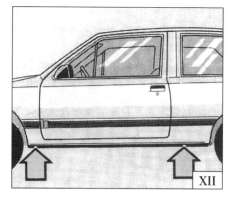

(XII) Make sure now that you know exactly where and how the car jack locates: The jacking-points on Novas are shown arrowed and are identical on both sides of the car. At each point there is a notch cut in the sill-edge which locates....

(XIII) ...with a spigot in the 'V'-shaped jack head. (Illustration, courtesy Vauxhall Motors Limited)

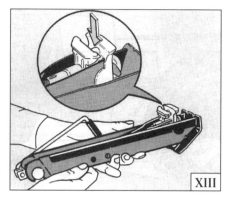

(XIV) Unfold and wind the handle clockwise to extend the jack, making sure it is kept as vertical as possible, although its angle will change as the jack is extended.

Remember to carry a piece of timber in the boot to place beneath the jack to spread the load and prevent the jack from sinking into soft ground. Once the car is raised, have the handbrake on and there are purpose-made chocks you can wedge each side of the wheel opposite to the one you are changing, to guard against the car rolling. In an emergency, use any old pieces of wood or bricks that you can find. Wind the jack handle until the required wheel is clear of the ground, remembering that if the tyre is flat, you need enough clearance for a wheel with a fully pumped up tyre - do not put any part of your body beneath a car which is supported only on a jack.

(XV) SAFETY FIRST! and INSIDE INFORMATION
Always place the spare wheel, or the wheel you've just removed, under the car: partly for safety to help guard against being crushed; partly so that if the car topples off the wheel-change jack (and they DO, especially on soft ground) you'll be able to reposition the jack and start again.

Once the required wheel is clear of the ground, fully undo the bolts, leaving one 'at the top' until last so you can get your balance and a secure grip before lifting away the wheel. Fitting the replacement wheel can be a bit of a struggle to try to locate the wheel while you attempt to align the bolt holes and insert at least one bolt with one hand while steadying the wheel with the other! Nip the bolts up finger-tight, then lower the wheel to the ground for final tightening, working diagonally, a little at a time, on each bolt: do them up as tight as you can, using all your strength if it's the car-kit wheelbrace, slightly less than full strength if it's the extended wrench.

making it easy! i) Because its difficult to locate wheels held on with bolts, have your local garage supply you with two pieces of threaded rod - wheel retaining bolts with heads cut off would be ideal. You can screw them into two of the holes in the hub, 'hang' the wheel on them while you put in the 'proper' wheel bolts to the other holes, then unscrew them with your fingers and fit the two remaining wheel retaining bolts. Remember to carry them with you! ii) You can also try levering the wheel up into place with a shovel, a length of wood or anything else you can lay your hands on, by the roadside.

ENGINE BAY LAYOUTS

FACT FILE: ENGINE BAY LAYOUTS

ENGINE BAY - PETROL

ENGINE BAY - DIESEL

Key:

A Oil filler cap
B Dipstick
C Coolant reservoir
D Windscreen washer reservoir
E Battery

F Brake fluid reservoir
G Air filter housing
H Fuel filter (diesel only)

Every 500 Miles, Weekly or Before Long Journeys

Every 500 Miles - The Engine Bay

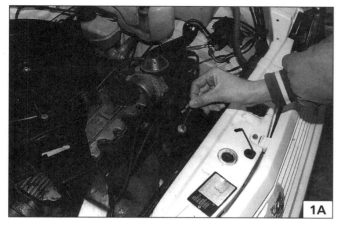

☐ **Job 1. Engine oil level.**

Check the engine's oil level with the car on level ground.

1A. On all cars the dipstick is found at the front of the engine, just behind the radiator - see *Engine Bay Fact File*, for your particular car. The top of the dipstick is painted yellow to help distinguish it. Lift out the dipstick, wipe it clean with a clean cloth, push it back in and lift it out again. Take a look at the level of the oil on the dipstick. You might have to do this three or four times before you can see a clear reading - the oil on the stick sometimes 'smears' as the stick is pulled out.

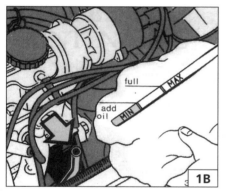

1B. This is a close-up view of the end of the dipstick; the oil level must be maintained above the 'MIN' mark. Approximately one litre will raise the level from the 'MIN' to the 'MAX' mark, as shown. (Illustration, courtesy Vauxhall Motors Limited)

1C. The diesel engine dipstick is marked differently, with 'FULL' and 'ADD' marks. (Illustration, courtesy Vauxhall Motors Limited)

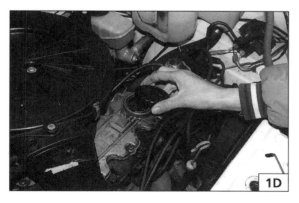

TOPPING UP WITH OIL

When topping-up is required, proceed as follows:

1D. On OHC petrol engines the oil filler cap is on the top-right of the cam cover - undo it by twisting anti-clockwise a quarter-turn.

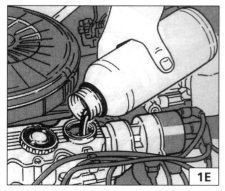

1E. On 1.0 OHV and diesel engines the filler cap is located at the left-hand end of the rocker cover - twist anti-clockwise to remove the petrol version, unscrew the diesel type. (Illustration, courtesy Vauxhall Motors Limited)

On all models, check the ground over which the car has been parked for evidence of oil or other fluid leaks. If any leaks are found, do not drive the car without first establishing where the leaks have come from - they could have come from a major failure in the braking system which will probably call for **SPECIALIST SERVICE** attention.

Job 2. Check coolant level.

SAFETY FIRST!
i) The coolant level should only be checked WHEN THE SYSTEM IS COLD. If you remove the pressure cap when the engine is hot, the release of pressure can cause the water in the system to boil and spurt several feet into the air with the risk of severe scalding. ii) Take precautions to prevent antifreeze coming into contact with the skin or eyes. If this should happen, rinse immediately with plenty of water.

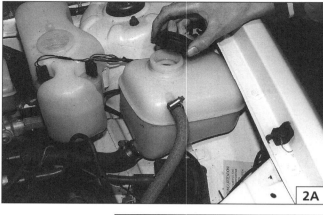
2A

2A. The coolant system expansion bottle on petrol-engined models is on the right-hand side of the engine bay as you stand in front of the car, see *Engine Bay Layouts* on *page 20*.

2B. On diesel engined models the reservoir is on the left-front corner of the engine bay. (Illustration, courtesy Vauxhall Motors Limited)

2B

If necessary, top up the system with a mixture of 50% antifreeze and water to the level mark on the expansion bottle, shown as 'KALT' on the reservoir (or German for 'Cold').

Job 3. Brake fluid level.

SAFETY FIRST!
i) If brake fluid should come into contact with the skin or eyes, rinse immediately with plenty of water. ii) It is acceptable for the brake fluid level to fall slightly during normal use, but if it falls significantly below the 'MIN' mark on the reservoir it indicates a leak or an internal seal failure. Stop using the car and seek specialist advice immediately. iii) If you let dirt get into the hydraulic system it can cause brake failure. Wipe the filler cap clean before removing. iv) You should only ever use new brake fluid from an air-tight container. Old fluid absorbs moisture and this could cause the brakes to fail when carrying out an emergency stop or other heavy use of the brakes - just when you need them most and are least able to do anything about it, in fact!

3A

3A. The transparent brake fluid reservoir is on the top of the master cylinder in front of the servo - there is no need to remove the cap unless the fluid level is below the MAX mark.

3B. If topping-up is necessary, wipe the top clean before removing the cap and be careful not to damage the wiring to the 'low-fluid-level' warning device. Top up the level to the 'MAX' mark on the side of the reservoir.

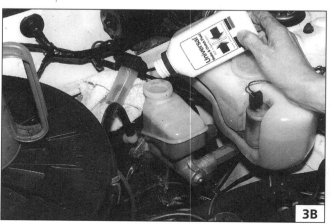
3B

making it easy! Should separate push-on connectors become disturbed, they can be replaced on either of the two terminals. Also, before lifting the cap clear of the reservoir, allow the fluid in the tube on the underside of the cap to drain back into the reservoir rather than around your engine bay.

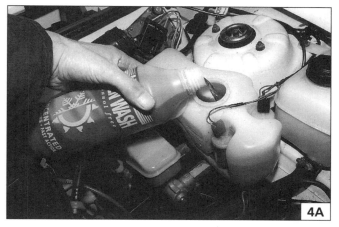

4A

Check that the brake fluid-level warning-light is operating, as follows: With the handbrake off - chock the wheels first and place the gear lever in first gear (or 'P' in the case of an automatic) - and the ignition switched on, lift the reservoir cap and its float clear of the fluid. The warning light on the dash should light up. If it does not, and the fluid level is satisfactory, have the circuit checked by a specialist without delay.

INSIDE INFORMATION: i) Check the ground on which the car has been parked, especially beneath the engine bay and each road wheel, for evidence of oil, clutch or brake fluid leaks. If any are found, investigate further before driving the car. ii) Brake fluid will damage painted surfaces if allowed to come into contact. Take care not to spill any but, if there is an accident, refit the master cylinder reservoir cap and wash off any accidental spillage immediately with hot soapy water.

☐ Job 4. Check windscreen wash level.

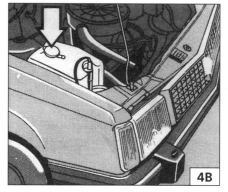

4B

4A. The screen wash reservoir is positioned on the right-hand side of the engine bay, as you look towards the rear of the car, and serves both windscreen and tailgate washers on hatchback models. The top is a simple push-fit cap. Screen wash additives are useful not only for cleaning the glass of 'traffic film', they also prevent the fluid freezing in cold weather - use as directed by the manufacturer.

4B. On models fitted with headlight wash/wipe systems, the reservoir is found on the left of the engine bay, just behind the headlight. (Illustration, courtesy Vauxhall Motors Limited)

Every 500 Miles - Around the Car

☐ Job 5. Check tyre pressures.

5. Use a reliable pressure gauge to check the pressure in each tyre, including the spare. Always check pressures with the tyres cold, never just after using the car which warms up the tyres and increases their pressures.

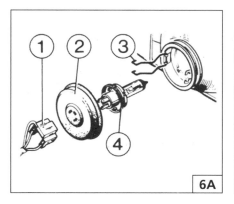

5

☐ Job 6. Check front lights.

6A

SAFETY FIRST!
i) It is important, for reasons both of safety and legality, that your car's lights work correctly and that the reflectors and lenses are in good condition. Replace faulty bulbs as soon as possible and get any damaged lens renewed. ii) If removing a headlight bulb, be aware that these items get extremely hot in use and are capable of burning fingers for some minutes after switching off; allow at least five minutes for the bulbs, and their holders, to cool before attempting to remove them. NEVER hold a headlight bulb while it is switched on - it will burn you before you can let it go!

Check the operation of the sidelights and headlights, on both full and dipped beam. If one sidelight, or one headlight beam fails to work on either side, the bulb has probably failed.

HEADLIGHTS

6A. These are the main parts of the headlight bulb/connector assembly: 1.- Connector & wires; 2. - Rubber dust cover; 3. - Spring clip; 4. - Bulb.

6B. **Removing the bulb:** From inside the engine bay, detach the connector and wires from the rear of the bulb, followed by the rubber dust cover.

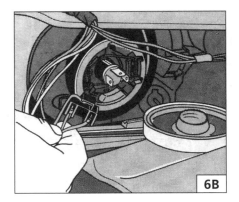

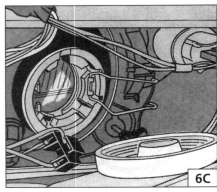

6C. Squeeze together the loops of the retaining clip and swivel it away to the side, allowing the bulb to be lifted out.

Refitting the bulb: Note there are three 'ears' attached to the flange of the bulb's base - these are spaced so that the bulb will only fit into the reflector the correct way round, i.e. when the three terminals at the rear of the bulb form an inverted 'U'.

> *making it easy!* If you touch a halogen headlight or driving light bulb with bare fingers, the microscopic transfer of grease will shorten its life. Handle with a piece of tissue paper if the original wrapping is no longer there. If the bulb is touched - no worries! Just wipe carefully clean with methylated spirit on a fresh, clean tissue or cloth.

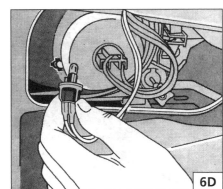

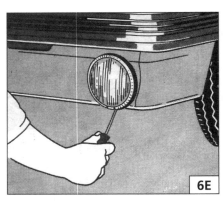

SIDELIGHTS

6D. Sidelights are integral with the headlight reflectors. The holder and the bulb into which it fits are both a simple push-fit.

FRONT FOG/AUXILIARY LIGHTS

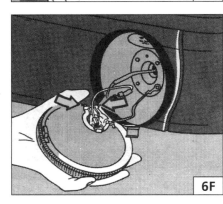

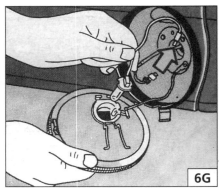

6E. If your car is fitted with front fog or driving lights, the bulb can be changed by first removing the small crosshead screw at the bottom of the rim.

6F. Lift out the light unit; the bulb, spring and connector are similar to those fitted to the headlight (see **6A**) but note the connector has only one wire connected to it. Be careful not to touch the bulb with bare fingers - hold it by the metal base.

6G. Squeeze the spring loops together and lift out the bulb, then detach the wire. Be sure to engage the lug on the bulb base with the recess in the reflector on reassembly.

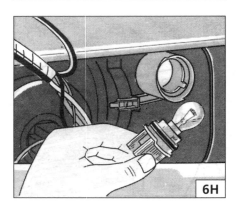

FRONT INDICATORS

CARS UP TO 1990

6H. The direction indicator bulb holder is removed from inside the engine bay and released by turning to the left; the bulb is a 'push-and-turn' bayonet fitting.

500 MILE/WEEKLY SERVICE

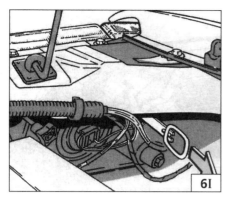

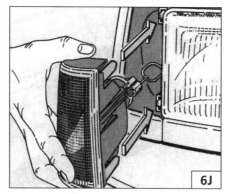

CARS FROM 1990

6I. The front indicator assembly is released from inside the engine bay by pulling on the looped retaining clip...

6J. ... which allows the assembly to be pulled forward; the bulb holder is turned anti-clockwise to release it, while the bulb is of the 'push-and-turn' type. (Illustrations, courtesy Vauxhall Motors Limited)

☐ **Job 7. Check side repeater indicators.**

7A. The outer lens is released by turning a quarter-turn to the left (anti-clockwise) and lifting it away.

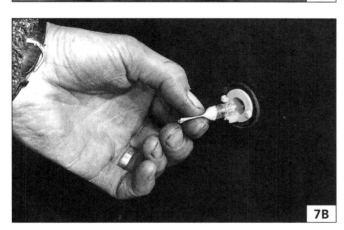

making it easy! 7B. The push-fit bulb is quite deeply recessed in the holder, leaving little on which to grip - if the bulb is defective and has to be replaced, apply a slip of masking tape to the bulb-glass, squeeze the excess into a small 'handle', as shown, and use this to withdraw the bulb.

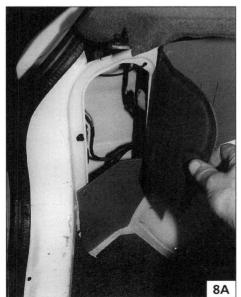

☐ **Job 8. Check rear lights and indicators.**

Check each of the rear lights in turn. On all models, tail light, indicator, reversing light and fog light bulbs are grouped together within the same bulb holder.

8A. The multi-bulb holder is located behind a trim panel which is released by turning a small button-catch.

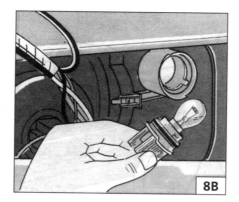

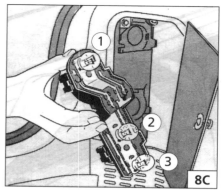

8B. Release the bulb holder by pulling gently on the two lugs shown being pinched between finger and thumb in the drawing. (Illustration, courtesy Vauxhall Motors Limited)

8C. Swing the bulb holder around so that the bulbs are exposed. The ratings and locations of the bulbs are as follows:

1. Tail and brake lights, 21/5 watt twin-filament bulb.
2. Indicator light - 21 watt bulb.
3. Reversing light on right hand-side; rear fog light on left hand-side - both 21 watt bulbs.

8D. The twin-filament side and brake light bulb has 'staggered' pins on its base so that the bulb can only be fitted one way.

□ Job 9. Check number plate light.

SAFETY FIRST!
Always disconnect the battery, especially before attemting to replace dash panel bulbs. See **FACT FILE - DISCONNECTING THE BATTERY.**

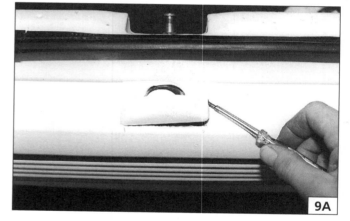

9A. This light is positioned in the rear bumper. Removal starts by prising the light gently upwards, using a small screwdriver to press in the spring catch at the side of the unit.

9B. By pressing the small 'tongue' at the end of the unit, the lens can be separated from the bulb holder.

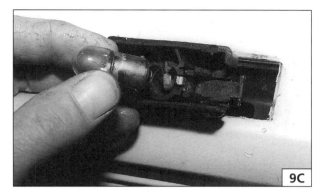

9C

9C. The 5 watt bulb is a 'push & twist' bayonet type.

☐ Job 10. Check interior light.

Check the interior light operates when either of the front doors is opened, or the lighting switch is pulled out when the doors are closed.

10A. The light unit is positioned in the car roof-lining, just behind the rear view mirror. Use a small screwdriver to carefully prise it from the recess. (Illustration, courtesy Vauxhall Motors Limited)

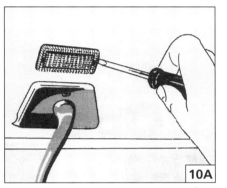

10A

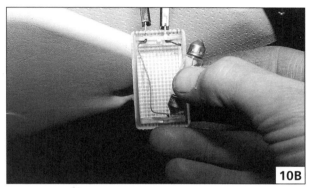

10B

10B. The bulb is of the 'festoon' type, with a contact at each end. It is held by the long sprung contact in the light unit and released by pulling lightly against the spring.

FACT FILE: FUSES

INSIDE INFORMATION: If a complete 'set' of bulbs fails to operate (and especially if other electrical components fail at the same time) check the fuses before suspecting any other fault. If a replacement fuse blows, you probably have a circuit fault. Seek specialist advice immediately. If the fuse protecting the circuit has not blown, it may be that a relay has failed. In this case, seek SPECIALIST SERVICE.

SAFETY FIRST!
Make sure that all the electrical circuits are switched off before removing or replacing a fuse. NEVER try to 'cure' a fault by fitting a fuse with a higher amperage rating than the one specified.

The fuses are colour coded, brown for 7.5 amp, red for 10 amp, blue for 15 amp, yellow for 20 amp, neutral or clear for 25 amp and green for 30 amp.

1

1. A 'blown' or defective fuse is indicated by a break in the wire (arrowed) which may appear melted.

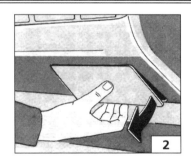

2

2. The fuse box is located to the right of the steering column, beneath a panel on the lower dashboard; the cover is retained by plastic lugs and simply pulls off.

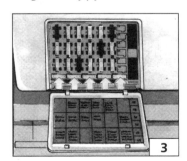

3

3. The underside of the cover gives a pictorial description of the circuits protected by each fuse, which are numbered. A more detailed description follows: (Illustrations, courtesy Vauxhall Motors Limited)

FUSE No.   CIRCUIT/ACCESSORY

1   Electric fuel pump (injection engines only).
2   Left-hand headlight main beam.
3   Right-hand headlight main beam.
4   Left-hand dipped beam; headlight range control motor (if fitted)
5   Right-hand dipped beam; rear fog light; headlight range control motor (if fitted).
6   Not used.
7   Direction indicators; brake lights.
8   Heated rear window.
9   Heater fan.
10 Radiator fan.
11 Electrically-operated door mirrors; electric front windows.
12 Front fog lights (if fitted).
13 Left-hand front parking light; left-hand rear light.
14 Right-hand front parking light; right-hand rear light; number plate light; instrument panel lights; engine compartment light (if fitted); headlights-on warning buzzer (if fitted).
15 Not used.
16 Interior light; boot/rear hatch light; hazard warning lights; clock; radio; central door locking (if fitted).
17 Windscreen wipers & washers; horn; tailgate wiper (if fitted).
18 Reversing light; cigar lighter; glove compartment light; fuel gauge; engine temperature gauge.

Job 11. Check windscreen wipers.

Lift the wiper blade away from the screen and examine the edge for damage or waviness which indicates that it is worn out. Give each blade a wipe with clean methylated spirit or replace.

BLADE RENEWAL

11A. Remove the blade by pulling it downwards away from the hooked end of the arm, then move the blade sideways...

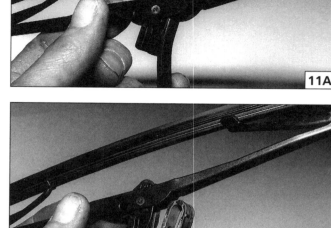
11A

11B. ...to allow the hook to pass through the gap in the blade. Fit the new blade by passing the hook through the gap, then push the connector up into the hook until it engages. Test the arm is securely held or there is a risk it might come off in use, resulting in damage to the windscreen.

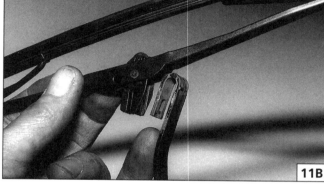
11B

Job 12. Check screen washers.

Check the aim of the washer jets on the windscreen, also the tailgate and headlights if washers for these are fitted to your car, and check the flow of fluid is sufficient. If one or other of the jets fails to work or directs the fluid to the wrong place (i.e. over the top of the car!) then it is likely the jet is blocked and/or the jet nozzle needs adjusting, as follows:

12. Use a safety pin to carefully clear the jets, and also to provide a means of directing the jet nozzle to where it is needed - ideally three-quarters of the way up the screen, towards the middle of the wiper arc.

The tailgate jet is similar to that on the windscreen; clear and adjust it in the same way.

If the washers refuse to work, but the pump can be heard to 'buzz' when operated and the jets are clear (and there is fluid in the reservoir!), it is possible the plastic/rubber pipes connecting the jets to the pump have come adrift. The pump is integral with the reservoir. Carefully trace the run of the pipes from the pump to the jets, making sure the pipe connections are in place.

12

making it easy! If the pump fails to operate, first check that the fuse (No.17 in the fuse box - see **FACT FILE - FUSES** after **Job 10**) hasn't 'blown', and that the wires to the pump are in place and the connections are clean and firm. If these items are found to be OK then the pump itself is probably defective - have it checked by your Vauxhall dealer.

Every 1,500 Miles - or Every Month, whichever comes first

Every 1,500 Miles - The Engine Bay

FACT FILE: DISCONNECTING THE BATTERY

Many vehicles depend on a constant power supply from the battery and you can find yourself in all sorts of trouble if you simply disconnect the battery on those vehicles. You might find that the car alarm will go off, you could find that the engine management system forgets all it ever 'learned' and the car will feel very strange to drive until it has re-programmed itself, and you could find that your radio refuses to operate again unless you key in the correct code. And if you've bought the car second-hand and don't know the code, you would have to send the set back to the manufacturer for re-programming. So, on later cars with engine management systems you must ensure that the vehicle has a constant power supply even though the battery is removed. To do so, you will need a separate 12 volt battery supply. You could put a self tapping screw into the positive lead near the battery terminal before disconnecting it, and put a positive connection to your other battery via this screw. But you would have to be EXTREMELY CAREFUL to wrap insulation tape around the connection so that no short is caused. The negative terminal on the other battery would also have to be connected to the cars bodywork.

A better way is to use something like the Sykes-Pickavant Computer Saver shown here. Clip the cables to your spare battery and plug into your cigarette lighter. (You may have to turn the ignition switch to the 'Auxiliary' setting to allow the

cigarette lighter to function).

You have to hold in the red button on the Computer Saver while inserting it into the cigarette lighter, and if two green lights still show after the button is released, you have a good connection and your battery can now be disconnected and removed.

Be sure not to turn on any of the car's equipment while the auxiliary battery is connected.

☐ **Job 13: Check battery electrolyte level.**

SAFETY FIRST!

i) The gas given off by a battery is highly explosive. Never smoke, use a naked flame or allow a spark to occur in the battery compartment. Never disconnect the battery (it can cause sparking) with the battery caps removed. ii) Batteries contain sulphuric acid. If the acid comes into contact with the skin or eyes, wash immediately with copious amounts of cold water and seek medical advice. iii) Do not check the battery levels within half an hour of the battery being charged with a separate battery charger because the addition of fresh water could then cause the highly acid and corrosive electrolyte to flood out of the battery.

13A

13A. Many vehicles were fitted from new with a sealed AC Freedom battery like that shown, but it is possible that yours may have a non-original item, fitted by a subsequent owner. If yours is the former type, then no maintenance is required. This section relates to the common type of replacement battery.

Remove the battery caps or covers and check the level of the electrolyte, i.e. the fluid inside each battery cell. You may find a small mirror handy for this, or a small torch to throw some light into the battery compartments.

making it easy! If you have difficulty seeing the electrolyte surface, tap the battery to make the liquid shimmer. The plates inside the battery should just be covered with electrolyte.

13B. If the level has fallen, top up with distilled water. NEVER use tap water, as it can destroy your battery. After replacing the covers, dry off the top of the battery. Check security of battery clamp at the base of the battery. If the terminals are furry with crystals or corroded, clean them by pouring boiling water over them. Dry the battery top and coat the terminals with Vaseline (petroleum jelly) or copper impregnated grease.

*INSIDE INFORMATION: i) Once water is mixed with acid inside the battery it won't freeze. So, in extremely cold weather, run the car (out of doors) so that you put a charge into the battery and this will mix the fresh water with the electrolyte, cutting out the risk of freezing and a cracked battery case. ii) If your battery persistently goes flat it may indicate a fault in the charging circuit, but it may be that the battery is nearing the end of its useful life. You can check the battery by measuring the specific gravity of the electrolyte - see **Job 81**.*

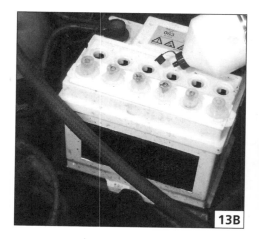

13B

Every 1,500 Miles - Around the Car

☐ Job 14. Check horn.

14. Operate the horn push to check that the horn sounds. If it does not, and the fuse has not blown, check the connections to the horn itself, which is mounted low down in front of the gearbox and accessible from beneath the front of the car. If the connections are poor, remake them, but remember that, with some circuits, one of the wires to the horn is live whenever the ignition is on. To be completely safe, disconnect battery before removing either cable from the horn, or seek **SPECIALIST SERVICE**.

14

☐ Job 15. Check tyre treads.

15. Check the tyres for tread depth, using a depth gauge and note that, in the UK, the minimum legal tread depth is 1.6 mm. Tyres are not at their safest at that level and you may want to replace them earlier. Also check both sides of each tyre for uneven wear, bulges or other damage to the side walls. Raise each wheel of the ground, using an axle stand, otherwise you won't be able to see the inside of each tyre properly, nor will you be able to check that part of the tyre which is in contact with the ground.

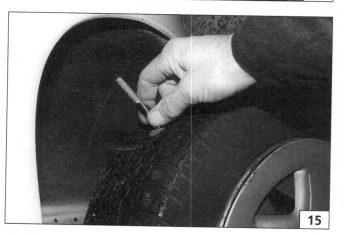

15

☐ Job 16. Check spare wheel.

The spare wheel lives in a compartment under the floor at the rear of the luggage compartment in saloons and hatchbacks. In the van, it lives under the rear of the load floor. Check the tyre pressure. We suggest that you keep it a few psi above the pressures of your road tyres and reduce it to the proper level if necessary should you have to use it. When allocating the wheel as a spare you should have checked that the tread depth was legal, as shown in **Job 15**.

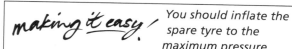
making it easy! You should inflate the spare tyre to the maximum pressure recommended for high speed or load running. The, if you have a puncture while on a journey, you'll be okay. It's always easier to carry a tyre pressure gauge with you and let some air out rather than put some in.

SAFETY FIRST!
Tyres which show uneven wear tell their own story, if only you know how to speak the language! If any tyre is worn more on one side than another, consult your main dealer or a tyre specialist. It probably means that your suspension or steering is out of adjustment - probably a simple tracking job but conceivably symptomatic of suspension damage, so have it checked. If a tyre is worn more in the centre or on the edges, it could mean that your tyre pressures are wrong but, once again, have the car checked. Incorrectly inflated tyres wear rapidly, can cause the car's handling to become dangerous and can even cause the car to consume noticeably more fuel. When checking your tyres, don't forget to include the spare.

☐ Job 17. Touch-up paintwork.

17. Touch-up stone chips with a small brush to prevent rust. If rust is already showing, treat first with a proprietary rust killer, following the instructions on the package. Allow new paint to harden before polishing.

☐ Job 18. Valet interior.

18. Regularly vacuuming the seats and carpets will not only make the car more pleasant to drive, but will remove a surprising amount of abrasive grit and dust, the main cause of 'baldness' in these items. For stains and grease-marks use one of the many domestic upholstery cleaning materials, although some severe stains can only be effectively removed by the use of white or methylated spirit - test these on an unseen area first though, to check for colour-fastness of the upholstery.

☐ Job 19. Improve visibility.

19. After leathering off the windows, go over them with a proprietary glass cleaner to get them sparkling clean. You will be surprised at the difference this makes. Also clean the door and interior mirrors and check them for any damage.

Every 3,000 Miles - or Every Three Months, whichever comes first

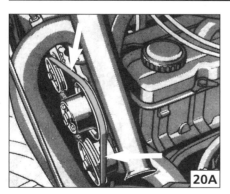

Every 3,000 Miles - The Engine Bay

First carry out Jobs 1 to 5.

☐ Job 20. Check alternator drive belt.

PETROL ENGINED MODELS WITHOUT POWER STEERING, UP TO 1990

20A. Check the tension of the alternator drive belt by deflecting it with firm finger or thumb pressure at a point halfway along the longest 'run' of the belt. The amount of movement should be no more than 12mm (0.5in.). Also check the general condition of the belt, looking for signs of cracking and frayed edges, and also for signs of 'polishing' of the belt's surface, which can indicate age and possibly imminent failure! (Illustration, courtesy Vauxhall Motors Limited)

SAFETY FIRST!
Disconnect the battery before working on drive belts so that the engine cannot inadvertently be started or turned over, causing personal injury.

20B. Tension the drivebelt (if necessary) by slackening the upper alternator bracket bolt shown - loosen it just sufficiently to allow movement of the alternator but maintaining a degree of 'grip'.

20B

>
> *making it easy!* 20C. Use a length of wood (such as the handle of a hammer) to apply sideways pressure to the alternator body (as near to the drive end bracket as possible) moving it away from the engine against belt tension. Providing the alternator-to-bracket bolt has been loosened just sufficiently to allow movement, the alternator should remain tensioned while the adjuster-stay nut and bolt are tightened.

However, if you find this procedure difficult (it takes practice!) ask an assistant to hold the wooden lever while you tighten the bolt. IMPORTANT NOTE: DON'T lever so hard that you crack the alternator casing - it's relatively brittle!

20C

☐ Job 21. Drain fuel filter.

DIESEL ENGINES ONLY

Drain the diesel fuel filter to remove any water residue.

> **SAFETY FIRST!**
> **Whenever you are dealing with diesel fuel, it's essential to protect your hands by wearing plastic gloves.**

INSIDE INFORMATION: The fuel filter on diesel engines is designed so that any water which passes through it will collect at the bottom of the filter housing, immediately above the drain plug. This means that any water present will be drained first and the drain plug can be closed as soon as fuel begins to flow. Under normal conditions, the amount of water likely to be present is usually very small, although under extreme conditions of high humidity or widely varying day-to-night temperatures, more will be present, so the careful diesel owner may wish to check the filter every 3,000 miles.

21

21. The fuel filter is located at the rear of the engine bay. Start by disconnecting the short length of hose from the bracket and allow it to hang down - place a container beneath it to catch any fuel and/or water that will drain off. Loosen the bleed screw at the top of the filter housing (top arrow) then loosen the bottom drain plug (lower arrow) to allow the contents of the filter to drain. Tighten the bleed and drain screws afterwards. (Illustration, courtesy Vauxhall Motors Limited)

☐ Job 22. Renew diesel engine oil.

DIESEL ENGINES ONLY

OPTIONAL: This job is specified by Vauxhall at 4,500 miles but with no time limit; we include it here regardless, but if your car only covers a small mileage, say 1,000 miles or less in three months, then you may want to include it in the six month checks described later in this chapter.

Refer to **Job 42** later in this chapter for precise instructions - the diesel engine is identical to the petrol version as far as oil changing is concerned and follows the same procedure.

☐ Job 23. Replace diesel engine oil filter.

OPTIONAL: This job is specified by Vauxhall at 4,500 miles with no time limit specified, but as above, we include it here.

Refer to **Job 42** later in this chapter for precise instructions - the diesel engine is identical to the petrol version as far as oil-filter changing is concerned and follows the same procedure.

24

☐ **Job 24. Check brake and fuel lines.**

SAFETY FIRST! AND SPECIALIST SERVICE
Fuel injection systems remain pressurised even when the engine is switched off and this requires a special procedure to make it safe - UNDER NO CIRCUM-STANCES loosen or remove fuel pipes on a fuel injection system. If pipework requires repair, take the car immediately to a fuel injection specialist or Vauxhall dealer.

24. Make a physical check of all the pipework and connections in the engine bay. Bend the flexible fuel lines in order to expose hairline cracks or deterioration which may not be immediately obvious. Look for signs of rust or tell-tale fluid marks on brake pipes and unions. Start the engine and check visually that there are no fuel leaks.

SAFETY FIRST!
As everyone is aware, petrol is highly flammable and only a small spark is necessary to ignite it, with potentially disastrous consequences. If a fuel leak, (however slight) is suspected or detected: don't smoke, switch off all car accessories (but don't disconnect the battery which often creates sparks as the terminals are removed) and mop-up any spilt or dripping fuel with rags which should by take immediately out of doors. Don't drive the car until professional advice is sought and the problem rectified.

25A

☐ **Job 25. Check air filter.**

ALL MODELS EXCEPT 1.6 LITRE INJECTION AND DIESEL ENGINES

25A. The round 'pancake' type air filter on these models is checked by first removing the three central bolts (early models) or cross-head screws (later types), then releasing the clips around the edge of the filter housing. The upper half of the housing can then be lifted away to reveal the filter itself. Check it is clean, and not clogged with dirt or deposits of oil from the crankcase breather pipe, otherwise renew it.

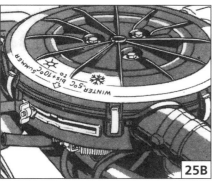

25B

25B. Additionally, on the 1.0 litre OHV engine, the air filter housing is provided with a flap to control the temperature of the air drawn into the engine. The flap has three positions - SUMMER, INTERMEDIATE and WINTER, controlled by a lever fitted with a wing nut which operates in a slot on the side of the housing. These positions correspond to the following temperatures:

SUMMER setting: above 0 degrees centigrade.
INTERMEDIATE setting: O deg down to -5 degrees C.
WINTER setting: below -5 degrees C.

To change the flap position, slacken the wing nut and slide it towards the appropriate setting, tightening afterwards. (Illustration, courtesy Vauxhall Motors Limited)

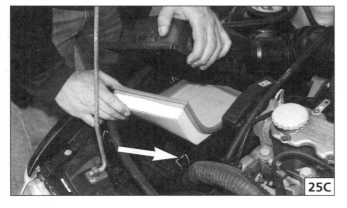

25C

FUEL INJECTION AND DIESEL MODELS ONLY

25C. The filter housing is situated in the lower-left front corner of the engine bay, as you look to the rear of the vehicle. The top cover is secured by four spring clips and, on later models, a cross-head screw. Remove the clips and screw (if fitted).

Every 3,000 Miles - Around the Car

☐ Job 26. Check wheel bolts.

Check the tightness of all wheel bolts. The wheel brace supplied with the car is merely intended for use in an emergency and we strongly recommend the use of a torque wrench for this job. This will avoid over-tightening the nuts and avoids the danger of stripped threads or over-stressed bolts.

INSIDE INFORMATION: To 'torque' the wheel nuts correctly, first slacken each nut and check that the threads aren't stiff or corroded, then tighten with the wrench to a torque of 9kgm (65 lb.ft).

☐ Job 27. Check handbrake adjustment.

27A. Apply the handbrake, without pressing the release knob at the end of the lever, and count the number of 'clicks' the lever goes through before the brake is firmly applied: the brake should ideally lock at between 2 and 4 clicks. If more or less than these figures, the cable can be adjusted as described in **Job 101**.

Raise the rear of the vehicle sufficiently to allow the rear wheels to turn and to provide sufficient working clearance, and support the body on axle stands. Fully release the handbrake and (on models from 1984) apply the footbrake firmly several times to ensure the automatic adjusters on each wheel are fully 'set' and the shoes centralised in the drums.

MODELS UP TO 1984

Ensure the rear brakes are adjusted correctly - see **Job 66** before proceeding; adjusting the shoes will also take-up some of the 'slack' in the handbrake cable and you may find adjustment of the cable is unnecessary after this is carried out.

27B. Apply the handbrake by two or three clicks of the ratchet, when it should just be possible to turn each wheel by heavy hand pressure. If one or other of the wheels is too stiff to turn, or turns freely, then adjustment may be necessary. However, the cause could be the result of wear or sticking of the mechanism, so check these before proceeding - see **Job 66**. Note that the wheels should most certainly be 'locked' at four or five clicks of the ratchet.

SPECIALIST SERVICE: Due to the design of the handbrake cables and the method of adjustment, a 'rolling-road' brake tester is required so that application of the handbrake results in an equal 'pull' on both sides of the car. Although an 'adjuster' is present on the rear torsion beam, mal-adjustment will produce unequal braking and instability, so we recommend the actual adjustment be carried out by a reputable garage or Vauxhall agent.

☐ Job 28. Check windscreen.

Check the windscreen for chips and scratches which are a potential MoT failure point depending on their location and size - see *Chapter 7, Getting Through the MoT*, for what is and is not acceptable according to UK regulations. Most small chips less than 10mm wide can be repaired by specialists, while light scoring can often be polished out by the same people.

☐ Job 29. Clean and lubricate aerial.

29. Clean each section of an extending aerial with a spray lubricant and work the aerial up and down a few times. Do not leave excess lubricant on the aerial sections as this will simply encourage the adherence of grit and dirt.

INSIDE INFORMATION: With electrically operated aerials it is especially important to keep the sections clean, otherwise the operating motor and/or gears will be over-stressed and quickly fail.

SAFETY FIRST!
Don't work beneath a vehicle supported only on axle stands with someone else sitting inside trying the handbrake. It's too risky that their movements will cause the vehicle to fall off the axle stands. Make sure that you are well clear of the raised vehicle when someone is inside it. Read carefully the information at the start of this chapter on lifting and supporting the vehicle.

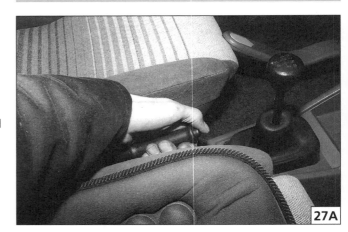
27A

27B

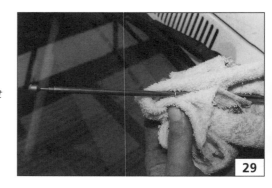
29

30A.

Every 3,000 Miles - Under the Car

☐ Job 30. Check exhaust system and mountings.

30A. Examine the silencers (as far as safe access will allow) for signs of corrosion, especially along seams and at the ends where the pipes are welded. Check the system joints where the pipe sections are joined together for tell-tale 'soot' marks indicating a leak.

> *making it easy!* If you suspect a leak but it's location isn't obvious, start the engine - car out of doors - and try pressurising the system by holding a piece of board or something similar so that it blocks off the tailpipe. Under pressure, the leak should be more noisy, enabling you to track down its position. Get an assistant to help you if you can, but remember an exhaust system can get very hot and touching the pipework can cause severe burns.

30B.

30B. If exhaust system mountings break, perish or come loose, the extra stresses on the exhaust system could cause the pipes or silencers to fracture. Always replace worn or damaged mountings before they break - it can save much hassle and expense later on. As well as a visual test, check the mountings by grasping the (cold) exhaust tailpipe with a piece of rag and 'shaking' it, listening for any rattles or bumps that indicate it is contacting the under-side of the car - usually the result of weak or damaged mountings.

SAFETY FIRST!
Never run your car's engine in an enclosed space, only ever out of doors. Exhaust gases can be toxic and an exhaust leak can allow gases into the car as you drive along. Check the condition and security of the entire exhaust system, looking carefully for any signs of corrosion on the pipes and silencers, or leakage at the joints. Replace gaskets if necessary.

☐ Job 31. Check brake and fuel lines.

31A. Carefully examine all the pipes under the car for signs of rust or weeping unions. Deep pitting indicates severe rusting and this, or even the slightest of leaks can render the car dangerous to drive. It must not be driven until the problem has been rectified. Also check the pipes are held securely in their clips, and that there is no physical damage to the pipes from incorrectly placed jacks or as a result of driving over obstacles and flattening the pipes.

31B. Bend all flexible hoses to show up signs of cracking rubber - if any are found, the hose should be replaced as soon as possible. The hoses should also be free from bulges or chafing marks.

INSIDE INFORMATION: Bend the hoses double, and check visually near the union ends for any signs of wear or damage. Also, have an assistant press hard on the brake pedal while the hoses are checked for bulging. Any hose not in perfect condition should be replaced as soon as possible.

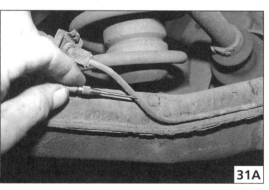

31A.

☐ Job 32. Check steering rack gaiters.

SAFETY FIRST!
This operation requires the steering to be moved from lock-to-lock so the use of axle stands is essential. Refer to Raising the Car Safely, at the beginning of this chapter for details of how to do

The steering rack gaiters - also sometimes called 'boots' - are made of convoluted rubber, their purpose being to prevent dirt and grit getting inside the steering rack mechanism while keeping the lubricant inside it, and at the

31B.

same time allowing the 'push-pull' motion of the steering arms as the steering wheel is turned.

After a few years of continual movement plus attack from stones, grit and other road dirt, the gaiter can split leading to dirt and water ingress, which will quickly ruin the rack mechanism.

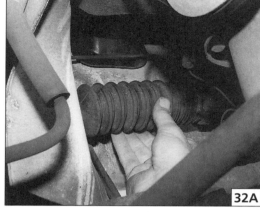

32A. The gaiters (there are two: left and right-hand) are located on the bulkhead behind the lower half of the engine; that shown is on the drivers' side of the car, viewed from beneath the wheel arch. With the steering turned on full lock (turned fully to the left or right) check the gaiter, looking for splits, chafing, perishing etc. Now turn the steering fully in the opposite direction and check the other gaiter in the same way.

32B. Make sure the gaiter securing clips are firm and doing their job. Clips can be metal bands either sprung or twisted into position, metal clips, or plastic bands commonly known as 'cable-ties'.

If one or both of the gaiters are defective, replace them as follows:

INSIDE INFORMATION: Renewing a steering rack gaiter isn't a particularly difficult job, but it does call for a special tool - viz. a 'ball-joint separator', and for the 'tracking' of the front wheels to be checked professionally afterwards via a **SPECIALIST SERVICE.**

First slacken the bolts of the wheel nearest the defective gaiter, before raising and supporting the front of the vehicle - see *Raising the Car Safely* on *Page 16* for details of how to do this safely. Remove the wheel completely.

Remove the track-rod-end as described in **Job 68B**.

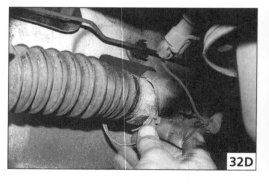

32C. The clips securing each end of the gaiter can now be removed, the small outer clip of the type shown can be released with pliers and passed over the gaiter.

32D. The larger tensioned metal-band type can be undone by levering the free-end of the clip upwards with a screwdriver, while the 'cable tie' type can simply be cut off with wire cutters.

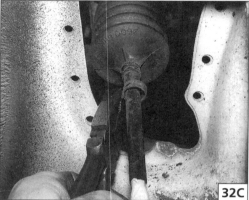

32E. The gaiter can now be slid-off along the steering arm, and a new one slipped into place. Note that no lubrication of the inner mechanism of the 'rack is necessary on this particular model but take care not to allow dirt or grit to settle on the exposed parts.

32F. Fit new clips, which should have been supplied with the new gaiter; replace the track-rod-end; fit the wheel and lower the vehicle to the ground, finally tightening the wheel-bolts.

IMPORTANT NOTE: The steering 'track' will need to be checked by a specialist, otherwise poor steering response and rapid tyre wear can result.

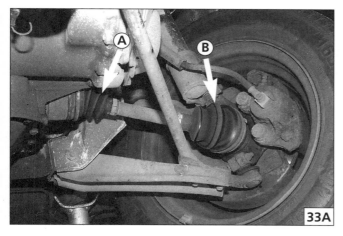

33A

33B

☐ Job 33. Check drive shaft gaiters.

33A. Check the inner ('A' in the photo) and outer (B) drive shaft gaiters. Check for condition of the rubber and for security of the fastenings at each end. Make sure there are no splits, pin-holes or signs of chafing. Any trace of grease leaking from the gaiter requires further investigation and probably replacement.

33B. Check both driveshafts in the same way, but note that as the outer joints are subject to a greater range of movement than the inner gaiters, wear is more common there. Put the steering on full lock while each gaiter is checked, so that the rubber is 'stretched' and any weakness or leak will be easier to spot.

SPECIALIST SERVICE: If there are any doubts as to the condition of the gaiters, or if they are obviously in need of replacement, consult your Vauxhall dealer for advice, as a number of special tools and equipment is required to change them.

☐ Job 34. Check underside of car for leaks.

Check along the car for any signs of fluid or oil leaks. Oil leaks are likely to come from the engine area and are probably a matter of gaskets or oil seals needing renewing. They should be cured because, apart from costing you a lot of money in oil, could cause low oil level with possible bearing failure. Some leaks are simple to cure, others not so simple. Decide, with the help of a workshop manual, if you feel competent to tackle any leaks you find. If not, seek early SPECIALIST SERVICE.

FACT FILE:
EMERGENCY GAITER REPAIR

33C. There are a number of 'easy-fit' gaiter replacement kits on the market, their main purpose being to enable the gaiter to be renewed without special tools or any dismantling.

33D. These gaiters are split longitudinally, which allows them to be simply placed over the joint, and then joined and sealed with a special cyano-acrylate glue. Fitting this type of gaiter successfully relies on absolute cleanliness as oil or grease will prevent the adhesive setting properly. Full instructions are supplied with each kit. (Illustration, courtesy Partco)

33C

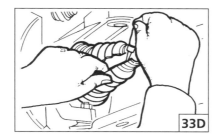

33D

☐ Job 35. Clean mud traps.

35. Use a strong water jet to clean away any build-up of mud and silt on the underside of the car, particularly the corners and extremities of the wheel arches.

Every 3,000 Miles - Road Test

☐ Job 36. Clean controls.

The door handles, steering wheel, switches and gear lever knob may well have become greasy from handling while you were carrying out the service. Clean them with a rag moistened with hot water and a little detergent.

35

making it easy! Sometimes, because the oil from a leak tends to spread, it is difficult to spot exactly where the leak is coming from. One way of finding it is to clean everything off with a de-greasing agent, dry it, then dust along the joint with talcum powder. When the engine is subsequently run, an oil leak will quickly show-up as a stain on the powder.

☐ Job 37. Check instruments and controls.

Switch on the ignition while sitting in the driving seat and check that all the warning lights which should come on, do come on. Warning lights which do not work are useless as warnings! Non-functioning may be just a case of a blown bulb, but it may be a symptom of deeper electrical trouble. If changing a bulb does not cure the problem, or if the warning lights fail to go out when they should, seek **SPECIALIST SERVICE** from an auto electrician. Check that all the switches are secure and working.

FACT FILE: ENGINE CONTROL INDICATOR

On later cars, the engine control indicator lights up when the ignition is switched on and remains illuminated during starting. Goes out shortly after engine starts to run.

The duration of injection, ignition, idling and overrun cut-off are controlled electronically.

If the indicator lights up, a fault has occurred. The electronic system switches to an emergency running programme so that driving may be continued. Consult a Vauxhall Dealer to remedy the fault.

Do not drive for a lengthy period with the engine control indicator illuminated, as this may damage the catalytic converter, increase fuel consumption and impare the vehicle's driveability.

If the engine control indicator lights up briefly and then goes out again this is of no significance. (Illustration, courtesy Vauxhall Motors Limited)

ENGINE CONTROL INDICATOR

☐ Job 38. Check throttle action.

38A. Operate the throttle pedal several times to check that it is smooth over its complete travel. A throttle pedal which is stiff or, worse still, which sticks, can be dangerous as well as making driving a misery. Apply a little oil to the pedal pivot arrowed. If your car has a manual choke control check the smoothness of operation of the choke knob.

38B. INSIDE INFORMATION: If neither throttle nor choke are as smooth as they should be, check the route of the cables to make sure there are no sharp bends or kinks and check that the inner cable isn't fraying where it comes out of the outer casing (arrowed). Later throttle cables with a nylon inner sleeve are much smoother in operation that the older steel sleeve sort. If the fault for a jerky or stiff throttle pedal or choke knob is not the cable, check the linkage at the carburettor for stiffness and lubricate if necessary.

☐ Job 39. Check clutch action.

Operate the clutch pedal several times with the engine switched off. The action of the pedal should be smooth, once the initial take-up of the clutch mechanism occurs - this can be felt as a resistance to the pedal after the first inch or so of movement. Repeat the test with the engine running and listen for any whine or 'scrubbing' noise from the gearbox area when depressing the pedal, which can indicate a worn clutch release bearing, or possible problem with the clutch plate itself.

39A. If the pedal action feels jerky, 'dry' or heavy, first try lubricating the pivots, located at the top of the pedal, and also at the clutch/gearbox as shown, with light oil.

39B. If the fault persists then the clutch cable can be suspected - the usual cause is fraying of the inner 'stranded' cable causing it to bind in the outer sheath (arrowed).

INSIDE INFORMATION: Replacing the clutch cable isn't a particularly difficult job in theory, but in practice the restricted working area in the upper reaches of the footwell, coupled with the need to use two hands (preferably three!) to manipulate the cable and automatic adjusting mechanism makes this an awkward and often frustrating job for the inexperienced! Don't forget - if you start the job but can't finish it, the car will be undriveable and could involve a costly tow-in charge to the nearest garage. Unless you are experienced or live next door to an understanding mechanic, seek SPECIALIST SERVICE for this item.

FACT FILE:
ROAD TEST: BRAKES AND STEERING

SAFETY FIRST!
Carry out the following tests only in daylight, in clear, dry conditions. Choose a quiet road when there are no other road users or pedestrians about. Use your mirrors to make sure there are no other vehicles following you before carrying out brake tests.

☐ Job 40. Road test: brakes and steering.

Only a proper brake tester at an MoT testing station can check the operation of the brakes accurately enough for the MoT test, but you can rule out some of the most obvious braking problems on a short road test in the following way. Always check the brakes at low speed first, before attempting to brake from higher speeds. Drive at about 20 mph, dip the clutch and, with your hands only lightly gripping the wheel, try braking first gently, then harder, though there is no need to do an 'emergency' stop. Ideally, the car should pull up in a perfectly straight line. If the steering wheel kicks in your fingers, if there are any 'clonks' or other noises from underneath, if the car drifts heavily to one side as you brake, or if the brake pedal does not feel firm in

operation, drive home very slowly and carefully to investigate further.

If all seems well, repeat the braking tests from a higher speed, say about 40 mph. Again, the car should, ideally, pull up in a straight line. If it drifts just gently to the left when you are on the nearside of the road, this may be due to road camber. Try to repeat the test on a non-cambered stretch of road or find a one-way street where you can try on the other side of the road to see if opposite camber has the same effect.

Check that the steering feels positive, does not kick back unduly over rough surfaces and that the car runs in a straight line when you are holding the steering wheel only lightly. Again, slight drifting may be due to road camber, but more persistent drifting needs investigating. Check that the steering self-centres when accelerating out of both left and right hand turns and, if you can find a suitably deserted stretch of road, pull the car from side to side to see that it straightens itself up. This check can be carried out at quite low speed, 15 to 20 mph is sufficient to show up any faults.

Braking and steering are a vital part of a car's safety. If you find any faults, or even if you are uneasy about anything, seek **SPECIALIST SERVICE** before you carry on using the car.

☐ Job 41. Check C.V. joints for noise (part of road test).

FRONT WHEEL DRIVE CARS ONLY

Before concluding the 'road' test (a deserted car park is more suitable for this check), put the car through a series of left and right-hand turns with the steering on full-lock, and listen for any knocking or deep 'clunks' from the front of the vehicle, especially under slight acceleration. Any such noise can indicate wear in the driveshaft constant-velocity (C.V.) joints - have them checked professionally by a reputable garage and don't delay having the joints replaced if defective.

Every 6,000 Miles or Every Six Months - whichever comes first

Every 6,000 Miles - The Engine Bay

First carry out Jobs 1 to 5 and 25 to 28.

☐ Job 42. Change engine oil and filter.

Probably the one service operation on which most DIY motorists will 'cut their teeth' is an engine oil change - that is emptying the old oil out through the sump drain plug situated beneath the engine and, later, pouring in a specified quantity of new oil through the oil filler, found at the top of the engine. And no matter how technically complex the engine, an oil change still remains basically a simple operation.

making it easy! Apart from small differences in location of the oil filter and the sump drain plug, the procedure is the same for all models. Before draining the sump, run the engine (if cold) for around five minutes to warm the oil slightly, so that it will drain more freely - but not so hot that it will scald. Use an oil drainage container to catch the oil as it drains from the sump - note that the oil will fall in an arc away from the drain hole, so position the container to allow for this. Spread newspaper on the floor beneath the engine bay to protect it from oil spills and drips.

SAFETY FIRST!
*Refer to the section on **ENGINE OILS** in **Chapter 1, Safety First**, before carrying out the following work. It is essential to wear rubber or plastic gloves since used engine oil can be carcinogenic. Oil drain plugs are often so tight that they seem to have been fitted by a gorilla with toothache. i) Take care that the spanner does not slip causing injury to the hand or head. (Use a socket or ring spanner - never an open-ended spanner - with as little offset as possible so that the spanner is near to the line of the bolt.) ii) Ensure that your spanner is positioned so that you pull downwards if at all possible. Take great care that the effort needed to undo the drain plug does not cause the vehicle to fall on you or slide off the ramps or axle stands - remember those wheel chocks! iii) Refer to information at the start of this Chapter on **Raising a Car Safely**.*

42A. This is the location of the oil drain plug on the great majority of Nova engines, viewed from under the car. As we stated previously, the plug will often be tight and require some force to move initially, when it may suddenly 'give' and offer little or no resistance - be careful not to rap your knuckles! Rubber or plastic gloves can compromise your grip on the spanner, so it may be wise to leave them off for the initial 'tug', but remember to don them immediately the plug has been slackened and before removing the plug completely, as some oil will inevitably spill onto your hands.

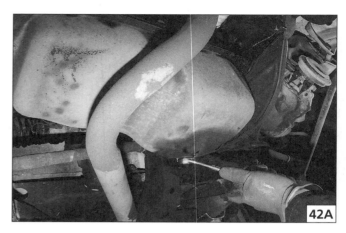
42A

42B. Once the plug has started to move in its thread it can be undone with the (gloved) fingers. Remember to hold onto the plug when fully unscrewed.

42C. Be ready to reposition your bowl - the angle of 'spurt' changes as the oil flows out of the sump! Allow at least ten minutes for the oil to drain completely.

42D. Remember to replace the drain plug once the oil has FULLY drained, and use a new copper or nylon washer which you can buy from the accessory shop or garage where you bought your oil. Buy it at the same time, then you won't forget it.

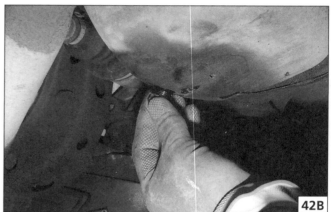
42B

making it easy! It isn't necessary to use excessive force when refitting the sump plug. Simply grip the spanner so that the thumb rests on the spanner head, thereby limiting the amount of leverage that can be applied; use 'firm' pressure only. Before refitting the plug, wipe around the drain hole with a piece of clean cloth to remove any dirt, and check that the sealing washer is fitted.

SAFETY FIRST!
DON'T pour the old oil down the drain - it's both illegal and irresponsible. Your local council waste disposal site will have special facilities for disposing of it safely. Moreover, don't mix anything else with it, as this will prevent it from being recycled.

OIL CARE
FOLLOW THE CODE

Also, see page 4.

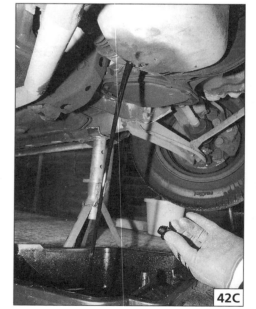
42C

42E. The oil filter is the familiar screw-on, throw-away thin metal cartridge type and can be reached either from above or from underneath the car. The easiest way to remove this type of filter is with a strap or chain wrench similar to that shown, which you can buy from any accessory shop.

42D

42E

42F. One full turn of the filter using the wrench is usually enough to get it started, after which it can be unscrewed by hand. Note that some oil loss will occur, so position an oil tray or container under the engine to catch it. It's also a good idea to place a cloth round the filter when unscrewing it to prevent the oil dribbling over your (gloved!) hand and down your arm! Clean the filter sealing face on the engine with a clean rag.

42G. Make sure the rubber sealing ring is properly fitted to the new filter, then apply a smear of clean engine oil to the ring to prevent it buckling as the filter is screwed home.

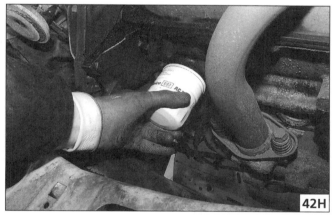

42H. Screw the new filter onto the threaded stub, taking care to avoid cross-threading. Most filters have tightening instructions printed in the casing, but essentially all filters are fitted by screwing on by hand only. When the sealing ring contacts the face on the engine, tighten it a further three-quarters of a turn and leave it - there's no need to tighten it any further as this will only distort the sealing ring and make it difficult to remove the filter next time.

42I. Lower the car to the ground, and pour in fresh oil gradually so as not to get a sudden air lock in the valve cover which can make the oil spurt out over the top. Dip the level occasionally, allowing time for the oil to drain down into the sump. After filling, run the engine for a few minutes to allow the oil to circulate and to fill the filter. Switch off and dip the level again, finally topping up if necessary. Check underneath the car, especially in the areas of the sump plug and filter, making sure that there are no oil leaks.

☐ Job 43. Clean and check spark plugs.

making it easy! 43A. Mark each plug lead with a spot of paint - typists' correction fluid is used by many mechanics as it is easy to apply and dries very quickly. Mark them from the drivebelt end of the engine in the sequence one, two, three and four 'dots'. (Identification of the plug leads is important as if incorrectly replaced, the engine will not run!)

43A

SAFETY FIRST!
You may minimise the risk of shock when the engine is running by wearing thick rubber gloves and by NEVER working on the system in damp weather or when standing on damp ground. Read **Chapter 1, Safety First!** *before carrying out any work on the ignition system.*

43B. Once this is done the plug caps can be pulled off. Be careful not to tug on the lead itself as you may pull it from the cap, which will remain on the plug!

43C. Using a suitably long spark plug spanner or socket extension, unscrew the spark plugs. They may be 'tight' to begin with so take care to keep the plug spanner or socket in line with the plug body, otherwise the porcelain insulator of the plug can break.

43B

INSIDE INFORMATION: If you are trying to remove a plug which gets ever tighter as you turn it, there's every possibility that it is cross threaded. Once out, it probably won't go back in again. Tighten it up again and take the car to a Vauxhall Dealer or specialist who may be able to clean up the threads with a purpose-made tool. If this can't be done, he will have to add a thread insert to your cylinder head. It pays to take great care when removing and fitting spark plugs, especially when dealing with aluminium cylinder heads!

43D. Clean the plug electrodes by vigorous use of a brass-bristled wire brush to remove any carbon deposits. If the electrodes of the plug look 'rounded' and worn (compare them to a new plug) they should be replaced.

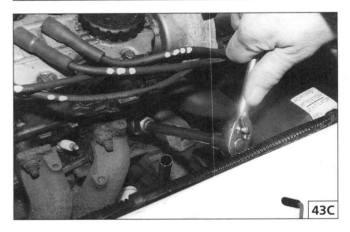
43C

43E. If using a flat feeler gauge select the 'blade' of the correct thickness (see *Chapter 8, Facts and Figures*) and slide it between the electrodes as shown. The gap between the two electrodes should provide a sliding fit, with no 'slack'. If necessary, adjust the gap using a pair of snipe-nosed (thin, pointed jaws) pliers, carefully bending the curved side-electrode towards or away from the tip of the centre electrode, until the feeler gauge fits the gap as described. Special gapping tools are available from accessory shops which make this easy and their use carries little risk of damaging the plug, which can occur if the electrode is clumsily moved by use of a screwdriver or pliers.

43D

43E

Replace the plugs when the gaps are correct, adding just a slight smear of grease to the threads to make future removal easier. There is no need to screw the plugs down with great force - just tighten them firmly.

making it easy! Leave the spark plug in the socket spanner while using the wire brush - this is kinder on the fingers and lessens the risk of dropping the plug and breaking it.

44A

☐ **Job 44. Clean and check ignition components.**

> **SAFETY FIRST!**
> **THE ELECTRONIC IGNITION SYSTEM INVOLVES VERY HIGH VOLTAGES!** *All manufacturers recommend that only trained personell should go near the high tension-circuit (coil, distributor and HT wiring) and it is ESSENTIAL that anyone wearing a medical pacemaker device does not go near the ignition system. Also, stroboscopic timing requires the engine to be running - take great care that parts of the timing lights or parts of you don't get caught up in the moving parts! Don't wear loose clothing or hair.*

*INSIDE INFORMATION: Two types of distributor have been fitted to the Nova, depending on engine and year of manufacture. They are either the Bosch, identified by its brown cap, or the Delco-Remy, which has a black cap. The latter type uses screws for securing the cap, while the Bosch uses spring clips - see **44A**.*

First check the position of the distributor on your engine by referring to the **Engine Bay Layouts** section at the beginning of this chapter.

44B

44C

44A. Undo the two cross-head screws (Delco-Remy) or spring clips (Bosch - shown here) and lift the distributor cap away. Clean the HT leads and check their exterior surfaces for signs of surface cracking, and loose connections where the leads fit on to the plug connectors and into the distributor cap.

44B. Clean the distributor cap inside and out and check for any signs of 'tracking' - burnt lines where carbon has lodged in a faint crack to provide a short circuit for the HT current. Any signs of tracking means that the cap could let you down with poor starting and bad running at any time as well as increasing your fuel consumption. Check also that the centre carbon brush still has plenty of length and that it is springy enough to bear on the centre of the rotor arm. Check the studs in the distributor cap for burning. Light burning can be cleaned up with fine glasspaper (better than emery paper because it does not leave any conducting dust behind).

44C. Check that the rotor arm fits firmly and not loosely on the centre cam/spindle of the distributor and check the end of it for burning. Again, light burning can be cleaned up but severe burning of either the cap studs or the rotor arm means renewal. (Illustration, courtesy Vauxhall Motors Limited)

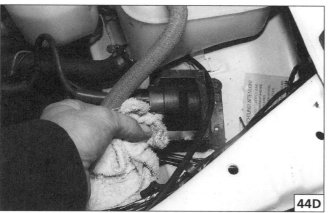

44D

44D. Clean the coil exterior and check for any signs of HT current tracking. Check that the HT lead, and the two low tension leads, are firm and secure.

44E. Clean the distributor cap exterior surfaces by spraying with water repellent fluid and wiping thoroughly with a cloth. This treatment will help prevent the build-up of dirt and condensation, both common causes of 'tracking' and poor starting

44F. Treat the high-tension (HT) leads in the same way, including the terminal ends and the spark-plug caps.

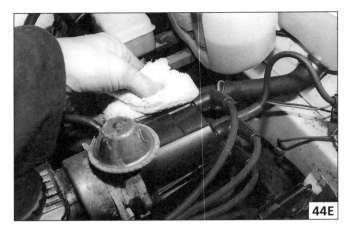

making it easy! If you have to renew either the HT leads or the distributor cap, renew the leads one at a time so you don't get them out of order. With a new cap, compare the position of the connection for number 1 cylinder with the old cap, using the depression where it locates on the body of the distributor as a reference point.

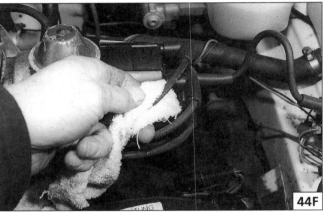

☐ Job 45. Check/adjust points dwell angle.

1.0 LITRE ENGINES ONLY

The contact-breaker (c.b.) points are located in the distributor, beneath the cap; their condition and adjustment is critical to the efficient running of the engine in terms of performance and fuel economy. It is advisable to carry out both a 'dwell' measurement as described below, and also a physical check on the actual condition of the points themselves.

INSIDE INFORMATION: While it is obviously possible to measure and adjust the contact breaker gap physically, as when new points are fitted for instance, such a method does not guarantee accuracy and the stated gap is regarded only as a starting-point so that the engine may be started and a more accurate 'dwell' measurement taken. Dwell meters are used with the engine running and therefore automatically take into account small (but significant) deviations and wear patterns in the distributor components and points, and they also require no dismantling of the engine to make a measurement.

45A. The type of multi-meter described in *Chapter 9, Tools and Equipment* will allow the dwell to be measured simply by attaching three wires, to the battery and coil, enabling an accurate reading to be taken without disturbing the distributor, and in a fraction of the time a physical measurement would take.

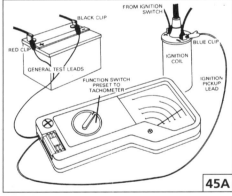

Connect the dwell meter as per the maker's instructions, start the engine, and note the reading given. If necessary, adjust the points gap as follows.

making it easy! Checking and adjusting the points requires the engine to be turned slowly by hand - not a particularly easy proposition given the close proximity of the crankshaft pulley to the inner wing panel, which makes use of a spanner on the pulley bolt awkward. A far easier method is to apply the handbrake firmly, select second gear and jack-up the right-hand (driver's side) wheel until just clear of the ground. Secure the car on an axle stand. Now, when the road wheel is turned by hand, the engine will also turn, due to the car being in gear.

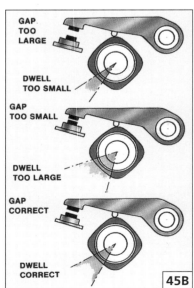

45B. It is important to measure the points gap when the heel of the moving contact arm is on the 'highest' part of the cam lobe - turning the engine (or road-wheel as above) will cause the cam to rotate to the required position. If the points are being adjusted using a dwell meter, note that reducing the gap increases the dwell, while increasing the gap reduces the dwell. (Illustration, courtesy Gunsons Ltd)

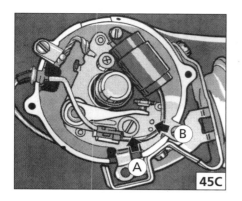

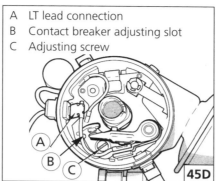

A LT lead connection
B Contact breaker adjusting slot
C Adjusting screw

45C

45D

AC-DELCO DISTRIBUTORS

45C. Adjust the points gap by slackening the screw 'A' (arrowed) just sufficiently to allow the fixed point to move on the baseplate. Then by inserting the tip of a screwdriver between the pips 'B' (arrowed) the fixed part of the points can be levered either towards or away from the sprung contact, thereby altering the gap between them. (Illustration, courtesy Vauxhall Motors Limited)

CHECK POINTS CONDITION

Prise the points apart with a small screwdriver and examine the faces of the contact areas, looking for signs of metal transfer between them (i.e a 'pip' on one and a 'pit' on the other). If this condition is present, the points need replacing - see **Job 72**.

BOSCH DISTRIBUTORS

45D. A small number of O.H.V. Novas were fitted with the Bosch distributor - the arrangement of these is very similar to the AC-Delco type and the points-renewal procedure is the same.

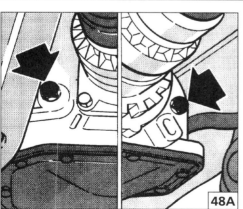

46

☐ Job 46. Lubricate distributor.

1.0 LITRE ENGINES ONLY

46. Apply a couple of drops of thin oil to the felt pad positioned in the centre of the cam, and dribble a few drops onto the advance/retard mechanism located beneath the baseplate on which the points are mounted. Finally, apply a small quantity of grease to the sides of the cam itself. IMPORTANT NOTE: Ensure no oil or grease comes into contact with the points themselves.

47

☐ Job 47. Lubricate clutch cable.

47. Apply a small quantity of grease to the clutch operating cable where the inner cable emerges from the outer sheath at the gearbox. Also grease the threads and locknut around the forked operating lever - this will prevent the threads corroding and make future adjustment easier.

☐ Job 48. Check gearbox oil.

A number of different gearbox types have been fitted to the Nova during its production life. However, the oil level plug on all of them is in one of two positions, as shown in **48A**.

INSIDE INFORMATION: To check the oil level, you will have to add a quantity of new oil. This is because simply removing the level plug and checking that oil issues from the hole will not determine the contents of the gearbox proper. The level plug is located on the differential casing which, while an integral part of the gearbox, contains oil that is kept at a higher level than that in the main gearbox, with the result that oil may well be present in the differential casing, but not in the gearbox adjacent to it, thereby giving a false indication of the level.

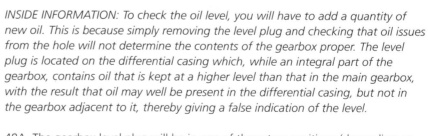

48A

48A. The gearbox level plug will be in one of these two positions (depending on type) adjacent to a driveshaft on the differential casing, either on the right or left-hand side of the casing. Remove it using a 17mm spanner, turned anti-clockwise. Some oil will ooze from the hole as the plug is removed, so have a drip tray ready to catch it. (Illustration, courtesy Vauxhall Motors Limited)

SAFETY FIRST!
*This job requires the vehicle not only to be raised but also to be level to the ground, in order for the operation to be effective. Therefore two sets of axle stands and a trolley jack will be required - see the **Raising the Car Safely** section at the beginning of this chapter for how to do this safely. The level/drain plug is likely to be tight so take care not to apply 'sideways' pressure to the spanner which could make the supported car unstable - pull or push the spanner in a down-or-upwards direction.*

48B. Looking down into the engine bay right-hand side, the oil filler also doubles as a vent for the gearbox, and as such may not readily be recognisable. It is removed with a 17mm open-ended spanner, as shown.

48C. Place the nozzle or pipe of the oil bottle into the hole and have an assistant squeeze the bottle gently so that oil flows into the gearbox, while you watch the level outlet for signs of oil starting to flow. When this occurs, replace the plug and stop filling - the level is now correct.

Tighten the level plug and replace the vent/filler. Finally, wipe any excess or spilt oil from the gearbox casing with rag.

☐ Job 49. Check and turn air filter element.

49. Remove the air filter top cover (refer to **Job 25** for particular types if different to that shown here) and check the condition of the paper element. Shake it carefully (away from the car!) to remove any loose debris or dust, and check for signs of oil fouling, which could indicate a blocked or defective breather pipe. Clean the filter housing of debris, but be careful not to allow any dirt to enter the open carburettor throat.

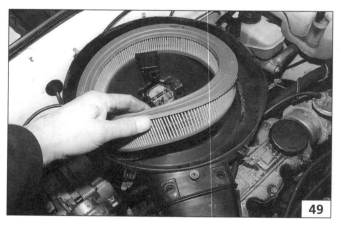

☐ Job 50. Lubricate throttle linkage.

50. Place a dab of grease on the throttle cable where the inner cable exits the outer sleeve, at the carburettor linkage, to help prevent water working its way in. Check the cable for any frayed strands or sharp kinks - if present the cable will need to be replaced as there is a danger of the throttle sticking 'open' when least expected.

51

☐ Job 51. Lubricate carburettor linkages.

51. Apply a few drops of light oil to the carburettor linkages and operating arm, allowing it to soak through the coil springs fitted to the spindles.

☐ Job 52. Adjust carburettor.

52A

SAFETY FIRST!
*Carburettor adjustment has to be carried out with a warm, running engine. Therefore: i) Watch out for rotating cooling fan and belt and do not wear loose clothing or jewellery and tie back long hair. ii) Take care that you do not burn yourself on the hot engine parts and/or exhaust manifolds. iii) Always work out of doors. DO NOT perform this check in your garage or any confined space - exhaust gases are highly poisonous and can kill within minutes! iv) Apply a strict No Smoking! rule whenever you are servicing your fuel system. Remember, it's not just the petrol that's flammable, it's the fumes as well. Overall, if you're not (justifiably) confident, give the job to someone who is fully competent. Some manufacturers recommend that only trained mechanics should carry out work on a vehicle's fuel system. Read **Chapter 1, Safety First!***

52B

INSIDE INFORMATION: i) This Job requires the use of gas testing equipment and a tachometer to check idle speed, if any meaningful results are to be obtained. Indeed, attempting to 'tune' a carburettor without this equipment is likely to result in increased fuel consumption and poor performance, except in the hands of experienced mechanics although, it has to be said, even they tend to use them anyway, for speed of use and accuracy! ii) The carburettor should be the last part of the engine tune-up procedure, as the general settings will be affected by the condition efficiency of the other engine components such as the ignition system.

First familiarise yourself with the carburettor fitted to your car, either the Weber 32 TL, Solex/Pierburg 1B1, or Solex/Pierburg 2E3. Pay particular attention to the location of the 'idle' (tick-over speed) and 'mixture' adjusting screws. Use the accompanying diagrams to determine where each screw is positioned.

52A. This is the idle speed adjustment screws on the Solex/Pierburg 1B1 carburettor...

52B. .... and here (arrowed) is the idle mixture screw.

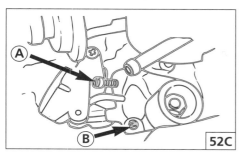

52C

52C. The Solex/Pierburg 2E3 carburettor. The idle-speed screw is 'A'; the mixture screw 'B'.

52D. The Weber 32 TL, showing the idle speed screw....

52E. .... and the mixture screw. (Illustrations, courtesy Vauxhall Motors Limited)

52D

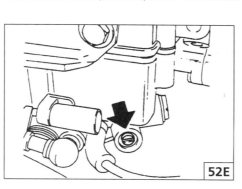

52E

ADJUST IDLE SPEED

Adjust the idle screw until the engine is running at the prescribed idle speed, see *Chapter 8, Facts & Figures.* Setting this accurately requires an rpm meter but, if you do not have one, set the engine to run at the slowest speed at which it is comfortable without stalling. Rev the engine to approximately 3,000 rpm for half a minute to clear and stabilise the carburettor and check the idle speed again. The mixture should not need adjusting at this service but, if you cannot get the engine to idle smoothly, the mixture may be inaccurate.

ADJUSTING THE MIXTURE

The small, recessed, mixture screw on all types of carburettor is turned clockwise to richen the mixture, anti-clockwise to weaken it. Only a small amount of movement is required to adjust the idle mixture - start by turning the screw a quarter-turn at a time, observing the effect on the gas-tester read-out for each movement - see **Job 54.**.

☐ **Job 53. Check idle speed.**

MODELS WITH PETROL FUEL INJECTION, AND DIESEL ENGINES

INSIDE INFORMATION: It is seldom necessary to adjust the idle speed on fuel injection systems and on models from 1989-on, this will also affect the mixture and it is very easy for the inexperienced to quickly put a car 'out of tune' simply by altering the idle speed setting. If the idle speed appears too high or low, have the car checked in a SPECIALIST SERVICE.

☐ **Job 54. Check exhaust emission.**

PETROL ENGINES ONLY

54. Since the introduction of relatively inexpensive test meters for exhaust emissions, such as the Gunson one shown here, mixture testing and adjustment has become feasible for home mechanics. Follow the instructions with the meter, remembering to rev the engine between each adjustment of the mixture screw to stabilise the carburettor. IMPORTANT NOTE: On the Bosch LE3-Jetronic fuel injection system used on the Nova GTE, the mixture adjustment screw is an Allen-headed screw under a tamper-proof plug on the air-flow metering unit. However, as it is very easy to cause damage by heavy-handed adjustment of this screw, we recommend that you check the exhaust emission and, if the mixture needs adjusting, leave it to **SPECIALIST SERVICE.**

1.4 LITRE INJECTION ENGINES

There is no provision for altering the mixture on the MULTEC single-point injection system used on the 1.4 litre engine. If the gas analyser indicates a faulty mixture, again refer to a **SPECIALIST SERVICE.**

☐ **Job 55. Check pipes and hoses.**

Check all the pipes and hose in the engine compartment, including fuel lines, vacuum pipes, breather pipes, etc. Look for signs of chafing, splitting or perishing of the surfaces, and also check all connections and unions for signs of leaks.

Every 6,000 Miles - Around The Car

☐ **Job 56. Check seat belts and mountings.**

56A. Examine the seat belts for chafing and tug hard at them to check their fixings to the body. With inertia seat belts, check the inertia lock by giving the belt a sharp tug. Fit each seat belt catch into its socket and check that it holds properly and frees easily when the catch is pressed. NEVER try to repair a seat belt or its catch, and do not mix catches and sockets from different belts. If you find anything faulty, replace the whole belt and socket.

56B. Check the lower belt fixings on three and five door cars and vans, as the belts can be vulnerable damage.

> ### FACT FILE: DIESEL ENGINES EMISSIONS
>
> Petrol emissions meters are NOT suitable for checking diesel exhaust emissions. With a diesel, allow the engine to idle for a few moments and then rev it and hold it at moderately high revs. There may be a puff of black smoke as you first raise the revs but this should clear. If black smoke persists, the injectors may need cleaning. Seek **SPECIALIST SERVICE.**

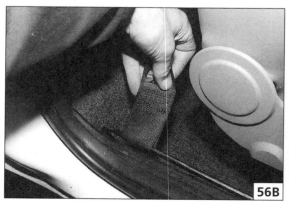

57

☐ Job 57. Check seat mountings.

57. Check the seats for security by trying to rock them and check the seat adjustment mechanism. Grease the runners lightly and wipe off any surplus to avoid soiling clothes and carpets. Check, if applicable, that the folding seat backs lock securely in the upright position and that the release catches work smoothly.

☐ Job 58. Check fuel filler-cap seal.

58. Check the sealing rubber (arrowed) on the fuel filler cap to make sure it is not damaged or badly worn. A worn seal here is an MoT failure.

58

☐ Job 59. Lubricate bonnet release.

INSIDE INFORMATION: It doesn't always figure highly, if at all, in service schedules, but there are a fair few moving parts on the motor car which would benefit from occasional oil-can lubrication. They will then work more smoothly, probably more quietly, and will certainly last longer. Here are just a few examples - but if you get into the habit of regularly 'carrying the can' around your car, you'll probably spot a few more!

59. Apply a few drops of oil to the bonnet release mechanism, dribbling a little through the aperture. Also apply a dab of grease to the cable-end and mechanism from beneath the slam-panel.

59

☐ Job 60. Lubricate hinges, locks, check straps.

60A. Door hinges are a prime area of neglect - the hinge-pins of Nova doors are hollow, similar to those shown, and require a plastic cap to be removed before a squirt of oil is added. Replace the cap afterwards!

60B. In some places you can use either grease or oil, as here on a door check strap, which if left unlubricated, dries out, rusts up, and not only retards smooth door opening and closing, but also causes those strident 'graunching' noises which are always an embarrassment - particularly in your drive-way late at night! An occasional 'lube' works wonders.

> *making it easy!* On older, or previously neglected door hinges, it could be beneficial to first douse them with penetrating fluid, following up with the oil can a little later, when the penetrating stuff has done its work.

60A

60B

60C. Aerosol water displacement fluid, using the can's slim 'accessory tube', is handy for penetrating stiff lock mechanisms, or door lock push-buttons, and helps prevent them freezing in winter.

60D. Van and hatchback tailgate hinges will benefit from a drop or two of oil as well, as will the tailgate lock and latch. Be careful not to put too much oil on the hinges, as it could seep past the seal and stain the headlining.

60C

☐ Job 61. Check shock absorber action.

61. Press down on each corner of the car in turn and release your weight. The suspension should 'bounce' back once or twice at the most. If it is easy to compress the springs, and the car 'bounces' several times when you release your weight, the shock absorbers may need renewing - seek **SPECIALIST SERVICE**.

☐ Job 62. Check wheel alignment.

It is important for the front wheels of a car to be properly adjusted, in terms of 'toe-in' or 'toe-out', often known as 'tracking'. This describes the preset amount of deviation, measured in degrees, of the front wheels from the straight-ahead position. An incorrect setting will affect the handling of the car and also cause the front tyres to wear unevenly - see *paragraph 24F, Chapter 7*. This service is quickly and cheaply carried out by most reputable tyre-fitting companies, so is a **SPECIALIST SERVICE**.

60D

Every 6,000 Miles - Under the Car

☐ Job 63. Check/renew front brake pads.

63A. You can check the pad thickness without removing the caliper. The maker's recommended minimum thickness for the friction material is 7mm but you may want to renew earlier than this because you won't be looking at the pads again for another 6,000 miles. It is normal for one pad to wear slightly more than the other but, if it appears that only one pad is doing the work and the other has hardly worn at all, it is a sign that the caliper is sticking. This means **SPECIALIST SERVICE**. Have the calipers checked by a garage. (Illustration, courtesy Vauxhall Motors Limited)

61

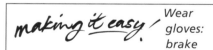 *making it easy!* Wear gloves: brake dust gets in cut and skin cracks and pores and can take ages to 'wear' out!

63A

SAFETY FIRST!
Raise the front of the car off the ground once again, after reading carefully the information at the start of this chapter on lifting and supporting the car. ii) Obviously, your car's brakes are among its most important safety related items. Do NOT dismantle or attempt to perform any work on the braking system unless you are fully competent to do so. If you have not been trained in this work, but wish to carry it out, we strongly recommend that you have a garage or qualified mechanic check your work before using the car on the road. See also the section on BRAKES AND ASBESTOS in Chapter 1, Safety First! for further information. Always start by washing the brakes with a proprietary brand of brake cleaner - brake drums removed where appropriate - never use compressed air to clean off brake dust. Always replace the brake pads and/or shoes in sets of four never replace the pads/shoes on one wheel only. After fitting new brake shoes or pads, avoid heavy braking - except in an emergency - for the first 150 to 200 miles (250 to 300 km).

REPLACING FRONT DISC PADS

CARS UP TO 1992 ONLY

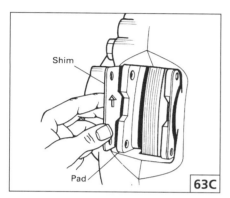

63B

INSIDE INFORMATION: i) A special pin-punch will be required to drift the pad retaining pins from the calipers. Because the pins are hollow, the punch requires a small 'step' to be included at the 'business' end that locates inside the pin, thereby keeping the punch central. These special punches are available from most good accessory shops and are worth purchasing - do not try to use a conventional 'straight' punch as there is a risk it will damage the retaining pin or become firmly and irretrievably jammed, requiring expert help. ii) ALWAYS replace disc pads in sets of four across the car: that is, both front wheels or both rear wheels at the same time. Failure to do this will result in unequal and dangerous braking, due to the imbalance in efficiency.

63B. Drive out the upper pad retaining pin, using the special punch, from the inside of the caliper as shown. The pins may well be corroded and stiff to move - if so, apply a little penetrating oil to the pins but, if the pads are to be used again, make absolutely sure no oil gets on to the pad surface.

As the upper pin is moved across, the two anti-rattle springs will be freed - be ready for this and take note of their position in relation to the pads and pins, then remove the lower pin.

Shim

Pad

63C

63C. By levering the outer pad away from the disc slightly, the pads can be removed from the caliper with pliers, along with their respective shims...

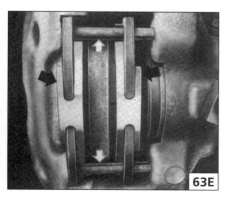

63D

63D. ...which must be retained for re-fitting. Scrape away any rusty scale from the pad housings using an old screwdriver, brushing away any loose debris afterwards with a small brush, but remember - DO NOT BREATH IN ANY DUST as it will contain potentially dangerous irritants.

INSIDE INFORMATION: In preparing to re-fit or renew the pads, wash any oil or grease from your hands so that you don't get it onto the friction materials. Also, wipe the disc surface with methylated spirit to remove any traces of oil, grease or dirt. In order to make room for new (obviously much thicker) disc pads, the caliper piston must be pushed back into the cylinder bore - one good reason why you have to be sure a piston's exposed dirt doesn't get pushed back into the cylinder bore along with the piston.

making it easy! As the pistons are pushed back into their bores the brake fluid level in the reservoir will rise accordingly, often to the point of over-flow! Be prepared for this by removing a quantity of fluid first, the easiest way of which is to draw-off the fluid using an old battery hydrometer, to 'suck' the fluid a little at a time from the reservoir.

Before reassembly, lightly smear a little special brake grease (NOT ordinary grease) around the top and bottom edges of the steel backing plate of the pads, being extra careful not to allow the grease to get onto the pads' friction material - use just a small amount of grease on each edge. Brake grease is available from your auto. accessory store.

63E. On reassembly, position the pads and shims (dark arrows) in the caliper housing and fit the bottom pin first, followed by the anti-rattle springs, then the top pin. (Pins are indicated by light arrows.) The springs will need to be tensioned as the top pin is tapped home. Remember to fit the pins from the outside of the caliper i.e. tap them home TOWARDS the engine side of the caliper, to finish flush with the caliper sides, and with the openings in the pins facing each other.

CARS FROM 1992 ONLY

A revised type of caliper was fitted to all models from 1992 which differs in the method of retaining the caliper and brake pads. The following sequence describes these operations, but reference should be made to the previous section for general information.

INSIDE INFORMATION: A 7mm Allen key will be needed to unscrew the often very-tight caliper retaining bolts and you will also need some form of 'tool' to retract the caliper piston into its bore. The latter can be improvised using a woodworking 'G' clamp or valve spring compressor tool and one of the old brake pads. ALWAYS replace disc pads in sets of four across the car: that is, both front wheels or both rear wheels at the same time. Failure to do this will result in unequal and dangerous braking, due to the imbalance in efficiency.

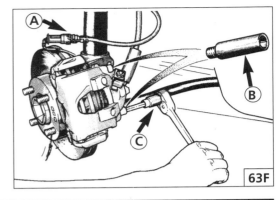

63F. First disconnect the brake wear indicator wiring, if fitted to your car, by pulling the connector (A) apart. The caliper is retained by two hollow bolts (B) for which the Allen key (C) is required.

INSIDE INFORMATION: Plastic caps are fitted to the dust-excluding tubes which surround the bolts - remove the caps first. The bolts themselves are likely to be very stiff to turn initially, but take care as they often release quite suddenly, 'skinning' the knuckles of the unwary!

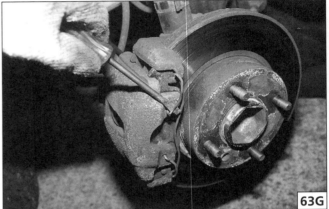

63G. This pad retaining spring is detached by levering-out one end of the spring to release the tension, when it can be lifted away.

63H. The caliper assembly can now be pulled forwards over the disc. Note that the outer pad may remain with the carrier bracket and require a sharp tap or two from a hammer to free it.

63I. If a wear-ridge is present on the outer edge of the disc you may find it necessary to lever the caliper carefully against the disc to retract the piston slightly. Use a screwdriver as shown, or a large pair of grips if available.

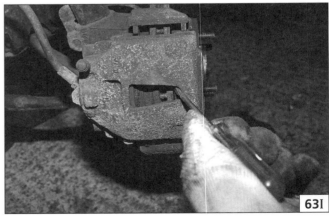

63J. The inner pad has a three-legged spring retaining it to the hollow piston - the pad usually comes away easily, but might need a tap from a hammer to free it if corroded.

63K. Spray brake cleaner over the carrier bracket, paying particular attention to the pad seatings and those areas not accessible when the pads are fitted.

63L. Wire brush the pad seatings on the bracket, removing any hard scale or rust by scraping with an old screwdriver or chisel.

63M. Retracting the piston is necessary when fitting new pads. This can be done earlier in the sequence when the caliper is still attached to the carrier, or now before cleaning. See **MAKING IT EASY!** panel earlier in this Job, regarding fluid level in the master cylinder reservoir.

63N. Check the piston rubber dust excluder for splits, chafing or perishing. If any sign of brake fluid is present a leak is indicated, and you should have the affected caliper inspected by a qualified specialist or Vauxhall dealer before using it.

63O. Reassemble the new pads to their seats and ensure the two raised steps on the piston face are positioned at the 12 o'clock and 6 o'clock positions - the pistons can be turned using the square shaft of a screwdriver, or a large pair of grips. Fit the caliper and bolts, replace the pad retaining spring and reconnect the wear indicator wiring. Do not over- tighten the sliding bolts (the correct torque figure is 30 Nm (22 lb/ft.) - firm hand pressure is sufficient.

☐ **Job 64. Check brake discs.**

64. Check the disc for signs of excessive corrosion, scoring, uneven wear, and ridges at the inner and outer edges of the pad contact area, arrowed in the photo. Some wear and light scoring is inevitable of course, but if there is more than a very small amount, then the disc will need renewing.

SAFETY FIRST!

If you are in any doubt as to the condition of the disc or discs, seek professional advice before using the car again. Corroded or pitted areas of the disc's working surface indicates a possible problem with the caliper, which may be partially seized. Additionally, deep scoring causes the pad friction material to contact only the 'peaks' of the ridges, thereby drastically reducing the area of contact, and subsequently reducing braking efficiency.

SPECIALIST SERVICE: Consult your Vauxhall dealer and have them examine the disc and measure it with a micrometer if scoring is evident. Badly scored or badly ridged discs will seriously reduce braking efficiency even with fully bedded-in pads. New pads would take for ever to bed-in on them and meanwhile braking efficiency could be virtually nil!

A light ridge at the very edge of the disc, if it's mostly a build-up of rust, can be carefully removed with a file - it's possible to feed the file (or a hefty old screwdriver) through a pad aperture, then steadying the file (or screwdriver blade) firmly against the ridge while you spin the disc.

☐ Job 65. Check/adjust/renew rear brake shoes.

CLEAN AND CHECK CONDITION

SAFETY FIRST! AND SPECIALIST SERVICE
Obviously, your car's brakes are among its most important safety related items. Do NOT dismantle or attempt to perform any work on the braking system unless you are fully competent to do so. If you have not been trained in this work, but wish to carry it out, we strongly recommend that you have a garage or qualified mechanic check your work before using the car on the road. See also the section on BRAKES AND ASBESTOS in Chapter 1, Safety First! for further information. Always start by washing the brakes with a proprietary brand of brake cleaner - brake drums removed, where appropriate - never use compressed air to clean off brake dust. Always replace the shoes in sets of four - never replace the shoes on one wheel only. After fitting new brake shoes, avoid heavy braking - except in an emergency - for the first 150 to 200 miles (250 to 300 km).

65A. Raise the rear of the car and support it on axle stands positioned beneath the axle cross-beam; remove both rear wheels and release the handbrake. Position a few sheets of newspaper beneath the drum to catch any brake dust that may be dislodged.

65B. Using a broad-bladed screwdriver, prise off the hub-nut dust cover. Don't try to remove it in one go, but turn the drum and 'work' the cap out of the recess.

65C. This split-pin retains the hub nut to the shaft, its free ends splayed to prevent it falling out - straighten the pin with pliers and remove it. (Buy a new one: don't re-use the old!)

65D. Use a suitably-sized socket to remove the nut, turning anti-clockwise.

65E. Move the drum from side-to-side a few times and this washer and the outer bearing will move outwards. Slide them off the stub axle and put them somewhere safe and clean - NOT on the floor!

65F. The drum should now be free to slide off the stub axle and over the shoes, BUT - in most cases it will be obstructed by the shoes due to a 'wear-ridge' on the drum...

65G. ...in which case place a screwdriver in the hole provided on the backplate and push the handle towards the front of the car - this applies pressure to the handbrake lever inside the drum and causes the shoes to contract slightly, allowing the drum to pass over them.

65H. Spray the brake components with brake cleaner to 'wash' away all traces of brake dust: NEVER use a brush or air-line to blow the dust away. Check the thickness of the lining material - the minimum thickness is specified as 0.5mm above the rivet heads, (or the backing plate, if the bonded-type - arrowed) but as the shoes may not be examined again for some time, they should be renewed if less than 3.0mm thick.

65I. This potentially dangerous brake dust has accumulated in the drum and is the usual cause of brake 'squeal'. Tap the drum on the newspaper to dislodge the dust, fold-up the 'paper and dispose of it straight away.

65J. After 'washing' the drum with brake cleaner, check the interior surface for excessive scoring, corrosion and deep 'wear-ridges', arrowed. If in doubt, take the drum to a specialist or a Vauxhall dealer for an expert opinion.

65K. Pull back the rubber gaiters at each end of the wheel cylinder and check there are no signs of brake fluid seeping past the piston - if there is, the cylinder will have to be replaced, a **SPECIALIST SERVICE job**.

Reassemble the drum and hub in reverse order, but note the following: after fitting the outer bearing and thrust washer, screw-on the hub nut by hand. Using a torque wrench, tighten the nut to 18 lb.ft while turning the drum, then slacken the nut just sufficiently to allow the thrust washer to turn when 'pushed' by the edge of a screwdriver. If the slots in the nut are not aligned with the hole in the stub axle, slacken (don't tighten) the nut by the minimum amount until the split-pin can be fitted (always use a new split-pin). Splay the free-ends of the pin, refit the dust cap, fit the wheel and lower the car to the ground. If new shoes have been fitted, apply the foot-brake and handbrake several times to allow the auto-adjuster to take up any free movement in the shoes.

IMPORTANT NOTE: Check for excess bearing play (see **Job 93**) after reassembly and again after about 100 miles (150km) of use. If there is excess play you can't get rid of, excess stiffness in spinning the wheel (which can be very dangerous!) or excess noise, have a specialist reassemble the hubs for you.

BRAKE SHOE REPLACEMENT

making it easy! 65L. Before dismantling brake shoes, but after the drum has been removed, make a careful record of where everything goes, especially brake shoe return springs. Make a careful sketch, take a couple of photographs (a Polaroid would be ideal!) or 'video' the assembly - it could turn out to be a life saver - literally!

Also, only work on one side at a time, so that you've always got the other one to refer to, but note that some components are 'handed' and each side of the car will be arranged as a mirror-image of the other.

65M. Release the spring clips on the shoe steady pins by holding the pin at the rear of the brake backplate and pushing against the spring with pliers, turn it through 90 degrees and allow it to pass over the holding-pin head.

65N. INSIDE INFORMATION: A useful tip is to cover the brake lining surfaces with masking tape to prevent contamination by grease, oil or dirt from the hands and other components.

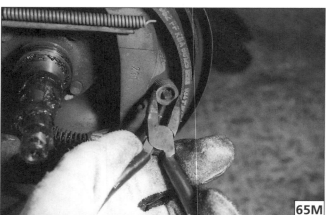

65O. Lever the bottom of one shoe away from the anchor plate, which will relieve the spring tension and allow the other shoe to be released.

65P. Unhook the handbrake cable from the operating arm on the rear-most brake shoe (arrowed). It will now be possible to lift the shoes away from the backplate in one piece for cleaning and re-assembly.

INSIDE INFORMATION: Try to remove the shoes in as near 'assembled' state as possible, to assist replacement. Place the assembly flat on the ground and build-up the new shoes a step at a time, transferring springs and adjuster in sequence. In this way you will avoid any confusion as to what part goes where, and can clean each part as it is dealt with.

65Q

65Q. This shows the arrangement of the auto-adjuster mechanism on the front shoe of the left-hand (passenger-side) brake assembly. It is permissible to apply a little brake grease to the auto-adjuster rod and click-wheel, but make absolutely sure none gets on to the lining surfaces.

65R. Clean the backplate with spray cleaner and a rag before fitting the new shoes. Remember to attach the handbrake cable connector to the respective shoe before assembling the components; otherwise the installation operation is a reversal of the above procedure. Take care not to allow oil or grease to contaminate the new shoes!

On completion, operate the handbrake several times, followed by the foot brake, to centralise the shoes and allow the automatic adjuster to take up any slack.

☐ Job 66. Adjust rear brakes.

CARS UP TO 1984 ONLY

66. Pre-1984 Novas have a basically similar layout, with the exception of the auto-adjuster mechanism - but they do have shoe retaining clips (arrowed). These might be of the same type as in **Job 65Q** or they might be those shown here, which you squeeze together and remove; or they might be a curved spring from under which the shoe has to be slid, the spring staying in place. Adjustment of the brakes is provided by a hexagon-headed adjuster found on the rear of the backplate, one adjuster for each shoe.

65R

Adjust each wheel as follows: turn one of the adjusters in whatever direction is required to lock the wheel then slacken it so that the wheel is just free to turn without 'binding' on the shoes; repeat this operation for the second adjuster, and then repeat on the other wheel. (Illustration, courtesy Vauxhall Motors Limited)

☐ Job 67. Check brake proportioning valve.

This component is fitted to the rear underside of the car, its purpose being to control the flow of hydraulic fluid to the rear brakes, depending on the load carried by the vehicle. It does this by a connection to the bodywork in the form of a sprung arm which is deflected at varying angles depending on the load - the greater the load, the more fluid is allowed to pass and therefore the greater braking effort applied to the rear wheels.

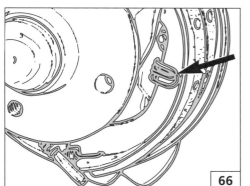

66

SPECIALIST SERVICE: Have this component checked by a reputable garage or Vauxhall dealer.

☐ Job 68. Check steering ball joints.

68A. Steering joints, or 'track-rod-ends' provide the link between the steering arms and the roadwheels. A small rubber boot covers the steering joint and forms part of the assembly and is vital to the life of the joint - any splits or cracks will allow the grease to escape and dirt to enter and ruin the joint.

68A

It's easier to check the joint if the front wheels are removed first. Refer to *Raising the Car Safely* at the beginning of this Chapter. Put the steering onto full lock so that each joint can be seen at the rear of the brake disc backplate. Check the condition and security of the protective boot on each track rod end. If split or damaged, the complete track rod end joint will have to be replaced.

RENEWING THE BALL JOINT

68B. The internally-threaded joint is fixed in position by a locknut - use one spanner to turn the nut and another to hold the square-ended joint, working them in opposing directions.

INSIDE INFORMATION: So that the 'tracking' of the front wheels can be retained, it is only necessary to slacken the locknut just enough to free the joint - half a turn of the 'nut is usually sufficient. However, if the locknut has to be removed to allow a steering gaiter to be fitted, mark its position by applying a dab of paint, or wrap a piece of tape around the steering arm so that the nut, when replaced, will return to its original position.

68C. Next undo the nut securing the joints' tapered pin to the forged steering arm of the hub assembly. A little easing oil may be necessary to allow the nut to pass over the outer threads of the pin, which often corrode and cause the nut to tighten as it is undone, with the risk of the pin being freed from its tapered seat and turning aimlessly with the nut. If this occurs it may be necessary to cut the nut from the pin using a hacksaw or nut-splitter. A new nut will be supplied with the new joint.

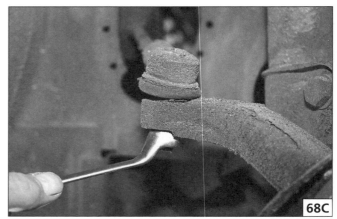

68D. A ball-joint removal tool is required to separate the tapered pin from its seat in the steering arm. DO NOT try to free the pin by hammering it - damage to the pin and seat will result.

68E. With the balljoint freed from its seat, unscrew the joint from the steering rack arm. Unless the steering rack gaiter is being removed, do not disturb the locknut...

68F. ...otherwise wrap a length of tape around the steering arm immediately behind and abutting the nut before unscrewing it - this will provide a 'mark' up to which the nut can be replaced, thereby maintaining the 'tracking' of the front wheels sufficiently to allow the car to be driven to a specialist, who can set the tracking accurately.

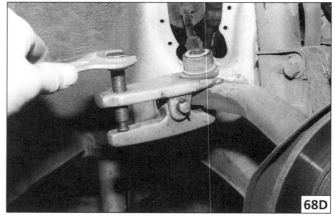

Before screwing-on a new joint, lightly grease the threads on the arm to make the joint easy to remove in the future.

SPECIALIST SERVICE: It is important to have the 'tracking' or wheel alignment check by a reputable garage after disturbing the steering joints in this way, to ensure the handling of the car remains safe and also to avoid uneven tyre wear.

Every 12,000 Miles or Every Twelve Months, whichever comes first

Every 12,000 Miles - The Engine Bay

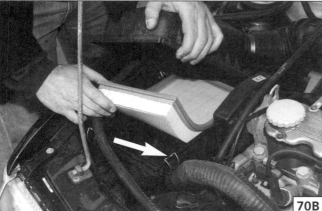
70A

☐ Job 69. Change air filter element.

If the element wasn't changed at the earlier 6,000 mile interval, now is the time to do it - even a partly-clogged element is likely to increase fuel consumption and cause unnecessary pollution.

Refer to **Job 49** for details of how to remove the filter housing cover.

☐ Job 70. Clean air filter housing.

70A. Undo the top cover, lift out the air filter and carefully remove any dust or debris (leaves, flies etc.) from the lower housing, taking care that none enters the carburettor intake situated in the centre of the housing - a vacuum cleaner with hose and nozzle is ideal for this task, if available.

70B. The air filter on diesel and fuel injection engines is located on the front/left of the engine bay. The cover is secured by four spring clips (one of them arrowed) and on later models, a screw.

70B

☐ Job 71. Check/adjust valve clearances.

1.0 LITRE PETROL ENGINES ONLY

The valve clearances must be set with the engine hot - that is, not so hot that you risk burning your fingers, but within half an hour of the engine having been run at operating temperature.

First remove the air filter housing by unscrewing the three bolts securing it to the carburettor and lift the housing away. Remove the spark plugs to make the engine easier to turn over.

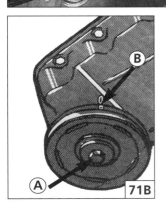
A 71A

71A. This is a plan view of the valve rockers - note the valves are numbered 1 to 8 from the left (crankshaft pulley) end; also note the order of the inlet (In) and exhaust (Ex) valves, which have different clearances. Valve sequence: Ex - In - In - Ex - Ex - In - In - Ex.

71B. Turn the engine (using a spanner fitted to the crankshaft pulley nut - A) until both valves of No.1 cylinder are closed (i.e. the rockers are 'slack') and the timing mark on the crankshaft is as shown (B). This puts No.1 cylinder at Top-Dead-Centre (T.D.C.) on its firing stroke.

With the engine in this position, the following valves can be adjusted.

1. (exhaust)
2. (inlet)
3. (inlet)
5. (exhaust)

Now turn the engine again through one complete revolution. You can now adjust the following valves.

4. (exhaust)
6. (inlet)
7. (inlet)
8. (exhaust)

IMPORTANT NOTE: Valves are counted from the crankshaft pulley/timing cover end of the engine.

71B

71C. See *Chapter 8, Facts & Figures*, for the correct clearances for your engine. Referring to the above sequence, insert a feeler gauge between the valve rocker and the valve stem - it should be a firm, sliding fit; if the clearance is too tight (small) or too loose (large) it can be adjusted using a socket spanner on the rocker securing/adjusting nut - clockwise to tighten, anti-clockwise to slacken.

After adjustment, turn the engine and re-check the clearances, following the same sequence. If the gaps are correct, replace the rocker cover (using a new gasket) and refit the air filter housing. (Illustration, courtesy Vauxhall Motors Limited)

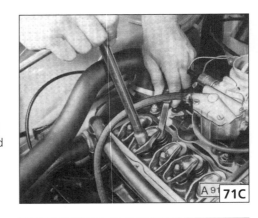

☐ Job 72. Renew contact breaker points.

1.0 LITRE PETROL ENGINES ONLY

AC-DELCO DISTRIBUTORS

72A. After removing the distributor cap, replace the points by removing the screw 'A' - be careful not to drop it! Release the spring-steel arm of the moving point from its post 'B' and disconnect the wires at 'C'. Fit new points in the reverse order, but first 'clean' the point faces of protective grease by sliding a piece of card or cloth between them.

After fitting new points it is necessary to check the ignition timing - see **Job 73**.

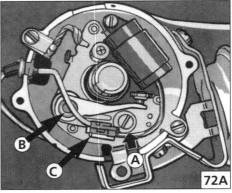

BOSCH DISTRIBUTORS

72B. A small number of O.H.V. Novas were fitted with the Bosch distributor - the arrangement of these is very similar to the AC-Delco and the points-renewal procedure is the same, except for the wire terminal 'A' which is a simple push-fit. The points securing screw is shown at 'B'.

After fitting new points it is necessary to check the ignition timing - **Job 73**.

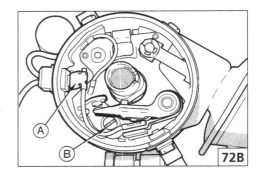

☐ Job 73. Check ignition timing.

INSIDE INFORMATION: To check or adjust the ignition timing with the required degree of accuracy calls for the use of a stroboscopic timing light similar to the Gunson's model shown here. Although a 'static' timing figure may be given in some workshop manuals, this is only a guide, mostly used to get an engine started after the distributor has been disturbed and the previous settings lost.

SAFETY FIRST!
THE ELECTRONIC IGNITION SYSTEM INVOLVES VERY HIGH VOLTAGES! All manufacturers recommend that only trained personnel should go near the high tension-circuit (coil, distributor and HT wiring) and it is ESSENTIAL that anyone wearing a medical pacemaker device does not go near the ignition system. Also, stroboscopic timing requires the engine to be running - take great care that parts of the timing lights or parts of you don't get caught up in the moving parts! Don't wear loose clothing or hair.

making it easy! 73A. Turn the engine by hand so that the timing marks can be highlighted with a dab of white paint or typist's correction fluid. This ensures the marks will be clearly visible when illuminated by the timing light.

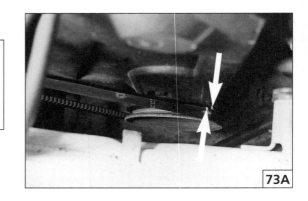

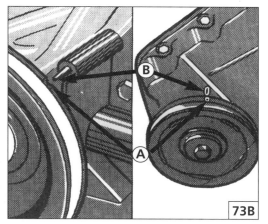

73B. The timing marks on OHC engines are shown on the left, those on OHV engines on the right, with 'A' denoting the pulley mark, and 'B' the pointer (OHC) or notch (OHV) on the engine.

73C. Timing checks and adjustments are made with the vacuum pipe disconnected at the distributor end and plugged with a suitable instrument, such as a small Phillips-type screwdriver or other suitable 'bung' such as the centre punch used here.

73D. Connect the timing light according to the makers' instructions, start the engine and let it tick-over at the correct idle speed (see *Chapter 8, Facts & Figures*) and point the flashing beam of the light at the timing marks. The strobe effect of the flashing beam 'freezes' the moving mark on the pulley and should appear stationary, adjacent to the static mark on the engine if the timing is set correctly. If the mark appears at the wrong place, the distributor will have to be slackened and turned to bring the marks into alignment, as follows:

> *SAFETY FIRST!*
> **Switch off the engine before slackening or turning the distributor. Very high voltages are present which can 'jump' through the insulation of HT leads and/or distributor cap, passing through the body to earth. This could be harmful or even fatal.**

OHV ENGINES ONLY

The distributor clamp bolt on OHV engines is located near the bottom of the distributor at the front of the engine. Slacken the bolt just sufficiently to allow the distributor body to be turned by hand, but not loose enough as to be disturbed when the bolt is tightened. Turn the distributor clockwise to increase the amount of 'advance', or anti-clockwise to reduce it. Tighten the clamp bolt when the desired setting is reached.

OHC ENGINES ONLY

73E. The distributor is retained by one bolt at the base of the body - shown with spanner fitted. Slacken the bolt but leave enough 'grip' to hold the distributor in position but enable it to move under firm pressure.

12,000 MILE SERVICE

73F. Turning the distributor clockwise increases the amount of 'advance', while anti-clockwise decreases it.

73G. Tighten the clamp bolts when the correct setting is achieved. In all cases, double-check the setting after the bolt has been tightened. If correct, disconnect the timing light, unplug and re-connect the vacuum tube to the distributor.

 **Job 74. Check coolant.**

74. Check the specific gravity of the antifreeze with a hydrometer. This is similar to the hydrometer for checking battery acid and can be bought at most accessory shops. Follow the instructions and, if the specific gravity is too low, add more antifreeze.

INSIDE INFORMATION: Remember that antifreeze, even in diluted form, will attack paintwork. Be particularly careful when flushing and if you have to disconnect the heater hoses. Any spilt antifreeze should be washed off immediately with plenty of cold water.

 **Job 75. Check vacuum hoses.**

75. Check the security of the vacuum hose from the inlet manifold (vacuum pump on diesel engines) to the brake servo. Bend it in your fingers. If it feels brittle, or if you hear any signs of cracking, the hose needs renewing. Also check the small diameter pipes that connect between the distributor vacuum-advance capsule and the inlet manifold, and also that from the manifold to the underside of the air filter housing (not applicable to 1.0 litre engines).

☐ **Job 76. Check/renew crankcase ventilation hoses.**

76. Squeeze the crankcase ventilation hose along its length, checking for signs of splitting, chafing and perishing. The hose will be found connecting the air filter housing to either the camshaft housing, as shown, or the oil separator canister fitted to the engine block. If the hose is damaged, or feels soft and spongy (a sign of internal perishing) replace it with a new length obtainable from your Vauxhall dealer.

73F

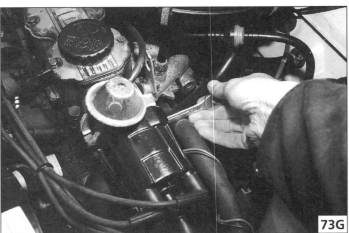

73G

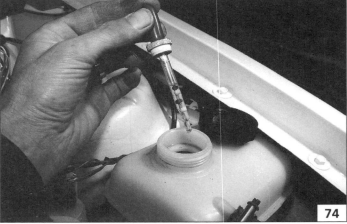

74

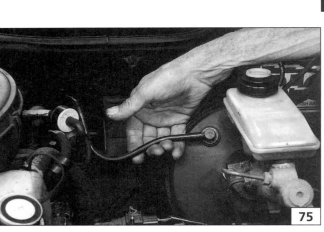

75

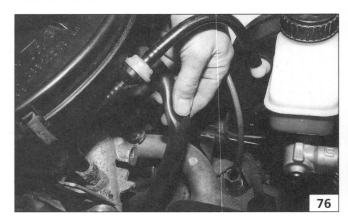

76

You can learn a lot about the condition of an engine from looking at the spark plugs. The following information and photographs, reproduced here with grateful thanks to NGK, show you what to look out for.

1. Good Condition

If the firing end of a spark plug is brown or light grey, the condition can be judged to be good and the spark plug is functioning at its best.

4. Overheating

When having been overheated, the insulator tip can become glazed or glossy, and deposits which have accumulated on the insulator tip may have melted. Sometimes these deposits have blistered on the insulator's tip.

6. Abnormal Wear

Abnormal electrode erosion is caused by the effects of corrosion, oxidation, reaction with lead, all resulting in abnormal gap growth.

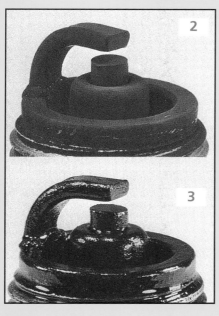

2. Carbon Fouling

Black, dry, sooty deposits, which will eventually cause misfiring and can be caused by an over-rich fuel mixture. Check all carburettor settings, choke operation and air filter cleanliness. Clean plugs vigorously with a brass bristled wire brush.

3. Oil Fouling

Oily, wet-looking deposits. This is particularly prone to causing poor starting and even misfiring. Caused by a severely worn engine but do not confuse with wet plugs removed from the engine when it won't start. If the "wetness" evaporates away, it's not oil fouling.

5. Normal Wear

A worn spark plug not only wastes fuel but also strains the whole ignition system because the expanded gap requires higher voltage. As a result, a worn spark plug will result in damage to the engine itself, and will also increase air pollution. The normal rate of gap growth is usually around 'half-a-thou.' or 0.0006 in. every 5,000 miles (0.01 mm. every 5,000 km.).

7. Breakage

Insulator damage is self-evident and can be caused by rapid heating or cooling of the plug whilst out of the car or by clumsy use of gap setting tools. Burned away electrodes are indicative of an ignition system that is grossly out of adjustment. Do not use the car until this has been put right.

☐ Job 77. Clean oil filler cap.

77. Clean the filler cap of any sludge and traces of old oil before refitting it. Also make sure the sealing ring on its inner side is in good condition, as some engines require the cap to provide an airtight seal for the emission control system to work properly.

77

☐ Job 78. Renew spark plugs.

PETROL ENGINES ONLY
Although not necessarily essential at this interval, renewing the spark plugs is considered advisable for reasons of economy and clean emissions. Refer to **Job 43** for details of this job.

☐ Job 79. Clean glow plugs.

DIESEL ENGINES ONLY

> **SAFETY FIRST!**
> **Whenever you are dealing with diesel fuel, it's essential to protect your hands by wearing rubber or plastic gloves.**

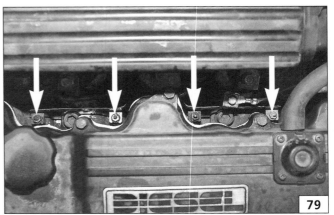

79

79. Disconnect the battery earth lead, disconnect the electrical lead to the bus bar joining the glow plugs, remove the nuts and washers from the glow plugs (arrowed) and remove the bus bar. Unscrew each glow plug in turn with a deep socket and clean the carbon off the end with a non-fluffy rag and clean diesel fuel or - better still - proprietary carburettor cleaner. After cleaning and replacing the plugs, reconnect the bus bar, the cable and the battery connection.

☐ Job 80. Clean/protect battery terminals.

Provided the battery is kept clean and dry and is not topped-up over generously, its terminals should also remain clean and sound - unless a generator fault is causing it to be over-charged, with consequent heavy 'gassing' from the cells.

80A

INSIDE INFORMATION: Often, it is electrolyte spillage or excess vapour which leads to the 'fungal growth' noted on the terminals of neglected batteries. It is a condition which, as well as the highly corrosive effect on nearby metals, such as the battery clamp and the battery tray, also causes poor electrical contact. In the extreme, the starter may fail to operate, or all electrics may apparently 'die'.

80A. If you have inherited a secondhand vehicle suffering from this problem, simply pouring hot water (or a mixture of hot water and domestic soda) over the terminals and any other affected parts, such as the battery strap or clamp, and the battery tray, will usually prove remarkably effective. Take care that you don't pour the hot water into the battery cells or onto nearby vulnerable components.

80B. Once all connections are clean and dry, a smear of petroleum jelly (such as 'Vaseline'), a proprietary battery jelly, or a copper-based grease, will guard against further corrosion and help to maintain good electrical contact.

80B

> **SAFETY FIRST!**
> **Be very careful to guard against 'short circuits' when working on battery terminals. The gas issuing from the cells, particularly when the battery is being charged, is extremely explosive and ignition by a careless spark can cause a truly horrific battery explosion.(A typical cause of accidental short-circuit is the bristles of a wire brush touching a battery terminal and a battery strap at the same time, or, similarly, a spanner being used to tighten a terminal nut also touching this strap or the car bodywork).**

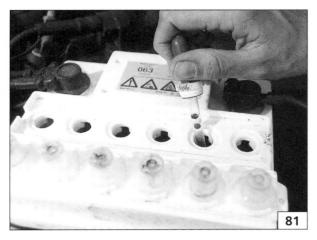

Job 81. Check battery specific gravity.

> *making it easy!* Use a coin to undo cell caps, rather than a screwdriver. The slots are very wide, made of soft plastic and just chew up if you try to use an ordinary screwdriver.

NOT AC-DELCO 'FREEDOM' BATTERIES

81. The 'specific gravity' of a battery is an indication of the state of charge of each battery cell and the battery's overall condition. Test it using a hydrometer (small ones like that used here are readily available from accessory shops) to 'suck' a small quantity of electrolyte into the glass tube - the state of charge is indicated by the number of beads that float in the liquid. Test each cell in turn and if one or more gives a significantly lower reading than the others, the battery may be faulty and should be checked by a battery specialist.

Job 82. Renew fuel filter.

CARBURETTOR PETROL ENGINES

> **SAFETY FIRST!**
> **Disconnect the battery before disturbing any of the fuel pipe joints or unions. A small amount of fuel is likely to be lost with this job so position a rag beneath the fuel pump to catch it.**

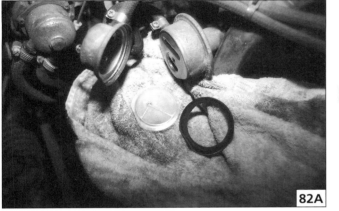

MODELS UP TO 1984

82A. The fuel filter is contained within the fuel pump and consists of a fine screen through which the fuel is drawn from the tank. To remove the filter for cleaning, remove the screw in the centre of the fuel pump and lift away the lid, revealing the screen filter and sealing rubber. Clean the filter in fresh fuel and replace, taking care that the sealing rubber is not distorted and is positioned correctly.

INSIDE INFORMATION: Fuel pumps were fitted to certain Novas with no facility for cleaning the filter - these are identified by having no centre securing screw.

MODELS AFTER 1985 ONLY

82B. The in-line fuel filter is located at the top of the engine, just behind the cam/valve cover. It is placed in the fuel supply line between pump and carburettor. It is non-cleanable and must be replaced. First undo the two fuel pipe securing clips at the filter.

82C. The filter is held in place on a small bracket and secured by two screws - remove these and discard the filter, fitting a new one in place. After tightening the fuel pipe clips run the engine and check for leaks.

INSIDE INFORMATION: Ensure that the arrow on the filter points in the direction the fuel will flow through it. Some filters work in either direction, in which case there will be no arrow.

FUEL INJECTION ENGINES ONLY

SAFETY FIRST!
*i) This Job requires the rear of the car to be raised sufficiently to give good working clearance beneath the fuel tank, necessitating the use of ramps or axle stands. Be doubly careful to ensure the stability of the car before venturing beneath it - see **Raising the Car Safely** at the beginning of this chapter for how to do this safely. ii) Fuel injection systems remain pressurised even when the engine is switched off and require special procedures to make them safe - UNDER NO CIRCUMSTANCES loosen or remove fuel pipes on a fuel injection system. If pipework requires repair, take the car to a fuel injection specialist or your Vauxhall dealer.*

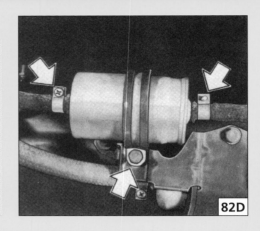

82D

82D. The fuel filter is located at the rear of the car, under the boot floor and behind the right-hand wheel arch. Position a container to catch the small amount of fuel that will inevitably be spilt and fit hose clamps to the inlet and outlet hoses, then undo the two hose clips, one at each end of the filter. On models up to 1992 the filter is free-hanging, while on later cars it is fixed by a bracket, as shown. A single screw holds the filter and bracket.

82E

82E. Before removing the hoses note which way the arrow stamped on the filter casing is pointing - in most cases it will be visible and pointing towards the pump, in the direction of travel. If there are no markings and the filter is to be replaced, mark one end so that it can be refitted correctly. If fitting a new filter, make sure its arrow points the same way as the original.

DIESEL ENGINES ONLY

FUEL FILTER DRAINING

82F. The fuel filter must be checked for possible water residue at every engine oil change: Drain it by first placing a container beneath the drain tube fitted to the bottom of the filter, then slackening the bleed screw (arrowed) at the top of the unit. Allow a small quantity of fuel to drain into the container and check it for signs of water, which will appear 'separated' from the fuel in blobs or layers. Continue draining until no water is evident. (Illustration, courtesy Vauxhall Motors Limited)

SAFETY FIRST!
i) Whenever dealing with diesel fuel, it's essential to protect your hands by wearing plastic gloves. ii) Keep diesel fuel away from the clutch and brakes, the starter motor and any rubber components. Protect Tarmac surfaces by putting down newspaper. IMPORTANT NOTE: Dirt is the enemy of fuel injection systems; even microscopic amounts can be disastrous. Clean thoroughly around the filter before dismantling and work with clean lint-free rags to wipe every component clean before re-assembling.

FILTER REPLACEMENT

82G. Position a container beneath the housing to collect the fuel that will inevitably be lost. Change the filter element by unscrewing the main body of the filter from the housing, which will allow the inner element to be removed. Fit the new sealing ring (supplied with the new element) and make sure it is properly seated, fit the new element and screw the canister into the housing. Turn the engine on the starter to purge the fuel system of air, and allow the engine to run for a minute or two, checking around the filter housing for leaks.

82F

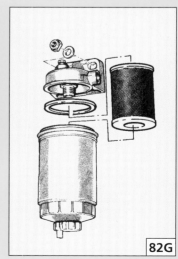

82G

☐ Job 83. Read stored engine fault codes.

FUEL INJECTION CARS FROM 1989 ONLY

The engine management systems fitted to these models has a facility to 'store' details of faulty components and other information useful to the service technician. Until recently these 'fault-codes' could only be accessed or read by Vauxhall dealers using very expensive equipment. However, Gunsons have introduced a code-reader suitable for D.I.Y. mechanics at a reasonable cost. The machine will help diagnose certain problems, but repair and adjustment procedures still need to be carried out by an experienced operator. Consult your Vauxhall dealer to read the codes and advise on any corrective measures necessary, whether or not you decide to read the codes yourself beforehand.

84

Every 12,000 Miles - Around the Car

☐ Job 84. Check toolkit and jack.

84. Inspect the toolkit, wipe tools with an oily rag to stop them rusting and lubricate the jack, checking that it works smoothly. Also, check that the spare wheel retaining bolt hasn't rusted in. Remove it and lubricate the threads with a dab of grease.

☐ Job 85. Check light seals.

Check the headlights, front indicators and rear light clusters for signs of water ingress, usually apparent as condensation on the inside of the lens. If present, either the weather seal has failed or mechanical damage such as stone chips is letting water in. Remove lenses so that you can check the seals. Renew them where possible and/or replace lenses.

☐ Job 86. Check door/tailgate seals.

Carefully examine the door seals for splits and cracks, and also the boot or tailgate seals, which often become damaged by heavy objects being dragged over them. Damaged seals will allow water to enter the interior of the car or luggage area - often the cause of internal corrosion. Replace any damaged seals as soon as possible.

☐ Job 87. Check headlight alignment.

It is possible to adjust your own headlights but not with sufficient accuracy to be safe or within the law. Badly adjusted headlights can be very dangerous if they don't provide you, the driver, with a proper view of the road ahead, or they dazzle oncoming drivers. Older drivers and those with poor eyesight can become disorientated when confronted with maladjusted headlights. **SPECIALIST SERVICE:** Have the work carried out for you by a garage with beam measuring equipment. Any MoT testing station in the UK will be properly equipped.

☐ Job 88. Renew wiper blades and arms.

Wiper blades don't last for ever, even though some people seem to think they do! It's a good policy to change them every year at least, not only on safety grounds but because a clear screen makes driving, especially at night, so much more comfortable. Refer to **Job 11** for details of how to change them.

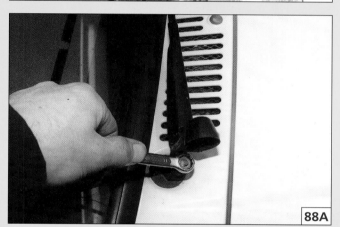

88A

88B

88A. The wiper arms can lose their tension and 'soften' over time, so change the complete arm periodically. They are removed by unscrewing the nut located beneath the flip-up plastic cover.

88B. The mounting boss is splined to match the drive spigot and allows the arm to be fitted at the correct angle to the screen.

12,000 MILE SERVICE

☐ Job 89. Check floors.

Lift the carpets and check for signs of rust and wetness on the floor underneath. If you find any, deal with it before any leaks are left for so long that you face the problem of seriously rusted metal as well. If you find any wetness, you will probably have to take the seats and the carpets right out to dry the carpets and any underfelt. Tracing leaks isn't the easiest of jobs, and sometimes the only way is to dry the floor thoroughly and then get someone play a hose on the underside of the car, round the doors and over the bonnet while you look inside.

INSIDE INFORMATION: Leaks through spot-welded seams may be just an indication of the original sealant having dried out and the problem. But it might just be the first sign of something more serious, like rusting. If you are in any doubt about the soundness of any part of the floor pan structure, seek SPECIALIST SERVICE at once. An early professional repair will save you pounds later on as well as ensuring that your car is structurally sound and safe. After any repair or re-sealing, give inside of the floor pan a coating of mastic such as body underseal. This doesn't normally dry right out but, when it is touch-dry, you can cover it with sheets of polythene to stop the carpets sticking to it.

☐ Job 90. Renew batteries in car alarm sender.

If your car is fitted with a remote control alarm system it is most galling to arrive at the car and find that the remote sender doesn't work and you can't get into your own car without setting off the alarm! Don't wait for the batteries to fail, renew them now.

☐ Job 91. Check wiring and terminals.

91. These items are by no means confined to the engine bay of course, but this is where the majority will be found. Terminals hanging by a thread or two could just be a breakdown waiting to happen - or even a fire. Your local accessory shop will stock standard-sized terminals and a crimping tool for fitting them.

☐ Job 92. Clean radiator exterior.

Modern radiators are finely engineered to fit the maximum amount of cooling surfaces into the smallest space, which means the spacing between the cooling 'tubes' or fins of the core are fine and prone to clogging. Dead flies, leaves, litter etc. can drastically reduce the effective cooling area of the radiator, so clean the core by directing a water jet from a garden hose through it - most effectively from the engine-bay side. A high-pressure jet isn't necessary and could damage the cooling fins, so keep the pressure down or use a spray attachment on your regular garden hose.

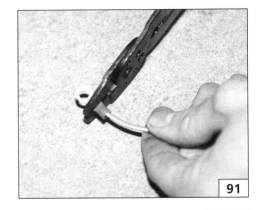

91

Every 12,000 Miles - Under the Car

☐ Job 93. Check wheel bearings.

93. Raise the front of the car just sufficiently for the wheels to be clear of the ground. Grip the top and bottom of the wheel and try to rock it with a push-pull motion, feeling for any sign of slackness or movement. If there is more than just the slightest suspicion of movement, have the wheel bearings checked by **SPECIALIST SERVICE**. Do the same for the rear wheels after releasing the handbrake. Also, spin each wheel, listening for any 'rumble' or roughness from the hub (but don't confuse this noise with the 'rubbing' sound commonly caused by the brake shoes contacting the drums slightly).

93

☐ Job 94. Check steering and suspension.

94A. With the front wheels just clear of the ground, grasp the wheel at the sides and try to turn it from side to side. If you feel free play, put the car up on axle stands and get someone to turn the wheels while you investigate where the free play is occurring. If it is in one of the steering ball joints, these can be renewed, see **Job 68**. If, however, the play is in the steering rack, seek **SPECIALIST SERVICE**.

Test the steering column by grasping the steering wheel and rocking it up-and-down and sideways. Excessive play needs to be investigated - seek professional advice.

94A

94B. With the front wheels still raised just clear of the ground, put a lever under the wheel and try to lever it upwards. If you get any free play it means wear in the suspension bushes or suspension strut. Seek **SPECIALIST ADVICE**.

Job 95. Check steering rack mountings.

95. Check the two clamps securing the steering rack to the bulkhead by grasping the steering rack and trying to rock it. If any play is felt, check the mounting bolts for tightness with a spanner. (Illustration, courtesy Vauxhall Motors Limited)

Job 96. Check front suspension units.

SAFETY FIRST!
*The front of the car needs to be raised sufficiently to allow the front suspension components to be checked - see **Raising the Car** at the beginning of this chapter for details of how to do this safely. Note that it will be necessary to position the axle stands under the chassis so that the suspension is free to 'hang' down, i.e. without bearing any of the car's weight.*

96. Check the front spring/shock absorber units (correctly termed 'MacPherson struts'), looking for badly corroded or broken springs. Make sure the drain holes in the lower spring seat-pan are clean and clear. Check the shock absorber inside the spring for signs of oil staining, indicating a failed unit - have it investigated and always renew shock absorbers in pairs, one each side of the car.

Job 97. Check front suspension bushes.

97. Check the rubber bushes at each mounting point of the front suspension components, looking for signs of splits, perishing or other damage. Check also the anti-roll bar bushes (arrowed).

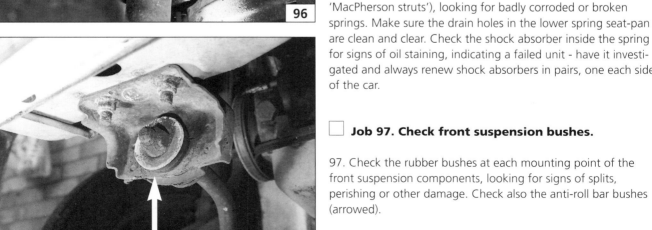

12,000 MILE SERVICE

☐ **Job 98. Check rear springs and-shock absorbers.**

SAFETY FIRST!
*The rear of the car needs to be raised sufficiently to allow the suspension components to be checked - see **Raising the Car** at the beginning of this chapter for details of how to do this safely. Note that it will be necessary to position the axle stands under the chassis so that the suspension is free to 'hang' down, i.e. without bearing any of the car's weight.*

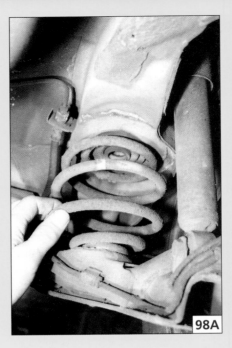

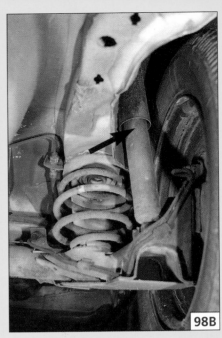

98A. Check the rear springs for signs of corrosion and breaks in the coil. Check also the rubber seating into which the spring fits.

98B. Examine the rear shock absorber (arrowed), looking for signs of staining which could indicate an oil leak. Grasp the damper and try to rock it - there should be little or no free play, but if there is, check the mounting bolts (99.A) and rubber bushes (99.B) for tightness and condition.

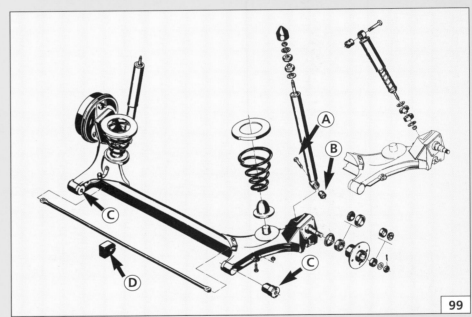

☐ **Job 99. Check rear suspension bushes.**

99. Check the axle pivot bushes (C) for splits and perishing, and check also the anti-roll bar rubber damper (D) located in the axle 'channel'.

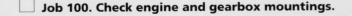

☐ **Job 100. Check engine and gearbox mountings.**

100. Examine the engine mountings for signs of perishing, splits, and cracks in the steel brackets. Use a large screwdriver or lever to check that the metal-rubber-metal 'sandwich' doesn't separate when pressure is applied. 'Rock' the engine fore and aft by pushing on the valve/camshaft cover - only a small amount of movement should be evident, otherwise seek SPECIALIST SERVICE.

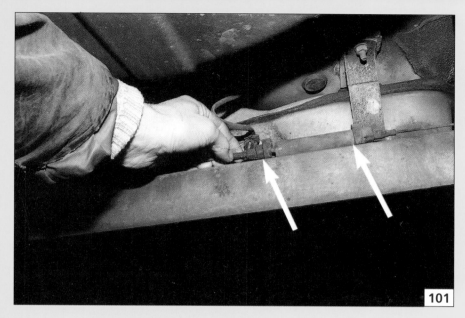

101

☐ Job 101. Check/lubricate hand-brake cable.

Check the cable outer sheath along its length for signs of chafing or other damage. Operate the handbrake lever and feel for any roughness in operation that may indicate a damaged or frayed inner cable.

101. Apply grease liberally to the handbrake equaliser where it slides along the rear axle (arrowed).

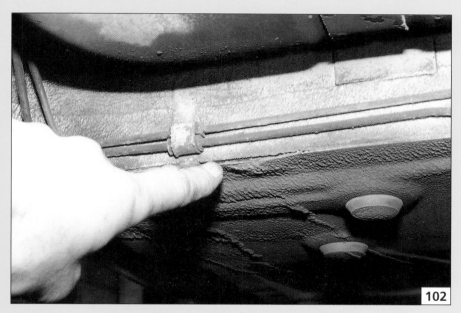

102

☐ Job 102. Check underside of body structure.

102. Examine the underbody structure for corrosion, particularly in the vicinity of welded joints and seams, and also for 'mechanical' damage caused, for instance, by driving over high kerbstones. Make good any damage to the 'underseal' coating using a wax-based product rather than a bitumen one, which will crack again.

103

☐ Job 103. Clear drainage holes.

103. Check and clear drainage holes in door bottoms, sills, boot/luggage area etc. Use a thin probe to poke the holes clear, while for a lasting job a vacuum cleaner and nozzle will clear most debris. Check also the nooks and crannies around the bulkhead at the rear of the engine bay , especially for leaves in autumn and winter - your vacuum cleaner is possibly the only thing that will shift them!

CHAPTER THREE

☐ **Job 104. Renew brake fluid.**

SPECIALIST SERVICE: Vauxhall recommend that brake fluid is changed annually on all models of all ages of their cars. This is best carried out by a reputable garage or Vauxhall dealer, who will have the necessary facilities to carry out the work thoroughly and safely.

Every 24,000 Miles - Or Every Two Years, whichever comes first

Every 24,000 Miles - The Engine Bay

☐ **Job 105. Replace coolant and clean expansion tank.**

105. The cooling system is drained at the radiator bottom-left outlet by unscrewing the clip and easing-off the hose. Place a container beneath to catch the old coolant. Replace the hose and clip and add the required amount of antifreeze (follow the manufacturers' guidelines regarding dilution) followed by clean water. Run the engine at tickover, noting the coolant level in the expansion tank and topping-up as air in the system is expelled and the coolant level drops. Finally, fit the radiator cap and allow the engine to reach operating temperature; cut the engine and check the coolant level again - if topping-up is still required, allow the engine to cool for at least twenty minutes before attempting to undo the cap, which should be done slowly to release any pressure before the cap is removed.

105

INSIDE INFORMATION: If necessary clean the expansion tank using a little detergent and an old dish-washing brush. Flush the tank afterwards with clean water.

☐ **Job 106. Replace coolant expansion tank cap.**

106. Renew the expansion tank cap (often still called the 'radiator' cap). The rubber sealing washer perishes or hardens over time, preventing the necessary pressure to accumulate in the system and therefore allowing the coolant to boil at a lower temperature.

106

☐ **Job 107. Renew drive belts.**

Renew the alternator drive belt - see **Job 20** for details of this item. Renewing it now could save an engine-stopping or even an engine-ruining breakdown at some time in the future if the belt breaks unexpectedly.

Every 36,000 Miles - or Every Three Years, whichever comes first

☐ **Job 108. Change gearbox oil.**

INSIDE INFORMATION: Vauxhall do not specify an interval for this job - in fact they don't specify this job at all in their servicing schedules and regard the occasional need to top-up as sufficient. Also, it has to be remembered that other repair procedures, such as drive-shaft renewal or repair, will cause a considerable loss of oil from the gearbox and, provided new oil is used to replenish the 'box, they consider this to be satisfactory. However, the extra-careful owner may feel happier to change the oil at regular intervals, especially as part of the 'catch-up' service on a newly-acquired used car. And since, by definition, all oil must deteriorate over a period of time, we recommend it.

SAFETY FIRST!
As with engine oil, gearbox lubricants contain many chemicals that your hands may be sensitive to, so always wear rubber gloves when carrying out work that may bring oil into contact with the hands.

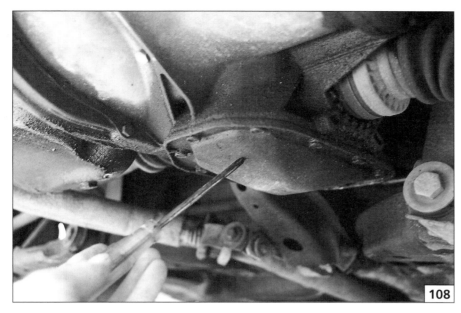

108. No drain plug is provided on the gearbox, so this 'sump' plate has to be removed to drain the oil. Position a suitable drip-tray beneath the gearbox and proceed to remove the screws, starting with the lowest. On loosening the last screw the plate should move sufficiently to allow the oil to drain. If the plate sticks to the gasket and maintains a seal, tap the lower edge of the plate with a wooden or hide mallet to jar it free. After draining fully, fit a new gasket to the sump before replacing it, then refill with fresh oil through the gearbox vent plug, see **Job 48B** for details and location.

☐ Job 109. Renew camshaft belt.

OHC ENGINES ONLY

The camshaft drive belt or 'cam-belt' performs the vital job of turning the camshaft in time with the crankshaft, from which it is driven. If it breaks, or the 'teeth' become stripped (the belt is made from rubber-reinforced fabric) then synchronisation will be lost and the camshaft-driven valves are likely to come into contact with the pistons, causing severe damage to the engine.

109A. Start by removing the camshaft belt cover so that you can at least inspect the belt for yourself.

109B. *SPECIALIST SERVICE & INSIDE INFORMATION: Vauxhall recommend the cam-belt be changed at 36,000 miles or FOUR years for all petrol engined cars, with diesels at 72,000 miles or eight years. We would recommend playing safe and sticking to 36,000 miles or THREE years for all cars. A cam-belt breaks without warning and, as stated above, an engine can be very severely damaged as the pistons hit the valves. Replacement is a job is best entrusted to a reputable garage or Vauxhall agent, who have the necessary facilities and skills to carry it out.*

☐ Job 110. Top-up rust-proofing.

110. Apply rust-proofing fluid/wax to the exposed areas of the car i.e. wheel arches and underside, where existing treatments are likely to be washed away by road grit and water. Apply rust-proofer to the box sections and door interiors too, although it isn't necessary to use as much fluid as the original treatment. See *Chapter 5, Rust-Proofing*, for details.

Every 48,000 Miles, or Every Four Years, whichever comes first

☐ Job 111. Renew HT leads, distributor cap and rotor arm.

111. Even though the HT leads, distributor cap and rotor arm may look OK, they can deteriorate with age. To ensure trouble-free starting and running it pays to renew them at this interval.

making it easy! Mark the old cap with typist's correction fluid to indicate which lead goes to which plug; remove the old cap and leads from the distributor and use the markings as a guide to fitting the new leads.

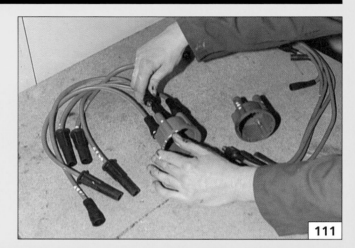

Every 72,000 Miles, or Every Six Years, whichever comes first

☐ Job 112. Renew glow plugs.

DIESEL ENGINES ONLY

112. Poor starting can be the bane of life for owners of older diesel engines. Replacing the glow plugs (one of them arrowed) at this stage can make a major difference. See **Job 79** for details.

☐ Job 113. Check and renew fuel injectors.

FUEL INJECTION PETROL AND DIESEL ENGINES

113. In time, and even with detergent fuels, injectors become carboned and do not work at their full efficiency. This may show up as poor starting or on an MoT exhaust emission test. Checking the spray pattern of injectors calls for specialised equipment, so this is a job for **SPECIALIST SERVICE**. (Illustration courtesy of V.L.Churchill)

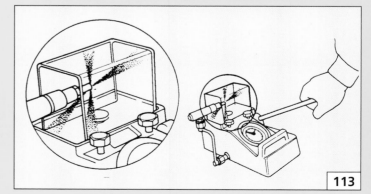

CHAPTER 4 - BODYWORK

In this Chapter, we show you how to make your car look its best. First, we demonstrate that your car's appearance can be improved beyond recognition by a couple of hours of work on a Sunday morning. Then, just in case a passing gate post should leap out at you, we explain how to carry out simple bodywork repairs at home.

PART I: THE BODY BEAUTIFUL

Have you ever looked in amazement at the condition of cars on a dealer's forecourt and wondered why your car doesn't look like that? Well, it can! It's all a matter of know-how and a bit of hard work - and using the techniques described in this Chapter, you'll find that your car can be made to look almost like new again, without using too many cans of elbow grease!

☐ I.1 Apply a thin coat of modern car polish, to give a far longer-lasting shine than old-fashioned waxes (though we've yet to find one that lasts as long as claimed!). Cover just one section of the car at a time and then, as soon as the wax dries

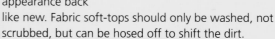

to a haze, buff off for a superb shine. You'll see the dull paint and oxides come off on the cloth as you buff.

I.1

making it easy! • As you polish, keep turning the cloth, always presenting a clean face to the surface of the paint - that's the secret of obtaining a clear shine with no rub marks. You'll need several clean cloths for polishing a whole car!

• Try removing a bug splat with a kitchen abrasive pad - the gentler sort made for non-stick pans - but only on glass and chrome; it'll ruin the shine on paintwork.

☐ I.2 Weekend trips in your car are likely to be cursed by the 'bugs on the bumper' syndrome, as well as black tar on the bodywork. Soak all the bug-splatted areas with soapy water first, while you wash the rest of the car, then come back later, when they've been softened. Rub off with cloth, rather than a sponge. Use a proprietary brand of tar remover to wipe off tar splash.

SOFT-TOP SPORTS CARS: If your vinyl soft-top has ingrained dirt, scrub it gently all over with a nail brush and soapy water. When dry, apply a good quality vinyl cleaner to bring the appearance back

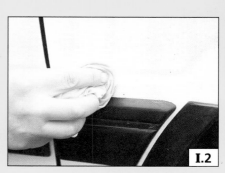

I.2

like new. Fabric soft-tops should only be washed, not scrubbed, but can be hosed off to shift the dirt.

☐ I.3 It's easy to forget that around a fifth of your car's 'bodywork' is in fact glass. Use purpose-made glass cleaner, or a clean wash leather, for sparkling results. Clouding on the inside (said to be the vapour from upholstery plastics!) cleans off in the same way.

I.3

BODYWORK

☐ I.4 Tyres are one of the most 'visual' parts of your car. There are proprietary tyre polishes and paints available, but be warned that the improvement in appearance goes the first time you drive on a wet road! A good cleaning with the wash sponge - *after* you've washed the rest of the car - is usually enough. Alloy wheels need a spray-on alloy wheel cleaner to shift stuck-on brake dust.

I.4

☐ I.5 *INSIDE INFORMATION: Many people just don't know what to do about dull plastic bumpers. Use a colourless trim cleaner and you'll find that just wiping it on will bring about a magical improvement. Several coats may be needed. (The old, black-coloured bumper polish makes a real mess of your hands, by the way!)*

☐ I.6 Even when an engine bay is clean, it often looks dirty. Use a spray-on cleaner to remove the heavy dirt and grease - best if you let it soak in to the worst areas. Use an old paintbrush in nooks and crannies. A vinyl protectant will then bring up a wonderful sheen to all of your hoses and pipes as well as all underbonnet paintwork.

I.5

> *making it easy!* If your engine is very oily, ask a local garage with a steam cleaner to hose off the worst of the 'grunge' before starting to clean up the engine bay. Paint any bare metal exposed by the steam cleaning, before it starts to rust.

☐ I.7 Choose a vinyl cleaner designed to put back the suppleness into vinyl and protect it from fading, as well as to remove dirt and grime and restore the appearance. If you hate the 'tacky' high gloss shine produced by some of them, look out for the low-gloss variety, giving a more natural finish.

INSIDE INFORMATION: If you can't get hold of low-gloss vinyl cleaner, try wiping over with a damp cloth before the cleaner has fully dried. This also 'wipes' away the worst of the gloss.

Rubber seals will last far longer if they are protected against the elements, by regular treatments with vinyl and rubber protectant. Scrape out dirt and grit from around the lower door seals then treat them all with several coats.

I.6

☐ I.8 Fabric seats and carpets will certainly benefit from cleaning with a proprietary brand of spray-on car upholstery cleaner - or a household upholstery cleaner. Follow the instructions carefully, take care not to soak cloth trim (it could cause shrinking) and the result will be carpets and cloth seats that look like new.

You can make leather more supple, and keep it cleaner and longer lasting by using a purpose-made brand of leather care. After use, the leather will feel soft and supple, because of the lanolin and mois-turisers that you will have added. At first, you may be surprised to see the colour of your leather go much darker but don't worry; that will pass as the leather cleaner dries out naturally.

I.7

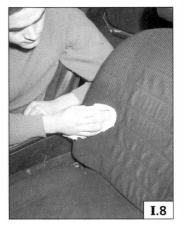

I.8

PART II: REPAIRING BODYWORK BLEMISHES

However well you look after your car, there will always be the risk of car park accident damage - or even worse! The smallest paint chips are best touched up with paint purchased from your local auto. accessory shop. If your colour of paint is not available, some auto. accessory shops offer a mixing scheme (including aerosols, in some cases) or you could look for a local paint factor in Yellow Pages. Take your car along to the paint factor and have them match the colour and mix the smallest quantity of cellulose paint that they will supply you with. Larger body blemishes will need the use of body filler.

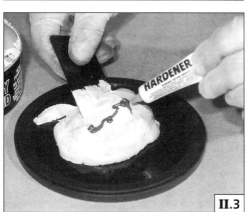

> **SAFETY FIRST!**
> **Always** wear plastic gloves when working with body filler, before it has set. Always wear a face mask when sanding filler and wear goggles when using a power sander.

II.1 The rear of this car's bodywork has sustained a nasty gash, the sort of damage for which you will certainly need to use body filler. The first stage is to mask off. Try to find "natural" edges such as body mouldings or styling stripes and wherever you can, mask off body trim rather than having to remove it.

II.2 Remove all paint from the damaged area and for about 25mm (1 in.) around the damaged area. Roughen the bare metal or surface with coarse abrasive paper - a power sander is best. Wipe over the area with white spirit (mineral spirit) and then wash off with washing-up liquid in water - **not** car wash detergent.

INSIDE INFORMATION: Rub the surrounding paintwork with cutting compound so that the new paint has a better chance of matching the old.

II.3 Mix the filler and hardener, following the instructions on the can. It's best to use a piece of plastic or metal rather than cardboard because otherwise, the filler will pick up fibres from the surface of the card. Mix thoroughly until the colour is consistent and no traces of hardener can be discerned.

II.4 You can now spread the filler evenly over the repair. If the damage is particularly deep, apply the paste in two or more layers, allowing the filler to harden before adding the next layer. The final layer should be just proud of the level required, but do not overfill as this wastes paste and will require more time to sand down.

II.5 It is essential when sanding down that you wrap the sanding paper around a flat block. You can see from the scratch marks that this repair has been sanded diagonally in alternate directions until the filler has become level with the surrounding panel, but you have to take care not to go deeply into the edges of the paint around the repair.

INSIDE INFORMATION: There will invariably be small pin holes even if the right amount of filler was applied first time. Use a tiny amount of filler scraped very thin over the whole repair, filling in deep scratches and pin holes and then sanding off with a very fine grade of sand paper - preferably dry paper rather than wet-or-dry because you don't want to get water on to the bare filler.

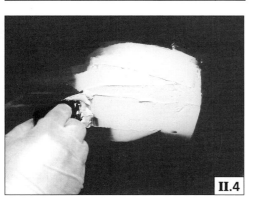

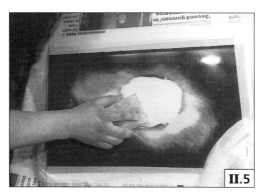

BODYWORK

☐ II.6 You can now use an aerosol primer to spray over the whole area of the repair but preferably not right up to the edges of the masking tape...

☐ II.7 ...and now use wet-or-dry paper, again on a sanding block, to sand the primer paint.

INSIDE INFORMATION: Don't sand fresh primer paint - leave it up to a day to harden off.

The filler is now protected from the water by the paint. If you do apply paint right up to the edge of the tape, be sure to 'feather' the edges of the primer, so that the edges blend in smoothly to the surrounding surface, with no ridges.

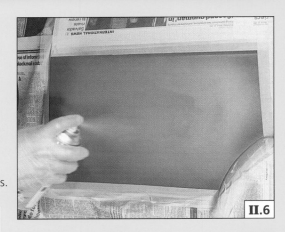
II.6

SAFETY FIRST!
Always wear an efficient mask when spraying aerosol paint and only work in a well-ventilated area, well away from any source of ignition, because spray paint vapour, even that given off by an aerosol, is highly flammable. Ensure that you have doors and windows open to the outside when using aerosol paint but in cool or damp weather, close them when the vapour has dispersed, otherwise the surface of the paint will "bloom", or take on a milky appearance. In fact, you may find it difficult to obtain a satisfactory finish in cold or damp weather.

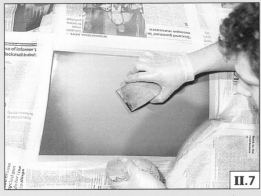
II.7

☐ II.8 Before starting to spray, ensure that the nozzle is clear. Note that the can must be held with the index finger well back on the aerosol button. If you let your finger overhang the front of the button, a paint drip can form and throw itself on to the work area as a paint blob.

making it easy! • *One of the secrets of spraying paint which doesn't run, is to put a very light coat of spray paint on to the panel first, followed by several more coats, allowing time between each coat for the bulk of the solvent to evaporate.*

• *Alternate coats should go on horizontally, followed by vertical coats as shown on the inset diagram.*

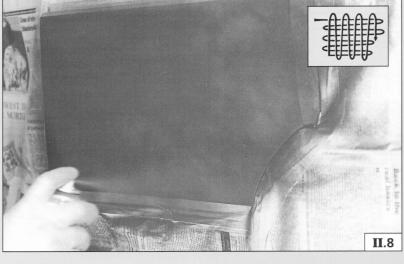
II.8

☐ II.9 After allowing about a week for the paint to dry, you will be able to polish it with a light cutting compound, blending the edges of the repair into the surrounding paintwork.

*INSIDE INFORMATION: Do note that if your repairs don't work out first time and you have to apply more paint on top of the fresh paint that you have already used, allow a week to elapse otherwise there is a strong risk of pickling or other reactions to take place. Also note that a prime cause of paint failure is the existence of silicones on the surface of the old paint before you start work. These come from most types of polish and are not all that easy to remove - they **won't** sand off!. Thoroughly wipe the panel down with white spirit before starting work and wash off with warm water and washing-up liquid to remove any further traces of the polish and the white spirit - but don't use the sponge or bucket that you normally use for washing the car otherwise you will simply introduce more silicones onto the surface!*

II.9

CHAPTER 5 - RUSTPROOFING

When mechanical components deteriorate, they can cost you a lot of money to replace. But when your car's bodywork deteriorates, it can cost you the car, if corrosion goes beyond the point where repairs are economical to carry out. Rust prevention should be regarded as a regular maintenance job, one which enables you to extend the life of your car by many years - and that will save you *real* money!

If you want to prolong its life, you'll have to inject rustproofing fluid into all the enclosed box sections and 'chassis' sections on your car. In many cases, you'll find holes already in place; in others, you'll be able to take off a cover, a piece or trim or a door lock in order to gain access. But in quite a few cases, you'll need to drill holes to gain an entry.

Don't be a drip!

*INSIDE INFORMATION: i) Place **lots** of newspaper beneath the car to catch the inevitable drips. ii) Some seat belts retract into a cavity that you will want to spray with fluid. Pull each belt out and hold it there until you have finished spraying the fluid. iii) All electric motors should be covered up with plastic bags so that none of the rustproofing fluid gets in and all windows should be fully wound up. iv) Ensure that all drain channels are clear so that any excess rustproofing fluid can drain out and also check once again that they are clear after you have finished carrying out the work to ensure that your application of the fluid has not caused them to be clogged up, otherwise water will become trapped, negating much of the good work you have carried out.*

making it easy! Decide on your drill size with reference to the size of the injector nozzle and the size of grommets that you can obtain for blanking the holes off again afterwards. You'll feel a bit foolish if you drill first, only to find that they don't make grommets to fit the holes you've drilled!

Choose Your Weapon

Those hand pump injectors that you can buy from DIY shops are often worse than useless. They don't usually make a proper spray, but simply squirt a jet of fluid that does nothing to give the all-over cover required. Make a dummy 'box section' out of a cardboard box - cut it and fold to make it about 10 or 15 cm square - and try a dummy run. Open up and see if it has worked. If you haven't obtained full misting of the fluid, you could be making the problem worse.

INSIDE INFORMATION: Rust strikes even harder in those areas that aren't properly covered!

Consider taking your car to a garage with suitable equipment and having them do the work for you. Full, professional injection equipment, as shown in the following picture sequence, will make the fluid reach much further and deeper than amateur equipment, and if you enlist the services of the best experts as featured here, you'll be able to benefit from their experience.

SAFETY FIRST!
*Before using rustproofer, read the manufacturer's safety notes. Keep rustproofing fluid off the exhaust or any other components where it could be ignited. Keep it away from brake components, covering them up with plastic bags before starting work. Follow **Chapter 1, Safety First!**, and advice at the start of **Chapter 3, Servicing Your Car** especially with regard to safe working beneath a car raised off the ground. Rustproofers all contain solvents. In a confined space, such as a garage, solvents can build up, creating both a health and a fire hazard. Wear an efficient face mask so that you don't inhale vapour and work out of doors, keeping out of confined spaces. Wear gloves and goggles, but if you do get any fluid in your eyes, wash out with copious amounts of water and immediately seek medical advice if necessary. If any welding has to be carried out on the vehicle within a few months of rustproofing being carried out, you must inform those who are carrying out the work because of the fire risk.*

Our thanks are due to Dinol Ltd for carrying out the work shown here, using Dinitrol rustproofing fluid.

☐ Job 1. Clean underbody.

1. You will have to hose off the underside of the body, paying particular attention to the undersides of the wings and wheel arches, before you can start to apply new rustproofing. Scrape off any hard, thick deposits of mud, and any old flaking body sealant under the car. One of the quickest ways to do the job is to use a power washer with a long lance. Many garages have this equipment for customer use in a wash bay and this is a very efficient way of doing the job. You will, however, still have to go underneath with a scraper afterwards as even a power jet won't take off flaking body sealant. You will also have to wait up to a week for the underside of the car to dry thoroughly (in warm, dry weather) before applying new rustproofing.

☐ Job 2. Equipment.

Gather together all the materials you need to do the job before you start. You will also need lifting equipment and axle stands.

making it easy! 2. A compressor-driven gun of this type won't break the bank - try your local trade parts factors - but you'll need to buy or hire a compressor. Results will be excellent.

Bear in mind the safety equipment you will need - referred to in *SAFETY FIRST!* - see **page 81**. You will need copious amounts of newspaper to spread on the floor because quite a lot of rustproofing fluid will run out of the box sections and other areas under the car and you may have to park your car over newspaper for a couple of days after carrying out this treatment. Remember that the vapour given off by the materials will continue for several days, so park your car in the open for a week or so if you can, rather than in an enclosed garage.

INSIDE INFORMATION: Tip from Dinol, the manufacturers of Dinitrol: Except in a heat wave, it is essential to stand the container of rustproofer in a tub of hot water to keep it fluid. Top up the tub from time to time with more hot water while you are working.

Not only will warm rustproofer penetrate seams better, it will flow through the applicator better and not clog so easily. Some people thin the rustproofer with white spirit, but warming it is better. Wash the gun and lances out with white spirit afterwards. If you let the rustproofer set, it is almost impossible to clean them.

Around the Car

☐ Job 3. Chrome trim and seams.

3. Some rustproofing fluids in aerosol cans are thin enough for injecting behind chromium trim strips and badges but some people find that they are inclined to leave a stain on the paintwork around the trim. As an alternative to a rustproofing fluid, you can use a water dispersant or a thin oil.

☐ Job 4. Doors.

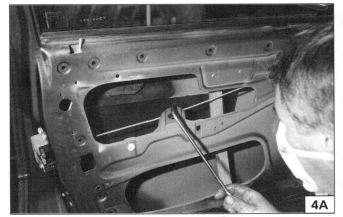

4A. Remove the trim panel and carefully "peel" away the clear plastic membrane that covers the door inner cavity. Insert the nozzle to cover all the inside of the door, making sure you get plenty of 'creeping' fluid into the steel joints, where water could collect and corrosion could occur. Naturally, the main problem is that moisture collects in the bottom of the doors and rots them out from the inside - use plenty of fluid here. If you don't want to remove the door trims, then fluid can be sprayed through the lower drain slots, but note that this will only provide protection for the lower surfaces and seams. If your car is fitted with door speakers, remove them first or the fluid could ruin them!

4B

4B. This how the bottom of the doors should look if you've done the job correctly! - excess fluid will issue from the drain slots in the door bottoms, which is why we recommend covering the ground beneath the car with newspaper.

Job 5. The 'A' post.

5. The 'A' post box-section is that part of the body immediately behind the front wings to which the front doors are hinged.
Access is gained by unscrewing the courtesy light switch securing screw and inserting a flexible nozzle as far as it will go, spraying as it is withdrawn. Feed the nozzle in both directions (up and down) so that all inner surfaces are covered, paying particular attention to the bottom of the section.

Job 6. The 'B' post (4 & 5-door models only).

Novas made from 1989 will have a grommet fitted to the lower 'B' post (the box section that connects the roof to the floor and to which the rear doors are hinged) which gives adequate access if a flexible nozzle is inserted and worked up into the post. Earlier models can be treated by removing the inner trim panel, which gives access to the post.

INSIDE INFORMATION: Think carefully before drilling holes to insert rustproofing fluid, especially in the "chassis", where there are numerous holes already. If you do drill a hole in steel, make sure that you file off the rough burrs and then apply an anti-rusting agent, followed by a coating of paint followed by a layer of wax.

Make sure the area you drill into is indeed hollow and not the inside of the car or luggage bay! Spend time looking out for wires or pipes. Disconnect the car's battery.

5

Job 7. The 'C' post.

7A. The 'C' post is that section of the bodywork up to which the rear doors close. To avoid drilling unnecessary holes on 4-door and 5-door models the 'C' post can be treated from inside the boot area, by passing the flexible nozzle up over the wheel arch and spraying in all directions...

7B. .... while on 2-door and 3-door cars access to both 'C' post and forward areas of the rear wheel arch can be treated by removing the side ashtray and inserting the nozzle. CAUTION: Take care to cover the seats with an old blanket or similar - rust-proofing fluid will stain upholstery and prove very difficult to remove!

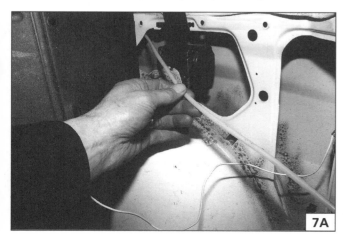

7A

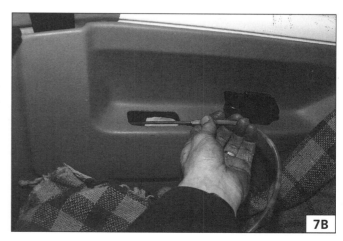

7B

RUSTPROOFING

Job 8. Tailgate/boot lid.

8. While it is better to remove the tailgate trim panel (the boot lid on saloon models is "open" already), with care it is possible to use the drain holes provided, as we have done here. Aim to apply the fluid to all the seams and strengthening ribs, and on tailgates 'wiggle' the nozzle up into the sides of the tailgate around the rear screen aperture. When spraying is complete, close the door/tailgate so that fluid drains down into the bottom seam. Make sure the drain holes remain clear on the bottom edge.

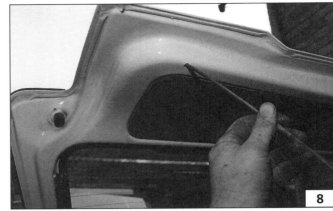
8

Job 9. Boot/luggage bay area.

9. Remove the pull-away side trims and work the nozzle into the space between the outer wing and the boot/luggage bay 'floor', paying particular attention to the lower joint which forms the wheel arch shown here. It is a good idea to remove the rear lamps also, in order to reach the box section beneath them and to adequately treat the upper corners of the wing. Insert the flexible nozzle into the box section that crosses the boot at the rear - holes provided for the wiring harness will give access to this section. Spray the spare wheel compartment (after removing the wheel!) but remember to wipe the excess fluid away before replacing it.

Job 10. Bonnet.

10. Apply fluid into all strengthening ribs and channels on the underside of the bonnet. Some models have a fibre-board insulation cover clipped to the underside - remove this first. Pay attention to the front, rear, and side-seams of the bonnet, making sure sufficient fluid is applied to penetrate the layers of metal. As with the tailgate, close the bonnet after application so that fluid runs down to the front seam.

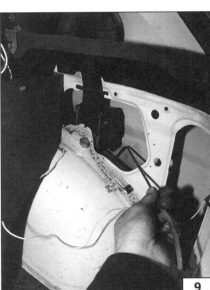
9

Job 11. Engine bay.

11A. Apply fluid to the joints between wings and body and to the wing fixing bolts/washers. Also apply fluid to the suspension tops, behind and beneath the front "slam" panel, down the seams between inner wing and bulkhead. Insert (see **Job 110** on page 76.) a flexible nozzle to the "apron" at the rear of the engine bay, reaching the seam beneath the panel where the windscreen is fixed, and around the wiper motor and heater blower box. At each end of the rear apron, work the nozzle up into the windscreen pillars, spraying as it is withdrawn.

11B. Apply fluid to the rear of the headlight apertures and the indicator lens assembly, and along the front 'slam' panel, making sure to get the fluid into all the little nooks and crannies formed in the panelwork.

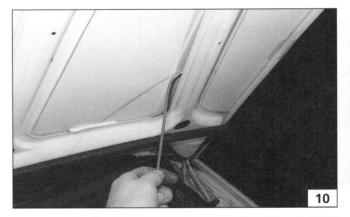
10

11A

11B

Under the Car

☐ Job 12. Cross members.

12A. Work the flexible nozzle along the cross-members and spray as it is withdrawn, paying particular attention to the end-seams where they join the inner wing "out-riggers" that travel forwards through the engine bay; use the flexible nozzle to treat these sections too, gaining access through the many drain holes already provided.

12B. The longitudinal strengthening members are similarly treated through the holes provided.

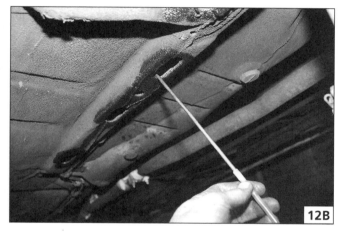

☐ Job 13. Sills.

13A. The sills are arranged with a central strengthening membrane so it is necessary to spray both inner and outer 'halves' of the assembly, to ensure coverage of the whole sill area. Drain holes are provided through which the flexible nozzle can be worked in both fore and aft directions, each time spraying as it is withdrawn.

13B. Access holes are already present on the inner sill panels. Make sure all the sill drain holes are clear by poking with a short length of stiff wire. Fluid should issue from all such holes, if you've applied sufficient!

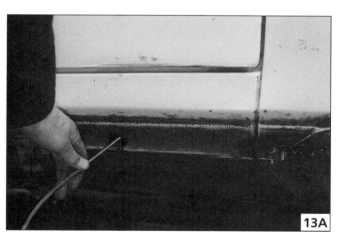

☐ Job 14. Rear 'chassis' sections.

14. Treat all the box sections, joints, seams, spring mountings etc. beneath the rear of the car, but take care not to get rustproofing fluid near the brakes, as this could result in brake failure.

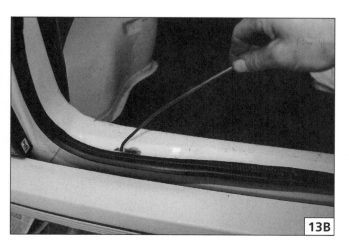

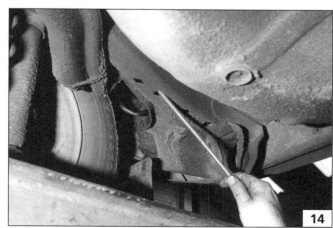

RUSTPROOFING

Job 15. Spray underside and wheel arches.

Get yourself prepared for this job! Disposable overalls or old clothes are a necessity and none more so than some form of headgear to protect your hair. Gloves and a face-mask are also essential.

15. First of all, the thinner, 'creeping' type of fluid is sprayed into and onto every seam. Then, it's time to cover the entire surface with the tougher type of protectant. For this process the thicker, black underbody fluid is used - note that this needs to be warmed by standing in a bucket of very hot water for twenty minutes or so before use. Make doubly sure that the car is safely raised and stable - this is no time to take chances - and ensure any floor protection is in place and secure. Spray the fluid while it is still warm and "thin", taking care to ensure an even coverage with no gaps. When spraying over fuel and brake pipes make at least two passes with the spraygun, at different angles, so that the fluid isn't masked by the pipes which would leave an unprotected "shadow" behind them. Start at the front of the car and work backwards, ending with the boot underside and spare wheel well.

Job 16. The wheel arches.

16A. Remove all four wheels and wrap plastic bags around the brake discs or drums, then spray the inner wheel arch surfaces. Pay particular attention to the outer wheel arch seams - spray "outwards" from inside the wheelarch to ensure good penetration and sealing. Spray also up into the coil spring recesses (suspension tops), varying the angle of the spray gun as the fluid is applied.

16B. If your car is fitted with plastic "inner splashguards" it's a good idea to remove them so that the fluid can be applied to the "hidden" seams and surfaces, because they can still get damp, and consequently will corrode. Alternatively, work the flexible nozzle up into the gap behind the splash-guards as shown, and apply plenty of fluid to the surfaces inside.

16C. Use these holes to treat the 'chassis' out-riggers at the front of the car, while the wheel is off and access is easy.

Finally, clean any fluid "overspray" from the body work, including the door sills where fluid will have dripped from the door drain holes. Use a good glass cleaner if fluid has found its way onto the glass (it usually does!), especially the windscreen. Also, clean the windscreen wiper blades, as traces of fluid will be smeared across the screen when the wipers are next used and you're unlikely to see much through it! The last job is to fit any grommets into holes you may have drilled - soak them in fluid before fitting, which will provide a very effective seal when the fluid turns to wax over the following week or so.

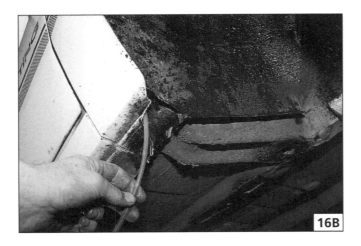

CHAPTER 6 - FAULT FINDING

Does this sound familiar? The vehicle refuses to start one damp Sunday morning. You decide that there must be no fuel getting through. By the time you've stripped the fuel pump and fuel lines and "unblocked" the fuel tank, it's time for bed. And the next day, the local garage finds that your main HT lead has dropped out of the coil! Something like that has happened to most of us!

Don't jump to conclusions: if your engine won't start or runs badly, if electrical components fail, follow the logical sequence of checks listed here and detailed overleaf, eliminating each "check" (by testing, not by "hunch") before moving on to the next. And remember that the great majority of failures are caused by electrical or ignition faults: only a minor proportion of engine failures come from the fuel system. Follow the sequences shown here - and you'll have a better chance of success in finding that fault. Before carrying out any of the work described in this Chapter please read carefully *Chapter 1, Safety First!*

PART I - PETROL ENGINED VEHICLES

Engine won't start.

1. Starter motor doesn't turn.

2. Is battery okay?

3. Check battery connections for cleanliness/tightness.

4. Have battery 'drop' test carried out by specialist.

5. Test battery with voltmeter or, preferable, with a hydrometer.

6. Can engine be rotated by hand?

7. If engine cannot be rotated by hand, check for mechanical seizure of power unit, or pinion gear jammed in mesh with flywheel - 'rock' car backwards and forwards until free, or apply spanner to square drive at front end of starter motor.

8. If engine can be rotated by hand, check for loose electrical connections at starter, faulty solenoid, or defective starter motor.

9. Starter motor turns slowly.

10. Battery low on charge or defective - re-charge and have 'drop' test carried out by specialist.

11. Internal fault within starter motor - e.g. worn brushes.

12. Starter motor noisy or harsh.

13. Drive teeth on ring gear or starter pinion worn/broken.

14. Main drive spring broken.

15. Starter motor securing bolts loose.

16. Starter motor turns engine but car will not start. See 'Ignition System' box.

Ignition system.

> **SAFETY FIRST!**
> *It is essential that you read **Chapter 1, Safety First!, The Ignition System** before carrying out work on this part of the car.*

(Carry out the following checks as appropriate. For example, some vehicles have contact breaker ignition while the majority of modern cars have electronic ignition. Only Step 17 can be carried out on cars with electronic ignition. If any faults are found - **SPECIALIST SERVICE**.)

17. Check for spark at plug (remove plug and prop it with threads resting on bare metal of cylinder block). Do not touch plug or lead while operating starter.

MODELS WITHOUT ELECTRONIC IGNITION ONLY

18. If no spark present at plug, check for spark at contact breaker points when 'flicked' open (ignition 'on'). Double-check to ensure that points are clean and correctly gapped, and try again.

19. If spark present at contact breaker points, check for spark at central high tension lead from coil. NOTE: Don't carry out this check with electronic ignition systems. An uncontrolled spark can, in some cases, seriously damage the ECU (Electronic Control Unit).

20. If spark present at central high tension lead from coil, check distributor cap and rotor arm; replace if cracked or contacts badly worn.

21. If distributor cap and rotor arm are okay, check high tension leads and connections - replace leads if they are old, carbon core type suppressed variety.

22. If high tension leads are sound but dirty or damp, clean/dry them.

23. If high tension leads okay, check/clean/dry/re-gap sparking plugs.

24. Damp conditions? Apply water dispellant spray to ignition system.

25. If no spark present at contact breaker points (cars without electronic ignition only), examine connections of low tension leads between ignition switch and coil, and from coil to contact breaker (including short low-tension lead within distributor).

26. If low tension circuit connections okay, examine wiring.

27. If low tension wiring is sound, is capacitor okay? If in doubt, fit new capacitor.

28. If capacitor is okay, check for spark at central high tension lead from coil. NOTE: DON'T carry out this check with electronic ignition systems. An uncontrolled spark can, in some cases, seriously damage the ECU (Electronic Control Unit).

29. If no spark present at central high tension lead from coil, check for poor high tension lead connections.

30. If high tension lead connections okay, is coil okay? If in doubt, fit new coil.

31. If spark present at plug, is it powerful or weak? If weak, see '27' (non-electronic ignition models only).

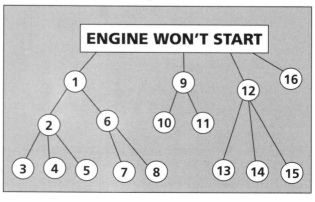

32. If spark is healthy, check ignition timing.

33. If ignition timing is okay, see 'Fuel System' box.

Fuel system.

FUEL INJECTED ENGINES ONLY

34. Do not disconnect fuel pipes to check fuel flow, as system is pressurised; check fuel pump operation by listening for "buzz" when ignition is switched on - buzz should last no more than 1 or 2 seconds; if longer, suspect fuel pump. If no buzz, suspect fuel pump relay - seek professional help.

NON FUEL INJECTED ENGINES ONLY

35. Check briefly for fuel at feed pipe to carb. See 36. If no fuel present at feed pipe, is petrol tank empty? (Rock car and listen for 'sloshing' in tank, as well as looking at gauge).

36. Check for a defective fuel pump. With outlet pipe disconnected AND AIMED AWAY FROM HOT EXHAUST COMPONENTS, ETC. as well as your eyes and clothes, and into a suitable container, turn the engine over (manual pump) or switch on ignition (electric pump) and fuel should issue from pump outlet.

37. If pump is okay, check for blocked fuel filter or pipe, or major leak in pipe between tank and pump, or between pump and carb.

38. If the filter is clean and the pump operates, suspect blocked carburettor jet(s) or damaged/ sticking float, or incorrectly adjusted carburettor.

39. If there is petrol in the tank but none issues from the feed pipe from pump to carburettor, check that the small vent hole in the fuel filler cap is not blocked and causing a vacuum. NOTE: On some cars there is no vent hole in the filler cap. Other arrangements are made for venting the tank. There are many systems - **SPECIALIST SERVICE.**

40. If fuel is present at carburettor feed pipe, remove spark plugs and check whether wet with unburnt fuel.

41. If the spark plugs are fuel-soaked, check that the choke is operating as it should and is not jammed 'shut'. Other possibilities include float needle valve(s) sticking 'open' or leaking, float punctured, carburettor incorrectly adjusted or air filter totally blocked. Clean plugs before replacing.

42. If the spark plugs are dry, check whether the float needle valve is jammed 'shut'.

43. Check for severe air leak at inlet manifold gasket or carburettor gasket. Incorrectly set valve clearances.

Engine lacks power.

44. Engine overheating. Check oil temperature gauge (where fitted). Low oil pressure light may come on.

45. Air cleaner intake thermostat not opening/closing at the correct temperatures. Replace or free-off as necessary.

46. If thermostat okay, check oil level. BEWARE - DIPSTICK AND OIL MAY BE VERY HOT.

47. If oil level okay, check for slipping fan belt, cylinder head gasket 'blown', partial mechanical seizure of engine, blocked or damaged exhaust system.

48. If engine temperature is normal, check cylinder compressions.

49. If cylinder compression readings low, add a couple of teaspoons of engine oil to each cylinder in turn, and repeat test. If readings don't improve, suspect burnt valves/seats.

50. If compression readings improve after adding oil as described, suspect worn cylinder bores, pistons and rings.

51. If compression readings are normal, checkfor mechanical problems, for example, binding brakes, slipping clutch, partially seized transmission, etc.

Engine stops suddenly.

52. Check for sudden ingress of water/snow onto ignition components, in adverse weather conditions. Sudden failure is almost always because of an ignition fault. Check for simple wiring and connection breakdowns.

Lights fail.

53. Sudden failure - check fuses.

54. If all lamps affected, check switch and main wiring feeds.

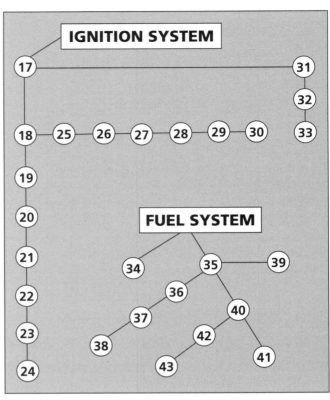

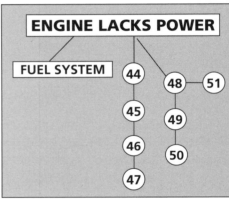

55. If not all lamps are affected, check bulbs on lamps concerned.

56. If bulbs appear to be okay, check bulb holder(s), local wiring and connections.

57. If bulb(s) blown, replace!

58. Intermittent operation, flickering or poor light output.

59. Check earth (ground) connections(s).

60. If earth(s) okay, check switch.

61. If switch okay, check wiring and connections.

Horn failure.

62. If horn does not operate, check fuse, all connections (particularly earths/grounds) and cables. Remove horn connections and check/clean. Use 12v test lamp to ascertain power getting to horn.

63. If horn will not stop(!), disconnect the horn and check for earthing of cable between button and horn unit and the wiring and contacts in the

*SAFETY FIRST! Before working on the fuel system, read **Chapter 1, Safety First!** Take special care to 1) only work out of doors, 2) wear suitable gloves and goggles and keep fuel out of eyes and away from skin: 3) if fuel does come into contact with skin, wash off straight away, 4) if fuel gets into your eyes, wash out with copious amounts of clean, cold water. Seek medical advice if necessary, 5) when testing for fuel flow, pump into a sufficiently large container, minimising splashes, 6) don't smoke, work near flames or sparks or work when the engine or exhaust are hot.*

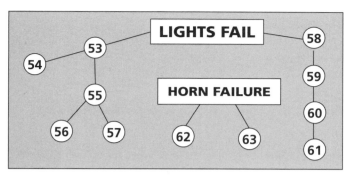

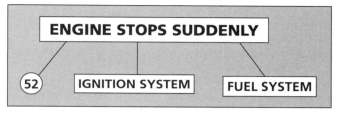

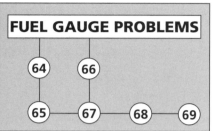

horn switch housing. **SPECIALIST SERVICE.** Horn wiring and connections are more complex than they appear at first. If necessary, have them checked by a specialist.

Fuel gauge problems.

64. Gauge reads 'empty' - check for fuel in tank!

65. If fuel is present in tank, check for earthing of wiring from tank to gauge, and for wiring disconnections.

66. Gauge permanently reads 'full', regardless of tank contents. Check wiring and connections as in '65'.

67. If wiring and connections all okay, sender unit/fuel gauge defective.

68. With wiring disconnected, check for continuity between fuel gauge terminals. Do NOT test gauge by short-circuiting to earth. Replace unit if faulty.

69. If gauge is okay, disconnect wiring from tank sender unit and check for continuity between terminal and case. Replace sender unit if faulty.

PART II - DIESEL ENGINE FAULT FINDING

SAFETY FIRST! Working on a diesel engine is no more dangerous than any other but remember that, when cranking the engine on the starter or even turning it over by hand, it could start. In theory the fuel cut-off valve should prevent this, but don't rely upon it.

Diesel fuel can cause skin disorders, so it's *essential* to use some form of barrier cream on your hands before starting work or to wear gloves. NEVER suck on a pipe in an attempt to draw up fuel.

INSIDE INFORMATION: When working on the fuel system, cleanliness is essential. Always wipe all unions clean before disconnecting, or even slackening them. The slightest trace of dust, water or any other contaminant can ruin the mirror-like finish on the 'internals' of the pump and injector plungers.

Engine won't start.

1. Starter Motor and Battery. Starter motor problems will be more or less the same as for petrol engines. However low cranking speeds

can prevent the engine from starting - see Check 11, Engine Condition.

2. Low pressure fuel system. The low pressure side of a diesel engined car fuel system is much the same as that in petrol versions comprising tank, filter and pump with interconnecting pipes. As such, you must check for the same kind of problems - air leaks into the system, fuel leaks from it and, of course, blockages.

3. No fuel in tank. If you run out of fuel, you will have to vent the system of air. The procedure for this can vary from model to model, but see the relevant section of *Chapter 3, Servicing Your Car*.

4. Fuel blockage. Usually if a lack of fuel is suspected, the first check will be at the bleed valve on the injection pump. Slacken this off and either operate the priming pump or crank the engine. No fuel coming out would indicate either an air leak or blockage, so repeat the test at the filter inlet. Any problems at this point would indicate a fault either at the tank itself, or between the tank and filter and would be much the same as those associated with a normal petrol system.

5. Fuel pump stop control. Check that the stop control solenoid at the pump clicks when the 'ignition' key is turned: If so you can assume it is working. If not, check for a 12 volt supply at the solenoid terminal ('ignition' on).

Other than actually running out of fuel, this is the most probable reason for lack of fuel at the injectors. A defective valve may also result in the engine continuing to run when switched off.

6. High pressure fuel system. *Safety First!* Beware very

high residual pressure in pipe when disconnecting even if engine not running! Pressure high enough for jet of diesel to penetrate skin - could cause blindness if it strikes the eye!

This part of the diesel engine's fuel system extends from the injection pump to the injectors. The pressures within the system are extremely high during the injection process (in the region of 300 bar) so care should be taken not to release any connections when the engine is running or being cranked on the starter motor. Checks on this part of the system are **SPECIALIST SERVICE** jobs other than the jobs shown below.

7. Injector pump faulty.

IMPORTANT NOTE: Testing the operation and output from the fuel injection pump requires specialist equipment. Do not attempt to strip it down yourself. Don't even remove it unless you are sure how to refit it and time it.

Some pumps are driven by a toothed belt, often the same one that drives the camshaft. As such they can suffer the same problems as with petrol engined cars - incorrect adjustment, overriding the teeth or complete breakage. Inspect the belt - if any problems, DON'T RUN THE ENGINE until you've had the belt replaced and the pump timed by a specialist.

8. Injectors faulty. As with the injection pump, specialised equipment is needed for checking the injectors. In some cases you can actually feel a light pulse on the injector feed pipe when injection takes place and the injector may also give a discernible grunt or buzz. However, neither is any indicator of a satisfactory injector spray pattern.

9. Injector feed pipes leaking. This would normally be pretty obvious with escaping fuel

leaving its mark. If only one injector is affected, the engine would probably start, but misfire and possibly emit black smoke. If the cause is a leaking union, then simply tightening it may sort out the problem. However, should the pipe itself be defective (cracked or split), the only answer is to renew it.

10. Glow plugs inoperative (cold engine). Glow plugs seldom go wrong, although after a considerable mileage, the heating elements may burn out. This would be unlikely to happen to all of the plugs at the same time, and if only one were affected, the engine would probably start but misfire on that cylinder until warmed up. Any failure affecting all of the plugs would probably be in the power supply. Symptoms of failure: engine slow to start; black smoke; misfiring until engine warm. Solution: replace any individual faulty plugs; check wiring if all are affected.

11. Engine condition. Combustion is achieved in diesel engines through heat generated by compressing air and anything which affects compression pressure - such as worn bores or 'leaking' valves - can result in poor starting or non-starting - much more so than with a petrol engine. Low cranking speeds may not have much effect on compression as such, but the consequent additional heat loss through the cylinder walls (due to the low piston speed) could also result in poor starting.

IMPORTANT NOTE: Do not use a petrol engine compression tester on a diesel engine - even assuming it could be held in place, because the high pressures involved would ruin it. Any such check should be left to the professionals. The same applies to checking valve clearances where any error could result in a valve striking the piston with consequent engine damage.

Engine misfires.

12. Water in fuel.

*INSIDE INFORMATION: The adverse effects of water in fuel are more pronounced in a diesel engined car than the petrol equivalent and, depending upon severity, may result in a misfire or the engine failing to start. Water may also damage the injection equipment. Many diesel cars have a water trap built into the main fuel filter which should be drained at regular intervals. See **Chapter 3, Servicing Your Car**.*

Unfortunately, if there is water in the system, it will all have to be drained of fuel - fuel tank, filter, fuel lines - and fresh fuel used. Dispose of scrap fuel responsibly at your nearest Local Authority disposal point.

13. Injection pump, injectors and engine condition. Most of the factors resulting in non-starting could also cause a misfire. See Checks 7, 8, 9 and 11.

Excessive smoke from exhaust.

14. Blue smoke. Results from oil being burnt in the combustion chamber. Causes similar to those for petrol engines - poor bore sealing,

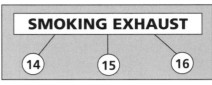

worn valve guides or faulty valve stem seals. NB Brake fluid leaking into the engine via a faulty brake servo will also produce blue smoke, but you will notice a slow, steady loss of brake fluid if this is the problem. SPECIALIST SERVICE: HAVE THE PROBLEM ATTENDED TO WITHOUT DELAY!

15. White smoke (steam). White smoke is usually steam and 'disappears' into the air. Usually caused by water (coolant) leaking into engine or exhaust although a cold engine on a cold or damp day will emit steam, and this is acceptable. Causes can be similar to those for petrol engines - cracked block, cracked cylinder head, defective head gasket.

16. Black smoke. Injection pump faults such as excessive fuel delivery, low fuel pressures and incorrect timing could all result in black smoke from the exhaust. Poor spray patterns, dribble and other injector faults are also possible causes, all of which will require professional assistance.

FACT FILE: EMERGENCY STARTING

Pushing or Towing

NOTE: This is not possible for vehicles with automatic transmission. Diesel engines: only attempt in warm weather or with a warm engine.

Turn off all unnecessary electrical load; switch on ignition and depress the clutch pedal. Select second or third gear; release the clutch when the car reaches a person's running speed.

Starting with Jump Leads

> *Safety First!*
> *This process can be dangerous and the following instructions must be followed to the letter. Also see **Chapter One, Safety First!** and the relevant part of **Chapter 3** for information on safe handling of car batteries.*

Ensure that the battery providing the jump start has the same voltage (12 volt) as the battery fitted to your car.

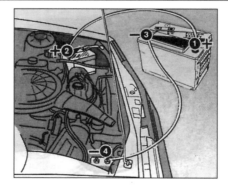

Do not lean over the battery during jump starting.

Switch off all unnecessary electrical loads and apply the hand brake. Auto. Transmission: Place gear selector in 'P'. Manual Transmission: Place gear shift lever in neutral.

Note that on some batteries and on battery connections, '+' (positive) terminals are coloured red and '-' (negative) terminals are coloured blue or black.

Run the engine of the vehicle providing the jump start (if battery fitted to vehicle).

(The following instruction numbers refer to the numbers on the drawing.)

1. Connect one end of the jump lead to the positive ('+') terminal of the battery providing the jump start.

2. Connect the other end of the same lead to the positive terminal on the car being started.

3. Connect one end of the other jump lead to the negative ('-') terminal on the 'slave' battery...

4. ...and the other end to the negative battery lead on the car, or to some bare metal in the car's engine bay.

Now try to start the car as quickly as is reasonably possible.

IT IS IMPORTANT that the leads are removed in the exact reverse sequence to that shown above. Keep hands, hair and loose clothing away from moving parts in both engine bays.

CHAPTER 7
GETTING THROUGH THE MOT

This Chapter is for owners in Britain whose vehicles need to pass the 'MoT' test. The Test was first established in 1961 by the then Ministry of Transport and it attempts to ensure that vehicles using British roads reach minimum standards of safety. Approximately 40 per cent of vehicles submitted for the test fail it, but many of these failures could be avoided by knowing what the vehicle might 'fall down on', and by taking appropriate remedial action before the test 'proper' is carried out.

It is true that the scope of the test has been considerably enlarged in the past few years, with the result that it is correspondingly more difficult to be sure that your vehicle will reach the required standards. In truth, however, a careful examination of the relevant areas, perhaps a month or so before the current certificate expires, will highlight components which require attention, and enable any obvious faults to be rectified before you take the vehicle for the test.

Getting Ahead

It is also worth noting that a vehicle can be submitted for a test up to a month before the current certificate expires - if the vehicle passes, the new certificate will be valid for one year from the day of expiry of the old one, provided that the old certificate is produced at the time of the test.

PART I: THE BACKGROUND

Keeping Up To Date

Alterations are being made to the Test on a regular basis - almost always making it tougher than it was before. It is MOST IMPORTANT that UK owners find out for themselves about any changes in the requirements that might have been made since this book was written. Your local MoT Testing Station should be able to help - if not, take your custom elsewhere! Also, non-UK owners should obtain information on the legal requirements in their own territory - and act accordingly.

Making A Good Impression

If your vehicle is muddy or particularly dirty (especially underneath) it would be worth giving it a thorough clean a day or two before carrying out the inspection so that it has ample time to dry. Do the same before the real MoT test. A clean vehicle makes a better impression on the examiner, who can refuse to test a vehicle which is particularly dirty underneath.

On the other hand, a clean vehicle makes a better impression and it will help the examiner to see what he is supposed to be examining. Generally, this will work in the owner's favour. For example, if a component or an area of underbody or chassis is particularly difficult to examine due to a build-up of oily dirt etc., and if the examiner is in doubt about its condition, he is entitled to fail that component because it was not possible for him to conclude that it reached the required standard. Had it been clean, it might well have been tested, and passed!

MoT testers do not dismantle assemblies during the test but you may wish to do so during your pretest check-up for a better view of certain wearing parts, such as the rear brake

> *SAFETY FIRST!*
> *The MoT tester will follow a set procedure and we will cover the ground in a similar way, starting inside the vehicle, then continuing outside, under the bonnet, underneath the vehicle, etc. When preparing to go underneath the vehicle, do ensure that it is jacked on firm level ground and then supported on axle stands or ramps which are adequate for the task. Wheels which remain on the ground should have chocks in front of and behind them, and while the rear wheels remain on the ground, the hand brake should be firmly ON. For most repair and replacement jobs under your vehicle these normal precautions will suffice. However, the vehicle needs to be even more stable than usual when carrying out these checks. There must be no risk of it toppling off its stands while suspension and steering components are being pushed and pulled in order to test them. Read carefully* **Chapter 1, Safety First!** *and the first part of* **Chapter 3, Servicing Your Car** *for further important information on raising and supporting a vehicle above the ground.*

shoes for example. See *Chapter 3, Servicing Your Car* for information on how to check the brakes.

Buying And Selling

This chapter provides a procedure for checking your vehicle's condition prior to its official MoT test. The same procedure could be equally useful to UK and non-UK owners alike when examining vehicles prior to purchase (or sale for that matter). However, it must be emphasised that the official MoT certificate should not be regarded as any guarantee of the condition of a vehicle. All it proves is that the vehicle reached the required standards, in the opinion of a particular examiner, at the time and date it was tested.

Pass The MoT!

The aim of this chapter is to explain what is actually tested on a vehicle and (if it is not obvious) how the test is done. This should enable you to identify and eliminate problems before they undermine the safety or diminish the performance of your vehicle and long before they cause the expense and inconvenience of a test failure.

Tool Box

Dismantling apart, few tools are needed for testing. A light hammer is useful for tapping panels underneath the vehicle when looking for rust. If this produces a bright metallic noise, then the area being tapped is solid metal. If the noise produced is dull, the area contains rust or filler. When tapping sills and box sections, listen also for the sound of debris (that is, rust flakes) on the inside of the panel. Use a screwdriver to prod weak parts of panels. This may produce holes of course, but if the panels have rusted to that extent, you really ought to know about it. A strong lever (such as a tyre lever) can be useful for applying the required force to suspension joints etc. when assessing whether there is any wear in them.

You will need an assistant to operate controls and perhaps to wobble the road wheels while you inspect components under the vehicle.

Age Related Checks

Two more brief explanations are required before you start your informal test. Firstly, the age of the vehicle determines exactly which lights, seat belts and other items it should have. Frequently in the next few pages you will come across the phrase "Cars first used ..." followed by a date. A vehicle's "first used" date is either its date of first registration, or the date six months after it was manufactured, whichever was earlier. Or, if the vehicle was originally used without being registered (such as a vehicle which has been imported to the U.K. or an ex-H.M. Forces model, etc.) the "first used" date is the date of manufacture.

Rust And Load Bearing Areas

Secondly, there must not be excessive rust, serious distortion or any fractures affecting certain prescribed areas of the bodywork. These prescribed areas are load-bearing parts of the bodywork within 30 cm (12 in.) of anchorages or mounting points associated with testable items such as seat belts, brake pedal assemblies, master cylinders, servos, suspension and

steering components and also body mountings. Keep this rule in mind while inspecting the vehicle, but remember also that even if such damage occurs outside a prescribed area, it can cause failure of the test. Failure will occur if the damage is judged to reduce the continuity or strength of a main load-bearing part of the bodywork sufficiently to have an adverse effect on the braking or steering.

The following notes are necessarily abbreviated, and are for assistance only. They are not a definitive guide to all the MoT regulations. It is also worth mentioning that the varying degrees of discretion of individual MoT testers can mean that there are variations between the standards as applied. However, the following points should help to make you aware of the aspects which will be examined. Now, if you have your clipboard, checklist and pencil handy, let's make a start...

The 'Easy' Bits

Checking these items is straightforward and should not take more than a few minutes - and could avoid an embarrassingly simple failure...

Lights

Within the scope of the test are headlights, side and tail lights, brake lights, direction indicators, and number plate lights (plus rear fog lights on all cars first used on or after 1 April, 1980, and any earlier cars subsequently so equipped, and also hazard warning lights on any vehicle so fitted). All must operate, must be clean and not significantly damaged; flickering is also not permitted. The switches should also all work properly. Pairs of lights should give approximately the same intensity of light output, and operation of one set of lights should not affect the working of another - such trouble is usually due to bad earthing.

Front fog and spot lights are not part of the MoT test (although their use is covered by *Construction and Use* regulations so that, for instance, spot lights should go out when headlights are turned off main beam) and won't be tested, provided they're not a physical hazard. Rear fog lights are part of the Test however. See later in this Chapter for details.

Indicators should flash at between 60 and 120 times per minute. 'Rev' the engine to encourage them, if a little slow (although the examiner might not let you get away with it!) Otherwise, renew the (inexpensive) flasher unit and check all wiring and earth connections.

Interior 'tell-tale' lights, such as for indicators, rear fog lights and hazard warning lights should all operate in unison with their respective exterior lights.

Headlight aim must be correct - in particular, the lights should not dazzle other road users. An approximate guide can be obtained by shining the lights against a vertical wall, but final adjustment may be necessary by reference to the beam checking machine at the MoT station. Most testers will be happy to make slight adjustments where necessary but only if the adjusters work. Make sure before you take the vehicle in that they are not seized solid!

Reflectors must be unbroken, clean, and not obscured - for example, by stickers.

Wheels And Tyres

Check the wheels for loose nuts, cracks, and damaged rims. Missing wheel nuts or studs are also failure points, naturally enough!

There is no excuse for running on illegal tyres. The legal requirement is that there must be at least 1.6 mm of tread depth remaining, over the 'central' three-quarters of the width of the tyre all the way around. From this it can be deduced that there is no legal requirement to have 1.6 mm (1/16 in.) of tread on the 'shoulders' of the tyre, but in practice, most MoT stations will be reluctant to pass a tyre in this condition. In any case, for optimum safety - especially 'wet grip' - you would be well advised to change tyres when they wear down to around 3 mm (1/8 in.) or so depth of remaining tread.

Visible 'tread wear indicator bars', found approximately every nine inches around the tread of the tyre, are highlighted when the tread reaches the critical 1.6 mm point.

Tyres should not show signs of cuts or bulges, rubbing on the bodywork or running gear, and the valves should be in sound condition, and correctly aligned.

Old-fashioned cross-ply and radial-ply tyre types must not be mixed on the same axle, and if pairs of cross-ply and radial-ply tyres are fitted, the radials must be on the rear axle.

Windscreen

The screen must not be damaged (by cracks, chips, etc.) or obscured so that the driver does not have a clear view of the road. Permissible size of damage points depends on where they occur. Within an area 290 mm (nearly 12 in.) wide, ahead of the driver, and up to the top of the wiper arc, any damage must be confined within a circle less than 10 mm (approx. 0.4 in.) in diameter. This is increased to 40 mm (just over 1.5 in.) for damage within the rest of the screen area swept by the wipers.

Washers And Wipers

The wipers must clear an area big enough to give the driver a clear view forwards and to the side of the vehicle. The wiper blades must be securely attached and sound, with no cracks or 'missing' sections. The wiper switch should also work properly. The screen washers must supply the screen with sufficient liquid to keep it clean, in conjunction with the use of the wipers.

Mirrors

Your vehicle must have at least two, one of which must be on the driver's side. The mirrors must be visible from the driver's seat, and not be damaged or obscured so that the view to the rear is affected. Therefore cracks, chips and discolouration can mean failure.

Horn

The horn must emit a uniform note which is loud enough to give adequate warning of approach, and the switch must operate correctly. Multi-tone horns playing 'in sequence' are not permitted, but two tones sounding together are fine.

Seat Security

The seats must be securely mounted, and the sub-frames should be sound.

Seat Belts

Seat belts must be in good condition (i.e. not frayed or otherwise damaged), and the buckles and catches should also operate correctly. Inertia reel types, where fitted, should retract properly.

Belt mountings must be secure, with no structural damage or corrosion within 30 cm (12 in.) of them.

Number (Registration) Plates

Both front and rear number plates must be present, and in good condition, with no breaks or missing numbers or letters. The plates must not be obscured, and the digits must not be repositioned (to form names, for instance).

Vehicle Identification Numbers (VIN)

Vehicles first used on or after 1 August, 1980 have to have a clearly displayed VIN - Vehicle Identification Number (or old-fashioned 'chassis numbers' for older cars) which is plainly legible. See *Chapter 2, Buying Guide* for the correct location on your vehicle.

Exhaust System

The entire system must be present, properly mounted, free of leaks and should not be noisy - which can happen when the internal baffles fail. 'Proper' repairs by welding, or exhaust cement, or bandage are acceptable, as long as no gas leaks are evident. Then again, common sense, if not the MoT, dictates that exhaust bandage should only be a very short-term emergency measure. For safety's sake, fit a new exhaust if yours is reduced to this!

PART II: THE CHECKLIST

You've checked the easy bits - now it's time for the detail! Some of the 'easy bits' referred to above are included here, but this is intended as a more complete check list to give your vehicle the best possible chance of gaining a First Class Honours, MoT Pass!

Inside The Vehicle

☐ 1. The steering wheel should be examined for cracks and for damage which might interfere with its use, or injure the driver's hands. It should also be pushed and pulled along the column axis, and also up and down, at 90 degrees to it. This will highlight any deficiencies in the wheel and upper column mounting/bearing, and also any excessive end float, and movement between the column shaft and the wheel. Look, too, for movement in the steering column couplings and fasteners (including the universal joint if applicable), and visually check their condition and security. They must be sound, and properly tightened.

In the case of cars (the majority) with steering racks, rotate the steering wheel in both directions to test for free play at the wheel rim - this shouldn't exceed approximately 13 mm. (0.5 in.), assuming a 380 mm. (15 in.) diameter steering wheel.

In the case of the smaller number of cars with steering boxes, free play at the wheel rim shouldn't exceed approximately 75 mm (3.0 in.), assuming a 380 mm (15 in.) diameter steering wheel.

In both cases where the steering wheel is larger or smaller the amount of permissible free play should be raised or lowered accordingly.

☐ 2. Check that the switches for headlights, sidelights, rear fog lights direction indicators, hazard warning lights, wipers, washers and horn, appear to be in good working order and check that the tell-tale lights or audible warnings are working where applicable.

☐ 3. Make sure that the windscreen wipers operate effectively with blades that are secure and in good condition. The windscreen washer should provide sufficient liquid to clear the screen in conjunction with the wipers.

☐ 4. Check for windscreen damage, especially in the area swept by the wipers. From the MoT tester's point of view, Zone A is part of this area, 290 mm (11.5 in.) wide and centred on the centre of the steering wheel. Damage to the screen within this area should be capable of fitting into a 10 mm (approx. 0.4 in.) diameter circle and the cumulative effect of more minor damage should not seriously restrict the driver's view. Windscreen stickers or other obstructions should not encroach more than 10 mm (approx 0.4 in.) into this area. In the remainder of the swept area the maximum diameter of damage or degree of encroachment by obstructions is 40 mm (approx. 1.6 in.) and there is no ruling regarding cumulative

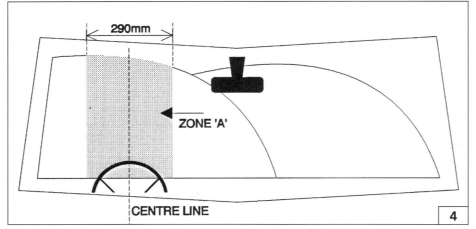

damage. Specialist windscreen companies can often repair a cracked screen for a lot less than the cost of replacement. Moreover, the cost of repair is often covered by comprehensive insurance policies. DIY repair kits are also available.

☐ 5. The horn control should be present, secure and readily accessible to the driver, and the horn should be loud enough to be heard by other road users. Gongs, bells and sirens are not permitted (except as part of an anti-theft device) and

multi-tone horns (which alternate between two or more notes) are not permitted at all. On cars first used after 1 August 1973, the horn should produce a constant, continuous or uniform note which is neither harsh nor grating.

☐ 6. There must be one exterior mirror on the driver's side of the vehicle and one other mirror - either an exterior mirror fitted to the passenger's side or an interior mirror. The required mirrors should be secure and in good condition.

☐ 7. Check that the hand brake operates effectively without coming to the end of its working travel. The lever and its mechanism must be complete, securely mounted, unobstructed in its travel and in a sufficiently good condition to remain firmly in the "On" position even when knocked from side to side. The 30 cm rule on bodywork corrosion applies in the vicinity of the hand brake lever mounting.

☐ 8. The foot brake pedal assembly should be complete, unobstructed, and in a good working condition, including the pedal rubber (which should not have been worn smooth). There should be no excessive movement of the pedal at right angles to its normal direction. When fully depressed, the pedal should not be at the end of its travel. The pedal should not feel spongy (indicating air in the hydraulic system), nor should it tend to creep downwards while held under pressure (which indicates an internal hydraulic leak).

☐ 9. Seats must be secure on their mountings and seat backs must be capable of being locked in the upright position.

☐ 10. The law requires all models to be fitted with seatbelts for the driver and front passenger. These have to be three-point lap and diagonal belts. Rear seat belts are a requirement for vehicles first used after 31 March 1987 with three anchorage points for the 'outer' passengers, and at least a lap belt only for the centre passenger position. Examine seat belt webbing and fittings to make sure that all are in good condition and that anchorages are firmly attached to the vehicle's structure. Locking mechanisms should be capable of remaining locked, and of being released if required, when under load. Flexible buckle stalks (if fitted) should be free of corrosion, broken cable strands or other weaknesses. Note that any belts fitted which are not part of a legal requirements may be examined by the tester but will not form part of the official test.

☐ 11. On inertia reel belts, check that on retracting the belts, the webbing winds into the retracting unit automatically, albeit with some manual assistance to start with.

☐ 12. Note the point raised earlier regarding corrosion around seat belt anchorage points. The MoT tester will not carry out any dismantling here, but he will examine floor mounted anchorage points from underneath the vehicle if that is possible.

13. Before getting out of the vehicle, make sure that both doors can be opened from the inside.

Outside The Vehicle

14. Before closing the driver's door, check the condition of the inner sill. Usually the MoT tester will do this by applying finger or thumb pressure to various parts of the panel while the floor covering remains in place. For your own peace of mind, look beneath the sill covering, taking great care not to tear any covering. Then close the driver's door and make sure that it latches securely and repeat these checks on the nearside inner sill and door.

Now check all of the lights, front and rear, (and the number plate lights) while your assistant operates the light switches.

15. As we said earlier, you can carry out a rough and ready check on headlight alignment for yourself, although it will certainly not be as accurate as having it done for you at the MoT testing station. Drive your vehicle near to a wall, as shown. Check that your tyres are correctly inflated and the vehicle is on level ground.

Draw on the wall, with chalk:
• a horizontal line about 2 metres long, and at same height as centre of headlight lenses.
• two vertical lines about 1 metre long, each forming a cross with the horizontal line and the same distance apart as the headlight centres.
• another vertical line to form a cross on the horizontal line, midway between the others.

Now position your vehicle so that:
• it faces the wall squarely, and its centre line is in line with centre line marked on the wall.
• the steering is straight.
• headlight lenses are 5.0 metres (16 ft.) from the wall.

Switch on the headlights' 'main' and 'dipped' beams in turn and measure their centre points. You will be able to judge any major discrepancies in intensity and aim prior to having the beams properly set by a garage with beam measuring equipment.

Headlights should be complete, clean, securely mounted, in good working order and not adversely affected by the operation of another lamp, and these basic requirements affect all the lights listed below. Headlights must dip as a pair from a single switch. Their aim must be correctly adjusted and they should not be affected (even to the extent of flickering) when lightly tapped by hand. Each headlight should match its partner in terms of size, colour and intensity of light, and can be white or yellow.

16. Side lights should show white light to the front and red light to the rear. Lenses should not be broken, cracked or incomplete. Stop lights must be red, of course.

17. Check your indicators, doing what the MoT tester will do: turn on side lights and apply the brake lights while ensuring that the indicators still work properly, and that none of the lights interfere with each other, causing dimness or intermittent failure. Check side repeater lights, too.

18. Vehicles first used before 1 April 1986 do not have to have a hazard warning device, but if one is fitted, it must be tested, and it must operate with the ignition switch either on or off. The lights should flash 60-120 times per minute, and indicators must operate independently of any other lights.

19. There must be two red rear reflectors - always fitted by the manufacturers, of course! - which are clean and are securely and symmetrically fitted to the vehicle.

20. Your vehicle must have at least one rear fog light fitted to the centre or offside of the vehicle. If there are two, they must be spaced an equal distance from the centre. It must comply with the basic requirements (listed under headlights) and emit a steady red light. Its tell-tale light, inside the vehicle, must work to inform the driver that it is switched on.

21. There must be registration number plates at the front and rear of the vehicle and both must be clean, secure, complete and unobscured. Letters and figures must be correctly formed and correctly spaced and not likely to be misread due to an uncovered securing bolt or whatever. The year letter counts as a figure. The space between letters and figures must be at least twice that between adjacent letters or figures.

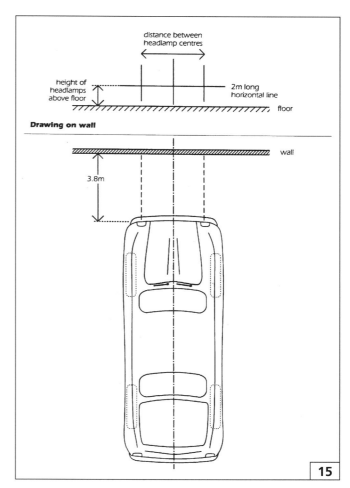

15

[ ] 22. Number plate lights must be present, working, and must not flicker when tapped by hand, just as for other lights. Where more than one light or bulb was fitted as original equipment, all must be working.

Wheels And Tyres

The MoT tester will examine tyres and wheels while walking around the vehicle and again when he is underneath it.

[ ] 23. Front tyres should match each other and rear tyres should match each other, both sets matching in terms of size, aspect ratio and type of structure. For example, you must never fit tyres of different sizes or types, such as cross-ply or radial, on the same 'axle' - both front wheels counting as 'on the same axle' in this context. If cross-ply or bias belted tyres are fitted to the rear of the car, you must not fit radial-ply tyres to the front. If cross-ply tyres are fitted to the rear, bias belted tyres should not be fitted to the front. (We recommend that you do not mix tyre types anywhere on the car.)

[ ] 24. Failure of the test can be caused by a cut, lump, tear or bulge in a tyre, exposed ply or cord, a badly seated tyre, a re-cut tyre, a tyre fouling part of the vehicle, or a seriously damaged or misaligned valve stem which could cause sudden deflation of the tyre. To pass the test, the grooves of the tread pattern must be at least 1.6 mm deep throughout a continuous band comprising the central three-quarters of the breadth of tread, and round the entire outer circumference of the tyre.

We are grateful to Dunlop/SP Tyres for the photographs and information in this section.

[ ] 24A. Modern tyres have tread wear indicators built into the tread groves (usually about eight of them spread equidistantly around the circumference). These appear as continuous bars running across the tread when the original pattern depth has worn down to 1.6 mm. There will be a distinct reduction in wet grip well before the tread wear indicators start to show, and you should replace tyres before they get to this stage, even though this is the legal minimum in the UK.

[ ] 24B. Lumps and bulges in the tyre wall usually arise from accidental damage or even because of faults in the tyre construction. You should run your hand all the way around the side wall of the tyre, with the vehicle either jacked off the ground, or moving the vehicle half a wheels revolution, so that you can check the part of the tyre that was previously resting on the ground. Since you can't easily check the insides of the tyres in day-to-day use, it is even more important that you spend time carefully checking the inside of each tyre - the MoT tester will certainly do so! Tyres with bulges in them must be scrapped and replaced with new, since they can fail suddenly, causing your vehicle to lose control.

24B

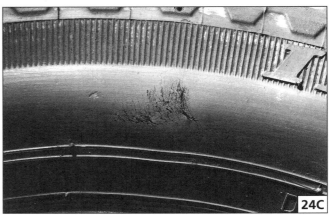

24C

[ ] 24C. Abrasion of the tyre side wall can take place either in conjunction with bulging, or by itself, and this invariably results from an impact, such as the tyre striking the edge of a kerb or a pothole in the road. Once again, the tyre may be at imminent risk of failure and you should take advice from a tyre specialist on whether the abrasion is just superficial, or whether the tyre will need replacement.

TWI

NEW TYRE   **ILLEGAL TYRE**   24A

24D. All tyres will suffer progressively from cracking, albeit in most cases superficially, due to the effects of sunlight. If old age has caused the tyres on your vehicle to degrade to this extent, replace them.

24D

24E. If the outer edges of the tread are worn noticeably more than the centre, the tyres have been run under inflated which not only ruins tyres, but causes worse fuel consumption, dangerous handling and is, of course, illegal.

Over-inflation causes the centre part of the tyre to wear more quickly than the outer edges. This is also illegal but in addition, it causes the steering and grip to suffer and the tyre becomes more susceptible to concussion damage.

24E

24F

24F. Incorrect wheel alignment causes one side of the tyre to wear more severely than the other. If your vehicle should hit a kerb or large pothole, it is worthwhile having the wheel alignment checked by a tyre specialist since this costs considerably less than new front tyres!

25. Road wheels must be secure and must not be badly damaged, distorted or cracked, or have badly distorted bead rims (perhaps due to "kerbing"), or loose or missing wheel nuts, studs or bolts.

26. Check the bodywork for any sharp edges or projections, caused by corrosion or damage, which could prove dangerous to other road users, including pedestrians.

27. Check that the fuel cap fastens securely and that its sealing washer is neither torn nor deteriorated, or its mounting flange damaged sufficiently to allow fuel to escape (for example, while the vehicle is cornering).

Under The Bonnet

28. The vehicle should have a Vehicle Identification Number fitted to the bodywork. This can be on a plate secured to the vehicle or, etched or stamped on the bodywork. See *Chapter 2, Buying Guide* for more information.

29. Check the steering rack or box for security by asking your assistant to turn the steering wheel from side to side (with the road wheels on the ground) while you watch what happens under the bonnet. Then, check for free play in the steering assembly as a whole. This is done by turning the steering wheel from side to side as far as possible without moving the road wheels - and measuring how far the steering wheel can be moved in this way. More than 75 mm (approx. 3 in.) of free play, on a steering box system, or 13 mm (approx. 0.5 in.), on a steering rack, at the perimeter of the steering wheel, due to wear in the steering components, is sufficient grounds for a test failure. Note that the free play is based on a steering wheel diameter of 380 mm (approx 15 in) and will be less for smaller steering wheels - which all of them virtually are! Also check for the presence and security of retaining and locking devices in the steering column assembly.

30. While peering under the bonnet, check that hydraulic master cylinders and reservoirs are securely mounted and not severely corroded or otherwise damaged. Ensure that the caps are present, that fluid levels are satisfactory and that there are no fluid leaks.

31. Also check that the brake servo is securely mounted and not damaged or corroded to an extent that would impair its operation. Vacuum pipes should be sound, that is, free from kinks, splits and excessive chafing and not collapsed internally.

32. Still under the bonnet have a thorough search for evidence of excessive corrosion, severe distortion or fracture in any load bearing panelling within 30 cm (12 in.) of important mounting points such as the master cylinder/servo mounting, front suspension mountings etc.

Under The Vehicle - Front End

☐ *33. SAFETY FIRST! On some occasions there is no alternative but for your assistant to sit in the vehicle whilst you go beneath. Therefore: 1) Place ramps as well as axle stands beneath the vehicle's structure so that it cannot fall. 2) Don't allow your assistant to move vigorously or get in or out of the vehicle while you are beneath it. If either of these are problematical, DON'T CARRY OUT CHECK 34 - leave it to your garage.*

☐ 34. Have an assistant turn the steering wheel from side to side while you watch for movement in the steering mechanism. Make sure that the rack or box mountings are secure, that the ball joints show no signs of wear and that the ball joint dust covers are in sound condition. Ensure that all split pins, locking nuts and so on are in place and correctly fastened, throughout the steering and suspension systems.

☐ 35. With each wheel raised in turn, spin the wheel listening for roughness in the bearings. There must be none.

☐ 36. Under the vehicle, check the condition of the front springs. Wearing goggles, use a stuff brush to clean off the mud and other debris so that you don't miss a hidden 'crack'. Make sure that all suspension mountings are sound.

☐ 37. Inspect the front shock absorbers. Their upper shrouds (outer casing) tend to rust. Any sign of leaks will cause failure of the test - look for weeping hydraulic fluid just below the lower edge of the upper shroud. Take a firm grip on the upper and lower shroud in turn with both hands and try to twist the damper to check for deterioration in the top and bottom mounting bushes.

☐ 38. With all four wheels on the ground, push down firmly a couple of times on each front wing of the vehicle, then let go at the bottom of the stroke. The vehicle should return to approximately its original level within two or three strokes. Continuing oscillations will earn your vehicle a 'failure' ticket for worn front shockers!

Under The Vehicle - Rear Suspension

☐ 39. Check the operation of the rear shock absorbers in the same way as the front (Check 38).

☐ 40. Check the rear wheel bearings as described in check 35.

☐ 41. Check the condition of the rear springs and suspension components as described in check 36.

☐ 42. Check the condition of the rear shock absorbers as described in check 37.

Braking System

☐ 43. The MoT brake test is carried out on a special 'rolling road' set-up, which measures the efficiency in terms of percentage. For the foot brake, the examiner is looking for 50 per cent; the hand brake must measure 25 per cent. Frankly, without a rolling road of your own, there is little that you can do to verify whether or not your vehicle will come up to the required figures. What you can do, though, is carry out an entire check of the brake system, which will also cover all other aspects the examiner will be checking, and be as sure as you can that the system is working efficiently.

IMPORTANT! See *Chapter 3, Servicing Your Car* for important information, including *SAFETY FIRST!* information before working on your vehicle's brakes.

☐ 44. The MoT examiner will not dismantle any part of the system, but you can do so. So, take off each front wheel in turn, and examine as follows:

Disc Brakes

Check the front brake discs themselves, looking for excessive grooving or crazing, the calliper pistons/dust seals (looking for signs of fluid leakage and deterioration of the seals), and the brake pads - ideally, replace them if less than approximately 3mm (1/8th in.) friction material remains on each pad - but check the recommendations in *Chapter 3*.

Drum Brakes

Remove each brake drum and check the condition of the linings (renew if worn down to anywhere near the rivet heads), the brake drum (watch for cracking, ovality and serious scoring, etc.) and the wheel cylinders. Check the cylinder's dust covers to see if they contain brake fluid. If so, or if it is obvious that the cylinder(s) have been leaking, replace them or - ONLY if the cylinder bore is in perfect condition - fit a new seal kit.

☐ 45. Ensure that the drum brake adjusters (where fitted) are free to rotate (i.e. not seized!). If they are stuck fast, apply a little penetrating oil (but if possible, only from behind the backplate; if you have to work inside the brake drum, take great care to avoid the risk of getting oil on the brake shoes), and gently work the adjuster backwards and forwards with a brake adjuster spanner. Eventually the adjusters should free and a little brake grease can be applied to the threads to keep them in this condition. Now rotate the adjuster until the brake shoes contact the drum (preventing the road wheel from turning), then reverse the adjustment just enough to allow the wheel to turn.

☐ 46. A similar procedure can be applied to the handbrake adjustment. Check that the handbrake applies the brakes fully, well before it reaches the end of its potential range of movement. Ensure that the handbrake lever remains locked in the 'on' position when fully applied, even if the lever is knocked sideways.

☐ 47. Closely check the state of ALL visible hydraulic pipework. If any section of the steel tubing shows signs of corrosion, replace it, for safety as well as to gain an MoT pass. Look too for leakage of fluid around pipe joints, and from the master cylinder. The fluid level in the master cylinder reservoir must also be at its correct level - if not, find out why and rectify the problem! At the front and rear of the vehicle, bend the flexible hydraulic pipes (by hand) near each end of each pipe, checking for signs of cracking. If any is evident, or if the pipes have been chafing on the tyres, wheels, steering or suspension components, replace them with new items, rerouting them to avoid future problems. Note also that where the manufacturers fitted a clip to secure a piece of pipe, then it must be present and the pipe must be secured by it.

☐ 48. Have an assistant press down hard on the brake pedal while you check all flexible pipes for bulges. As an additional check, firmly apply the foot brake and hold the pedal down for a few minutes. It should not slowly sink to the floor (if it does, you have a hydraulic system problem). Press and release the pedal a few times - it should not feel 'spongy' (due to the presence of air in the system). Now check the operation of the brake servo by starting the engine while the brake pedal is being held down. If all is well, as the vacuum servo starts to work, the pedal should move a short distance towards the floor. Check the condition of the servo unit and its hoses - all MUST be sound. If there is the risk of any problems with the braking system's hydraulics, have a qualified mechanic check it over before using the vehicle.

☐ 49. A test drive should reveal obvious faults (such as pulling to one side, due to a seized calliper piston, for example), but otherwise all will be revealed on the rollers at the MoT station...

Bodywork Structure

A structurally deficient vehicle is a dangerous vehicle, and rust can affect many important areas, including the sills, any 'outriggers' and the floorpan. Examine these areas carefully.

☐ 50. Essentially, fractures, cracks or serious corrosion in any load bearing panel or member (to the extent that the affected sections are weakened) need to be dealt with. In addition, failure will result from any deficiencies in the structural metalwork within 30 cm (12 in.) of the seat belt mountings, and also the steering and suspension component attachment points. Repairs made to any structural areas must be carried out by 'continuous' seam welding, and the repair should restore the affected section to at least its original strength.

☐ 51. The MoT examiner will be looking for metal which gives way under squeezing pressure between finger and thumb, and will use his wicked little 'Corrosion Assessment Tool' (i.e. a plastic-headed tool known as the 'toffee hammer'!), which in theory at least should be used for detecting rust by lightly tapping the surface. If scraping the surface of the metal shows weakness beneath, the vehicle will fail.

☐ 52. Note that the security of doors and other openings must also be assessed, including the hinges, locks and catches. Corrosion damage or other weakness in the vicinity of these items can mean failure. All doors must latch securely. It must be possible to open both front doors from inside and outside the vehicle and rear doors from the outside only.

Exterior Bodywork

☐ 53. Look out for surface rust, or accident damage, on the exterior bodywork, which leaves sharp/jagged edges and which may be liable to cause injury. Ideally, repairs should be carried out by welding in new metal, but for non-structural areas, riveting a plate over a hole, bridging the gap with glass fibre/body filler or even taping over the gap can be legally acceptable, at least as far as the MoT test is concerned.

Fuel System

☐ 54. Another recent extension of the regulations brings the whole of the fuel system under scrutiny, from the tank to the engine. The system should be examined with and without the engine running, and there must be no leaks from any of the components. The tank must be securely mounted, and the filler cap must fit properly - 'temporary' caps are not permitted.

Emissions

☐ 55. In almost every case, a proper 'engine tune' will help to ensure that your vehicle is running at optimum efficiency, and there should be no difficulty in passing the test, unless your engine or its ancillaries are well worn.

All petrol engines are subject to the 'visual smoke emission' test. The engine must be fully warmed up, allowed to idle, then revved slightly. If smoke emitted is regarded by the examiner as being 'excessive', the vehicle will fail. Often smoke emitted during this test is as a result of worn valve stem seals, allowing oil into the combustion chambers during tickover, to be blown out of the exhaust as 'blue smoke' when the engine is revved. In practice, attitudes vary widely between MoT stations on this aspect of the test.

☐ 56. For diesel-engined vehicles a 'smoke' test also applies. Again, the engine must be fully warmed up, and allowed to idle, before being revved to around 2,500 rpm for 20 seconds (to 'purge' the system). If dense blue or black smoke is emitted for more than five seconds, the vehicle will fail. In addition, the exhaust smoke is tested. Problems will require **SPECIALIST SERVICE.**

FACT FILE: VEHICLE EMISSIONS

PETROL ENGINED VEHICLES WITHOUT CATALYSER

Vehicles first used before 1 August 1973
- visual smoke check only.

Vehicles first used between 1 August 1973 and 31 July 1986
- 4.5% carbon monoxide and 1,200 parts per million, unburned hydrocarbons.

Vehicles first used between 1 August 1986 and 31 July 1992
- 3.5% carbon monoxide and 1,200 parts per million, unburned hydrocarbons.

PETROL ENGINED VEHICLES FITTED WITH CATALYTIC CONVERTERS

Vehicles first used from 1 August 1992 (K-registration on).

All have to be tested at an MoT Testing Station specially equipped to handle cars fitted with catalytic converters whether or not the vehicle is fitted with a 'cat'. If the test, or the garage's data, shows that the vehicle was not fitted with a 'cat' by the manufacturer, the owner is permitted to take the vehicle to a Testing Station not equipped for catalysed cars, if he/she prefers to do so (up to 1998-only). Required maxima are - 3.5% carbon monoxide and 1,200 parts per million, unburned hydrocarbons. The simple emissions test (as above) will be supplemented by a further check to make sure that the catalyst is maintained in good and efficient working order.

The tester also has to check that the engine oil is up to a specified temperature before carrying out the test. (This is because 'carbs' don't work properly at lower temperatures - ensure *your* engine is fully warm!)

DIESEL ENGINES' EMISSIONS STANDARDS

The Tester will have to rev your engine hard, several times. If it is not in good condition, he is entitled to refuse to test it. This is the full range of tests, even though all may not apply to your car.

Vehicles first used before 1 August, 1979

Engine run at normal running temperature; engine speed taken to around 2500 rpm (or half governed max. speed, if lower) and held for 20 seconds. FAILURE, if engine emits dense blue or black smoke for next 5 seconds, at tick-over. (NOTE: Testers are allowed to be more lenient with pre-1960 vehicles.)

Vehicles first used on or after 1 August, 1979

After checking engine condition, and with the engine at normal running temperature, the engine will be run up to full revs between three and six times to see whether your engine passes the prescribed smoke density test. (For what it's worth - 2.5k for non-turbo cars; 3.0k for turbo diesels. An opacity meter probe will be placed in your car's exhaust pipe and this is not something you can replicate at home.) Irrespective of the meter readings, the car will fail if smoke or vapour obscures the view of other road users.

IMPORTANT NOTE: The diesel engine test puts a lot of stress on the engine. It is IMPERATIVE that your car's engine is properly serviced, and the cam belt changed on schedule, before you take it in for the MoT test. The tester is entitled to refuse to test the car if he feels that the engine is not in serviceable condition and there are a number of pre-Test checks he may carry out.

CHAPTER 8 - FACTS & FIGURES

This Chapter serves two main purposes. In Part I, we aim to provide you with a guide to all the major production changes that have taken place, and in Part II, we supply the 'Facts and Figures' you will need when servicing your car. The information on 'Capacities and Settings' will make essential reading when you come to carrying out servicing, since you will then need to know things like the correct spark plug gap, torque settings and a whole host of other adjustments and measurements.

PART I - MAJOR MILESTONES

Apr. 1983 - Nova introduced as completely new model. Available with 1.0 litre OHV, 1.2 and 1.3 litre OHC engines in 2-door saloon and 3-door hatchback bodies.

July 1983 - 5-speed gearbox made available on 1.3 SR model only.

Jan. 1984 - GL specification introduced on 1.2 saloon and hatchback models, featuring improved trim and instrumentation.

May 1984 - Special Edition 'Swing' hatchback introduced; 5-speed gearbox now available as optional extra on all models.

June 1985 - 4-door saloon introduced with 1.0 and 1.2 litre engines; 5-door hatchback introduced with all engine size options except 1.0 litre. New 'Merit' designation introduced with 1.0 and 1.2 litre engines - model similar to 'base' but with improved trim and equipment.

Jan. 1986 - 5-speed gearbox now standard on all 1.3 litre models.

May 1986 - Special Edition 'Antibes' introduced with 1.2 litre engine and 3-door hatchback body style.

Aug. 1986 - 1.0 litre models now available in 5-door body style. Trim and equipment improvements made on all models.

Apr. 1987 - Special edition 'Club' introduced as 3-door hatchback with 1.2 engine and 4-speed gearbox.

July 1987 - Special edition 'Antibes' re-launched with 3-door body, 1.2 engine and 5-speed gearbox as standard.

Aug. 1987 - 2-door 1.2L saloon discontinued. Trim improvements made to other models. 1.3GL model discontinued.

June 1988 - GTE model with 1.6 litre fuel-injected engine, uprated suspension and brakes launched. Also 1.0 litre 'Gem' and 1.2 litre 'Diamond' special editions announced.

Jan. 1989 - Special edition 'Flair' introduced with 1.2 litre engine and 3-door body.

Sept. 1989 - 1.3 SR and 1.3L models discontinued. New

turbodiesel 1.5 litre introduced with 5-speed gearbox a standard.

Oct. 1989 - New 1.4 litre engine introduced in 'L' and SR designations.

June 1990 - Special edition 'Fling' announced, and 'Diamond' model re-introduced.

Nov. 1990 - Whole range revised - model list now comprises: 1.0 litre Trip & Merit; 1.2 litre Merit, Luxe and Flair; 1.4i Merit; 1.4 Luxe, Flair & SR; 1.5 Turbo-diesel Merit; 1.6 GSi.

Van introduced, with 1.2 litre petrol or 1.5 normally-aspirated diesel engines; 5-speed gearbox optional on petrol model, standard on diesel.

Mar. 1991 - Catalytic converter option available on 1.4i Luxe and Flair models.

May 1991 - Limited edition 'Spin' announced with 1.0 litre engine and three-door body style.

June 1991 - Limited edition 'Sola' announced with 1.2 litre engine and three-door body style.

Oct. 1991 - Limited edition 'Life' announced with 1.0 litre engine and three or five-door body style. New 1.5 litre normally aspirated diesel engine introduced. 1.0 litre engined Van announced.

Dec. 1991 - 1.0 litre Van discontinued - only 8 examples built.

Feb. 1992 - 1.2 litre engines now have fuel injection and catalytic converter. 1.4 litre SRi announced.

Mar. 1992 - Special edition 'Fun' introduced in hatchback and saloon body styles.

June 1992 - Special edition 'Expression' introduced, with 1.2 litre injection-engine in three-door hatchback and saloon form.

Feb. 1993 - Van models discontinued.

Mar. 1993 - Nova range discontinued - replaced by new 'Corsa'.

PART II - CAPACITIES AND SETTINGS

General - All Models

BULB TYPES (All 12 volt)

Headlights - 60/55w Sidelights - 4w
Indicators - 21w
Brake/Tail lights - 21/5w
No. Plate light - 10w
Reverse light - 21w
Courtesy lights - 10w
Fog lights - 55w
Rear Fog lights - 21w

TYRE PRESSURES

All models EXCEPT 1.6 litre variants:
Normal - 25psi front & rear
High speeds - 28psi front & rear

1.6 litre Engined Models:
Normal - 26 front, 23 rear
High speed - 28 front, 25 rear.

BRAKING SYSTEM

Brake disc thickness - 10 mm (non-ventilated): 20 mm (ventilated)
minimum disc thickness - 9 mm (non-ventilated): 18 mm (ventilated)
minimum pad thickness including backing plate - 7.0 mm
Brake drum internal diameter - 200 mm
Brake drum internal diameter after resurfacing - 201 mm
minimum brake shoe thickness - 0.5 mm (above rivets)

TORQUE WRENCH SETTINGS:	lbf/ft	Nm
Wheel bolts/nuts	66	90
Spark plugs	15	20

FUSES

See *FACT FILE: FUSES* in *Chapter 3 page 27*.

Model-Specific Settings

NOVA 1.0 1983 TO 1992

Engine Type - 10S OHV
Cubic Capacity - 993cc
Firing Order - 1-3-4-2
Compression ratio - 9.2:1
Valve clearances: (Engine HOT)
inlet - 0.15 mm
exhaust - 0.25 mm
Carburettor type - Weber 32TL
Idle speed - 900 to 950 rpm
CO percentage - 1.0 to 1.5 %
Cooling system pressure cap setting - 1.2 to 1.4 bar.

ELECTRICS

Contact breaker points gap - 0.40 mm (min)
Dwell angle - 50+/- 3 Spark plug type - Champion RL82YC
Spark plug gap - 0.7 mm
Ignition timing (stroboscopic) - 10 +/- 2 BTDC at 700 to 1000 rpm

CAPACITIES:

Engine oil including oil filter: 2.75 litres
Cooling system (inc. heater): 5.5 litres
Transmission (manual): 4 speed - 1.7 litres; 5 sp 1.8 litres
Brake fluid: 0.4 litre
Fuel tank: 42 litres

NOVA 1.2 1983 TO 1990

Engine Type - 12ST OHC (1983 to 90)
Cubic Capacity - 1196cc
Firing Order - 1-3-4-2
Compression ratio - 9.2:1
Carburettor type - Solex/Pierburg
Idle speed - 900 to 950 rpm
CO percentage - 1.0 to 1.5%
Cooling system pressure cap setting - 1.2 to 1.4 bar

ELECTRICS

Contact breaker points gap - ELECTRONIC
Spark plug type - Champion RN7YC
Spark plug gap - 0.7 mm
Ignition timing (stroboscopic) - 10 +/- 2 BTDC @ tickover

CAPACITIES:

Engine oil including oil filter: 3.0 litres
Cooling system (inc. heater): 6.1 litres
Transmission (manual): 1.7 litres (4sp): 1.8 litres (5 sp)
Fuel tank: 42 litres

NOVA 1.2 1990 TO 1992

Engine Type - 12NV O.H.C. (1990 to 1993)
Cubic Capacity - 1196cc
Firing Order - 1-3-4-2
Compression ratio - 9.2:1
Valve clearances: HYDRAULIC
Carburettor type - Solex/Pierburg 1B1
Idle speed - 900 to 950 rpm
CO percentage - 1.0 to 1.5%
Cooling system pressure cap setting - 1.2 to 1.4 bar

ELECTRICS

Contact breaker points gap - ELECTRONIC
Spark plug type - AC CR42CXLS
Spark plug gap - 0.7 to 0.8 mm
Ignition timing (stroboscopic) - 10 +/- 2 BTDC @ tickover

CAPACITIES:

Engine oil including oil filter: 3.0 litres
Cooling system (inc. heater): 6.1 litres
Transmission (manual): 1.7 litres (4sp) 1.8 litres (5 sp)
Fuel tank: 42 litres

NOVA 1.2i (CATALYST) 1990 TO 1993

Engine Type - C12NZ (Catalyst) 1990 to 1993

Cubic Capacity - 1196cc
Firing Order - 1-3-4-2
Compression ratio - 9.1:1
Valve clearances: Hydraulic adjusters
Carburettor type - Multec CFI Fuel Injection
Idle speed - 900 to 950 rpm
CO percentage - 0.5 to 1.0%
Cooling system pressure cap setting - 1.2 to 1.4 bar

ELECTRICS

Contact breaker points gap - ELECTRONIC
Spark plug type - AC CR42CXLS
Spark plug gap - 0.7 to 0.8 mm

CAPACITIES:

Engine oil including oil filter: 3.0 litres
Cooling system (inc. heater): 6.1 litres
Transmission (manual): 1.7 litres (4spd); 1.8 litres (5 spd).
Brake fluid: 0.4 litres
Fuel tank: 42 litres

NOVA 1.3 1983 TO 1989

Engine Type - 13SB O.H.C.

Cubic Capacity - 1297cc
Firing Order - 1-3-4-2
Compression ratio - 9.2:1
Valve clearances: HYDRAULIC
Carburettor type - Solex /Pierburg 1B1 or 2E3
Idle speed - 900 to 950cc
CO percentage - 0.5 to 1
Cooling system pressure cap setting - 1.2 to 1.4 bar

ELECTRICS

Contact breaker points gap - ELECTRONIC
Spark plug type - Champion RN7YC
Spark plug gap - 0.7 to 0.8 mm
Ignition timing (stroboscopic) - 10 deg +/- 2 @ tickover

CAPACITIES:

Engine oil including oil filter: 3.0 litres
Cooling system (inc. heater): 6.1 litres
Transmission (manual): 1.8 litres
Fuel tank: 42 litres

NOVA 1.4 1989 TO 1992

Engine Type - 14NV O.H.C. (1989 to 1993)

Cubic Capacity -1389cc
Firing Order - 1-3-4-2
Compression ratio - 9.4:1
Valve clearances: HYDRAULIC
Carburettor type - Pierburg 2E3
Idle speed - 900 to 950 rpm
CO percentage - 0.5 to 1.0 %
Cooling system pressure cap setting - 1.2 to 1.4 bar

ELECTRICS

Contact breaker points gap - ELECTRONIC
Spark plug type - AC CR42CXLS
Spark plug gap - 0.7 to 0.8 mm
Ignition timing (stroboscopic) - 5deg +/- 2 @ tickover

CAPACITIES:

Engine oil including oil filter: 3.0 litres
Cooling system (inc. heater): 6.1 litres
Transmission (manual): 1.8 litres (5spd)
Fuel tank: 42 litres

NOVA 1.4i (CATALYST) 1990 TO 1992

Engine Type - C14NZ OHC

Cubic Capacity - 1389 cc
Firing Order - 1-3-4-2
Compression ratio - 9.4:1
Valve clearances: HYDRAULIC
Carburettor type - Multec CFI Injection
Idle speed - 830 to 99o rpm
CO percentage - 0.4 max.
Cooling system pressure cap setting - 1.2 to 1.4 bar

ELECTRICS

Contact breaker points gap - ELECTRONIC
Spark plug type - AC CR42CXLS
Spark plug gap - 0.7 to 0.8 mm
Ignition timing (stroboscopic) - 5 deg +/- 2 @ 700 to 1000 rpm

CAPACITIES:

Engine oil including oil filter: 3.0 litres
Cooling system (inc. heater): 6.1 litres
Transmission (manual): 1.7 litres
Fuel tank: 42 litres

NOVA 1.6i 1988 TO 1993

Engine Type - E16SE OHC

Cubic Capacity - 1598 cc
Firing Order - 1-3-4-2
Compression ratio - 10.0:1
Valve clearances: HYDRAULIC
Carburettor type - Bosch LE Jeyronic fuel ignition
Idle speed - 900 to 950 rpm
CO percentage: 0.2 to 0.85 %
Cooling system pressure cap setting - 1.2 to 1.4 bar

FACTS & FIGURES

ELECTRICS

Contact breaker points gap - ELECTRONIC
Spark plug type - AC CR42CXLS
park plug gap -0.7 to 8

CAPACITIES:

Engine oil including oil filter: 3.5 litres
Cooling system (inc. heater): 6.1 litres
Transmission (manual): 1.8 litres
Fuel tank: 42 litres

NOVA 1.6i (CATALYST) 1990 TO 1992

Engine Type - C16NZ (OHC) 1990 to 1993
Cubic Capacity - 1598 cc
Firing Order - 1-3-4-2
Compression ratio - 9.2:1
Valve clearances: HYDRAULIC
Fuel Injection type - GM Multec CFI
Idle speed - 800 to 850 rpm
CO percentage - 0.4 max.
Cooling system pressure cap setting - 1.2 to 1.4 bar

ELECTRICS

Contact breaker points gap - ELECTRONIC
Spark plug type - AC, CR42CXLS
Spark plug gap - 0.7 to 0.8 mm
Ignition timing (stroboscopic) - 10 deg +/- 2 @ tickover

CAPACITIES:

Engine oil including oil filter: 3.5 litres
Cooling system (inc. heater): 6.1 litres
Transmission (manual): 1.8 litres
Fuel tank: 42 litres

NOVA 1.6i (MPi) 1990 TO 1992

Engine Type - C16SEI (OHV) 1990 to 1992
Cubic Capacity - 1598 cc
Firing Order - 1-3-4-2 Compression ratio - 10.0:1
Valve clearances: Hydraulic
Fuel Injection type - Bosch Motronic M1.5
Idle speed - 800 to 850 rpm
CO percentage - 0.4 max.
Cooling system pressure cap setting - 1.2 to 1.4 bar

ELECTRICS

Contact breaker points gap - ELECTRONIC
Spark plug type - AC, CR42CXLS
Spark plug gap - 0.7 to 0.8 mm
Ignition timing (stroboscopic) - 10 deg +/- 2 @ tickover

CAPACITIES:

Engine oil including oil filter: 3.5 litres
Cooling system (inc. heater): 6.1 litres
Transmission (manual): 1.8 litres
Fuel tank: 42 litres

DIESEL ENGINES

NOVA 1.5 D 1992 TO 1993

Engine type: 15D
Cubic capacity: 1488cc
Firing order: 1-3-4-2
Compression ratio: 23.0:1
Glow plug type: 12 14 310 (5 volt)
Idle speed: 780 to 840 rpm
Valve clearances (cold) -
inlet: 0.15 mm
exhaust: 0.25 mm

CAPACITIES:

Engine oil including oil filter: 3.75 litres
Cooling system (inc. heater): 6.4 litres
Transmission (manual): 1.8 litres
Fuel tank: 42 litres

NOVA 1.5TD 1989 TO 1993

Engine type: 15DT
Cubic capacity: 1488 cc
Firing order: 1-3-4-2
Compression ratio: 22.0:1
Glow plug type: 12 14 309; 12 14 310 from 1990
Idle speed: 800 to 900 rpm
Valve clearances (cold):
inlet: 0.15 mm
exhaust: 0.25 mm

CAPACITIES:

Engine oil including oil filter: 3.75 litres
Cooling system (inc. heater): 6.4 litres
Transmission (manual): 1.8 litres
Fuel tank: 42 litres

CHAPTER 9 - TOOLS & EQUIPMENT

Although good tools are not cheap, if you reckon their cost against what you would otherwise spend on professional servicing and repairs, your arithmetic should show you that it doesn't take long to recoup your outlay - and then to start showing a profit!

In fact, there is no need to spend a fortune all at once - most owners who do their own servicing acquire their implements over a long period of time. However, there are some items you simply cannot do without in order to properly carry out the work necessary to keep your car on the road. Therefore, in the following lists, we have concentrated on those items which are likely to be valuable aids to maintaining your car in a good state of tune, and to keep it running sweetly and safely and in addition we have featured some of the tools that are 'nice-to-have' rather than 'must have' because as your tool chest grows, there are some tools that help to make servicing just that bit easier and more thorough to carry out.

Two vital points - firstly always buy the best quality tools you can afford. 'Cheap and cheerful' items may look similar to more expensive implements, but

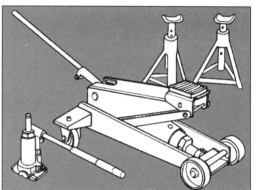

experience shows that they often fail when the going gets tough, and some can even be dangerous. With proper care, good quality tools will last a lifetime, and can be regarded as an investment. The extra outlay is well worth it, in the long run.

Over the years, there have been various nut/bolt/spanner designations. For many years British cars standardised on 'AF', a designation referring to the measurement 'across the flats' of the hexagon nut or bolt head, while the 'foreigners' were 'Metric'. While there are still many 'AF' cars around, all modern cars are 'Metric' of course, apart from American cars. (For the record, 'metric' sizes are also measured across their flats!). Be sure you know which designation applies to your car before you start buying. Your local motor accessory store should be able to advise, or you could all your local main dealer to make sure, if necessary.

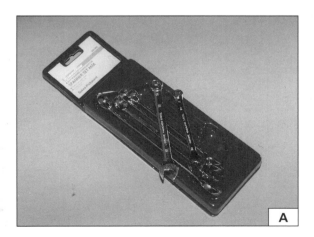

SPANNERS:

A. The two common types of spanner are the ring and the open-ended. The ring spanner grips practically all round the bolt, and is preferable where the bolt is really tight, for an open-ended spanner, merely straddling two flats of the bolt, could slip. On the other hand, the open-end is often quicker and easier to use - so this set of 'Combination' spanners, a ring at one end, open-ended the other, is a nice compromise!

All the tools featured here are available from your local High Street auto-accessory store or Super Store. Any special tools needed for your car are referred to in Chapter 3.

TOOLS & EQUIPMENT

B. While the 'flatness' of the combination spanners (or of a conventional open-ended spanner) is often useful, there are occasions when only the offset, or 'swan neck' of the conventional ring spanner will do the job - like when having to operate over the top of one bolt in order to undo another.

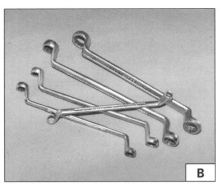

Unlike the combination spanners, the conventional ring and open-ended spanners will have a different size at each end.

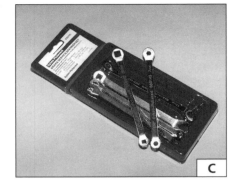

Usually, the AF sizes will rise in sixteenths of an inch, and the metrics by one millimetre - the following sizes will probably cover most of your needs:
AF - 3/8 x 7/16, 1/2 x 9/16, 5/8 x 11/16, 13/16 x 7/8
Metric - 10 x 11, 12 x 13, 14 x 15, 16 x 17

C. The sturdy specialist brake spanner used, for brake adjusters or bleed nipples, is undeniably a wise buy, as mentioned in the brake servicing text. You might not need the set as shown here, but you can choose individual sizes to suit your car, such as 1/4 in. square x 11/32 in. square or 1/4 in. hexagonal x 5/16 in. AF, or perhaps 8 x 10mm hexagonal - there are others.

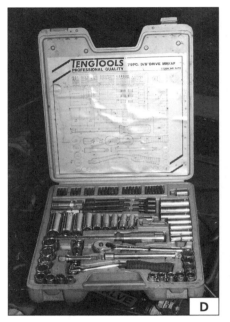

D. A basic socket set should figure highly on your shopping list, for it will cover your basic spanner sizes and can often solve difficult access or extra-leverage problems. This one is a fairly sophisticated set, and includes a number of useful extras, such as spark plug spanners and Allen key and screwdriver bits. Don't buy more than you need, however, and don't be tempted by cheap, nasty - and often dangerous - market stall socket sets.

E. A torque wrench was also once a luxury, but nowadays it's practically essential, with specific torque settings quoted for many of the nuts and bolts used in modern car engineering. The example shown will cater for most applications, including adjustable wheel-bearing hub nuts, but even the next size up (30-150 lb/ft) in the DIY range will still fall short of the 200-odd lb/ft specified for some hub nuts!

F. If you still need a plug spanner, and particularly if your engine features deep-set spark plugs, this Sykes-Pickavant 'extra long plug wrench', combining both 10mm and 14mm sizes, could be a boon. Some plugs are set deeper than the average length of a socket-set spark plug spanner, and if the socket set's extension bar is prone to leaving the spanner socket stuck on the plug, then you could have a problem ...

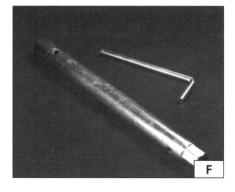

SCREWDRIVERS:

G. You will need a selection of screwdrivers, both flat-bladed and cross-headed, long ones, short ones, slim ones, fat ones ...

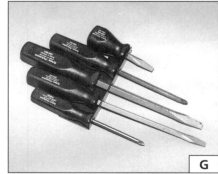

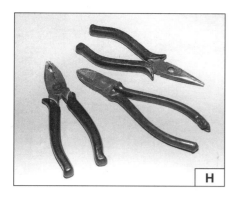

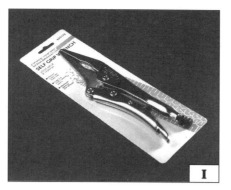

PLIERS:

H. Ordinary combination (or 'engineers') pliers are needed for general work, while a long-nosed pair are handy where access is tight. Their cutting edges are useful for stripping cable insulation, or for snipping wire or trimming split-pin lengths, but you might prefer a pair of specialist side-cutter pliers for such work.

I. Jolly useful as an extra pair of hands, or for gripping such as a rusty nut or bolt really tightly, is a self-grip wrench. This is a long-nose example, but there are also ordinary straight-jaw and round jaw versions.

SUNDRIES:

J. You'll need hammers, including the useful 1lb ball-pein type, plus a hefty copper hammer and maybe a soft (plastic-headed) hammer, too.

K. The wire brush should have brass bristles and as well as an ordinary set of feeler gauges, an 'ignition set' covers most plug and points gap sizes, and includes a points file and a spark plug gap setting tool.

L. You may need a grease gun (although virtually no modern cars have grease points) but you *will* want an oil can, and an oil funnel, and a container of sufficient capacity into which the engine oil can be drained.

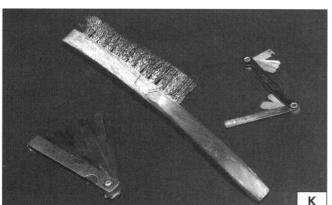

M. You may also need a drain plug 'key' suitable for your car unless all the drain plugs are 'bolt'-type hexagons.

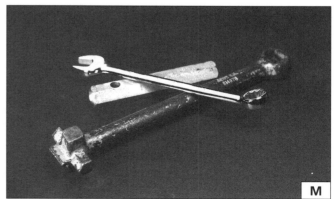

N. Well worthwhile, since some oil filters can be cussedly tight, is some sort of oil filter wrench - this chain-type is a nice example. In extreme cases, even these wrenches can fail to get a grip, in which case, drive an old screwdriver right through the filter and twist it loose.

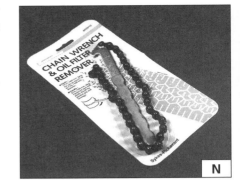

O. A separate set of hand-held Allen keys is a good idea (they come in metric or Imperial sizes), and an adjustable spanner and a 'Junior' hacksaw will have their uses.

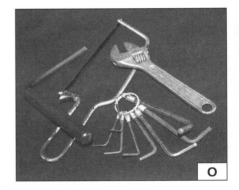

P. For your weekly maintenance checks, you'll need a tyre pressure gauge, tyre tread depth gauge and a footpump - which might, like the example here, have an integral pressure gauge. And whether you're wheel-changing at home or roadside, you will welcome the extremely useful Sykes-Pickavant 'Wheelmaster' wrench, which can be extended to give enough leverage to shift those wheel nuts or bolts that the average car-kit wheelbrace wouldn't even look at - see the wheel-change routine at the start of Chapter 3. Remember to carry the extendable wrench with you in the car!

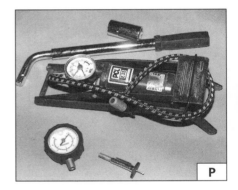

LIFTING:

Q. While the jack supplied with the car *might* be OK for emergency wheel-changes, you would soon tire of trying to use it for servicing operations. Here, you need a good trolley jack, and one of the latest on the market is this 2-ton lifting capacity 'Lift and Lock' example which, as its name suggests, has a built-in fail-safe locking device in the event of hydraulic failure.

R. No matter what sort of jack you use, it is ESSENTIAL that you should not venture beneath a car supported on a jack alone. Having raised it, you need to support it safely and securely. What you need now is definitely NOT house bricks (or any other such potentially dangerous items!) but rather axle stands or wheel-ramps. Adjustable-height stands are essential and both axle stands and ramps should be produced by a 'name' manufacturer, for safety's sake. If you don't need the wheels off, it can be argued that the ramps offer better stability - though you'll benefit from some assistance when it comes to driving upon them. See the start of *Chapter 3*.

TUNING AIDS:

S. As we have said earlier in this chapter and within the servicing sections, the tuning aids that are now available to the DIY market have become practically invaluable 'musts' for the dedicated home mechanic. Any of the Gunson's collection shown here would soon prove their worth. Top of the tree, of course, is their 'Gastester Professional' - don't let its designation suggest that it's not for DIY use, for although it's expensive a group of friends sharing its cost would find their outlay well worth the benefits offered by the unit's Exhaust Gas 'CO' functions, plus its Voltage, Dwell and RPM modes. If it's pure 'multi-meter' you're after, then their 'Digimeter 320' is a tidy little hand-held unit, with clear digital read-outs for such as Volts (DC and household AC) and Amps, Ohms, rpm, and Dwell (degrees and per cent), and its sophistication extends to Frequency, Period and Pulsewidth testing (handy for fuel injection systems), as well as Diode, Resistance and Continuity testing. Also by Gunson's is the powerful 'Timestrobe' xenon timing light, the now not so new, but still novel 'Colortune' and (not shown) the 'Carbalancer'. The latter two devices are virtually invaluable when it comes to car-burettor tuning.

APPENDIX 1
RECOMMENDED LUBRICANTS
& ESSENTIAL FLUIDS

Castrol has a broad range of top-quality oils, greases and other essential fluids, and they will all figure in the 'Recommended' list appended to the handbooks issued by the major motor manufacturers.

ENGINE OIL

PETROL ENGINES.

GTX (15W/50): The 'superior' multigrade engine oil that is certainly suitable for newer vehicles requiring an SAE 15W/50 or 20W/50 viscosity oil, but which is particularly appropriate for older technology engines and high-mileage vehicles, where working clearances might be higher than average.

GTX Protection Plus (15W/40): Suits newer vehicles, including turbo-charged, where this viscosity is recommended. Very low phospherous content to prolong catalyst life.

GTX Magnatec (10W/40): "The unique moleculare attraction protects your engine from the moment you turn your key, providing complete, continuous protection at all times," says Castrol.

Models up to 1990
Castrol GTX 15W/50

Models from 1990-on
Castrol GTX, GTX Protection Plus 15W/40 or Magnatec

DIESEL ENGINES.
GTD (15W/40): Specially formulated for the particular demands of all diesel engines, including turbo-charged.

All diesel models, including turbo
Castrol GTD 15W/40

GEARBOX OIL

MANUAL TRANSMISSIONS
Castrol Syntrax Universal

AUTOMATIC TRANSMISSION
Castrol Dexron R III

POWER STEERING

Castrol Dexron R III

BRAKE FLUID
Vehicles without ABS
Castrol Universal Brake Fluid:

Vehicles fitted with ABS
Castrol Super Disc 5.1

WHEEL BEARINGS
Castrol LM grease

DOOR LOCKS & HINGES
Castrol Everyman

ELECTRICAL CONNECTIONS
Castrol DWF

NUT & BOLT RELEASE
Castrol Easing Oil

COOLING SYSTEM
Castrol Anti-freeze & Summer Coolant

CASTROL ANTI-FREEZE: Recommended for use in petrol or diesel engine cooling systems, with aluminium or cast engines. Its formulation of mono ethylene glycol and corrosion inhibitors makes it suitable for all-year-round use, and because it contains no phosphate it is reckoned that the problems of deposits in some modern uprated engines are eliminated. A 33 per cent concentration will protect down to minus 17 degrees C.

APPENDIX 2
SPECIALISTS & SUPPLIERS
FEATURED IN THIS BOOK

All of the products and specialists listed below have contributed in various ways to this book. All of the consumer products used are available through regular high street outlets or by mail order from specialist suppliers.

A E Clegg Ltd, Hallow Service Station, Main Road, Hallow, Worcs. Tel: 01905 640228
Vauxhall main dealer.

**Dinol (GB) Limited, Dinol House, 98 Ock Street, Abingdon, Oxford, OX14 5DH.
Tel: 01235 530677**
Suppliers of Dinitrol rust proofing fluids, and are equipped to carry out rustproofing on vehicles.

Gunson Ltd, Coppen Road, Dagenham, Essex RM8 1NU. Tel: 0181 984 8855.
Electrical and electronic engine tuning equipment.

**NGK Spark Plugs (UK) Ltd, 7-8-9 Garrick Industrial Centre, Hendon, London, NW9 6AQ.
Tel: 0181 202 2151.**
Top quality spark plugs.

**SP Tyres UK Ltd, Fort Dunlop, Birmingham, B24 9QT.
Tel: 0121 384 4444.**
Manufacturers of Dunlop tyres.

**Sykes-Pickavant Group plc, Kilnhouse Lane, Lytham St Annes, Lancs, FY8 3DU.
Tel: 01253 721291**
Wide range of hand tools and specialist equipment, some of which were used in this book.

**Vauxhall Motors Ltd., Griffin House, P O Box 3, Osborne Road, Luton, Bedfordshire, LU2 0SY.
Tel: 01582 21122**
See your local main dealer in Yellow Pages for Vauxhall parts.

Waste Oil Disposal
There are 1,300 listed waste oil disposal sites in the UK alone. PLEASE don't foul the environment by tipping waste oil into the drains or the ground. Find your nearest oil disposal point by running the National Rivers Authority in the U.K. on **FREEPHONE 0800 663366.**

APPENDIX 3
SERVICE HISTORY

This Chapter helps you keep track of all the servicing carried out on your vehicle and can even save you money! A vehicle with a Service History is always worth more than one without, and you can make full use of this section, even if you have a garage or mechanic carry out the work for you. It enables you to specify the jobs you want to have carried out to your vehicle and, of course, it enables you to keep that all-important Service History. And even if your vehicle doesn't have a 'history' going back to when it was new, keeping this Chapter complete will add to your vehicle's value when you come to sell it. Mind you, it obviously won't be enough to just to tick the boxes: keep all your receipts when you buy oil, filters and other consumables or parts. That way, you'll also be able to return any faulty parts if needs be.

Buying Parts

Before carrying out a service on your car, you will need to purchase the right parts. Please refer to **Chapter 2, Buying Guide** for information on how to buy the right parts at the right prices and for information on how to find your car's 'identity numbers'; information that you will need in order to buy the right parts, first time!

Month, whichever comes first, is repeated at each one of the following Service Intervals. The same applies to the **6,000 Miles or Six Months** interval: much of it is repeated at **12,000 Miles or Twelve Months.** Every time a Job or set of Jobs is 'repeated' from an earlier Interval, we show it in a tinted area on the page. You can then see more clearly which jobs are unique to the level of Service Interval that you are on.

The Job Lists

Wherever possible, the Jobs listed in this section have been placed in a logical order or placed into groups that will help you make progress on the car. We have tried to save you too much in the way of unnecessary movement by grouping jobs around areas of the car. Therefore, at each Service Interval, you will see the work grouped into Jobs that need carrying out in The Engine Bay, Around The Car or Under The Car.

You'll also see space at each Service Interval for you to write down the date, price and seller's name every time you buy consumables or accessories. And once again, do remember to keep your receipts! There's also space for you to date and sign the Service Record or for a garage's stamp to be applied.

As you move through the Service Intervals, you will notice that the work carried out at say, **1,500 Miles or Every**

You will also find that all the major Intervals, right up to the 'longest', contain Jobs that are unique to that Service Interval. That's why we have continued this Service History right up to the **36,000 Miles or every Three Years** interval. So now, you will be able to service your car and keep a full record of the work, in the knowledge that your car has been looked after as well as anyone could wish for!

Important Note!

The Service Jobs listed here are intended as a check list and a means of keeping a record of your vehicle's service history, *not* as a set of instructions for working on your car. It is most important that you refer to **Chapter 3, Servicing Your Car** for full details of how to carry out each Job listed here and for essential SAFETY information and, see also, **Chapter 1, Safety First!**.

EVERY 500 MILES, WEEKLY OR BEFORE A LONG JOURNEY

This list is shown, complete, only once. It would have been a bit much to have provided the list 52 times over for use once a week throughout the year! Each job is, however, included with every longer Service list from 3,000 miles/Three Months-on so that each of the 'weekly' Jobs is carried out as part of every service.

Every 500 Miles - The Engine Bay

☐ Job 1. Engine oil level.

☐ Job 2. Check coolant level.

☐ Job 3. Brake fluid level.

☐ Job 4. Check windscreen wash level.

Every 500 Miles - Around the Car

☐ Job 5. Check tyre pressures.

☐ Job 6. Check front lights.

☐ Job 7. Check side repeater indicators.

☐ Job 8. Check rear lights and indicators.

☐ Job 9. Check number plate light.

☐ Job 10. Check interior light.

☐ Job 11. Check windscreen wipers.

☐ Job 12. Check screen washers.

EVERY 1,500 MILES - OR EVERY MONTH, WHICHEVER COMES FIRST

These Jobs are similar to the 500 Mile Jobs but don't need carrying out quite so regularly. Once again, these Jobs are not shown with a separate listing for each 1,500 miles/1 Month interval but they are included as part of every 3,000 miles/Three Months Service list and for every longer Service interval.

Every 1,500 Miles - The Engine Bay

☐ Job 13. Check battery electrolyte level.

Every 1,500 Miles - Around the Car

☐ Job 14. Check horn.

☐ Job 15. Check tyre treads.

☐ Job 16. Check spare wheel.

☐ Job 17. Touch-up paintwork.

☐ Job 18. Valet interior.

☐ Job 19. Improve visibility.

EVERY 3,000 MILES - OR THREE MONTHS, WHICHEVER COMES FIRST

All the Service Jobs in the tinted area have been carried forward from earlier service intervals and are to be repeated at this service.

Every 3,000 Miles - The Engine Bay

First carry out all Jobs listed under earlier Service intervals as applicable.

☐ Job 1. Engine oil level.

☐ Job 2. Check coolant level.

☐ Job 3. Brake fluid level.

☐ Job 4. Check windscreen wash level.

☐ Job 13. Check battery electrolyte level.

☐ Job 20. Check alternator drive belts.

☐ Job 21. Drain fuel filter.

☐ Job 22. **DIESEL ENGINES ONLY** Renew diesel engine oil.

☐ Job 23. **DIESEL ENGINES ONLY** Replace diesel oil filter.

☐ Job 24. Check brake and fuel lines.

☐ Job 25. Check air filter.

Every 3,000 Miles - Around The Car

First carry out all Jobs listed under earlier Service intervals as applicable.

- [ ] Job 5. Check tyre pressures.
- [ ] Job 6. Check front lights.
- [ ] Job 7. Check side repeater indicators.
- [ ] Job 8. Check rear lights and indicators.
- [ ] Job 9. Check number plate light.
- [ ] Job 10. Check interior light.
- [ ] Job 11. Check windscreen wipers.
- [ ] Job 12. Check screen washers.
- [ ] Job 14. Check horn.
- [ ] Job 15. Check tyre treads.
- [ ] Job 16. Check spare wheel.
- [ ] Job 17. Touch-up paintwork.
- [ ] Job 18. Valet interior.
- [ ] Job 19. Improve visibility.

- [ ] Job 26. Check wheel bolts.
- [ ] Job 27. Check handbrake adjustment.
- [ ] Job 28. Check windscreen.
- [ ] Job 29. Clean and lubricate aerial.

Every 3,000 Miles - Under the Car

- [ ] Job 30. Check exhaust system and mountings.
- [ ] Job 31. Check brake and fuel lines.
- [ ] Job 32. Check steering rack gaiters.
- [ ] Job 33. Check drive shaft gaiters.
- [ ] Job 34. Check underside of car for leaks.
- [ ] Job 35. Clean mud traps.

Every 3,000 Miles - Road Test

- [ ] Job 36. Clean controls.
- [ ] Job 37. Check instruments and controls.
- [ ] Job 38. Check throttle action.
- [ ] Job 39. Check clutch action.
- [ ] Job 40. Road test: brakes and steering.
- [ ] Job 41. Check C.V. joints for noise (part of road test).

Date serviced:...

Carried out by: ....
Garage Stamp or signature:

Parts/Accessories purchased (date, parts, source) ....

....

....

....

....

EVERY 6,000 MILES - OR EVERY SIX MONTHS, WHICHEVER COMES FIRST

All the Service Jobs in the tinted area have been carried forward from earlier service intervals and are to be repeated at this service.

Every 6,000 Miles - The Engine Bay

First carry out all Jobs listed under earlier Service intervals as applicable.

- [ ] Job 2. Check coolant level.
- [ ] Job 3. Brake fluid level.
- [ ] Job 4. Check windscreen wash level.
- [ ] Job 13. Check battery electrolyte level.
- [ ] Job 20. Check alternator drive belts.
- [ ] Job 21. Drain fuel filter.
- [ ] Job 22. **DIESEL ENGINES ONLY** Renew diesel engine oil.
- [ ] Job 23. **DIESEL ENGINES ONLY** Replace diesel oil filter.
- [ ] Job 24. Check brake and fuel lines.

- [ ] Job 42. Change engine oil and filter.
- [ ] Job 43. Clean and check spark plugs.
- [ ] Job 44. Clean and check ignition components.
- [ ] Job 45. Check/adjust points dwell angle.
- [ ] Job 46. Lubricate distributor.
- [ ] Job 47. Lubricate clutch cable.
- [ ] Job 48. Check gearbox oil.
- [ ] Job 49. Check and turn air filter element.
- [ ] Job 50. Lubricate throttle linkage.
- [ ] Job 51. Lubricate carburettor linkages.
- [ ] Job 52. Adjust carburettor.
- [ ] Job 53. Check idle speed.
- [ ] Job 54. Check exhaust emission.
- [ ] Job 55. Check pipes and hoses.

Every 6,000 Miles - Around the Car

First carry out all Jobs listed under earlier Service intervals as applicable.

- [ ] Job 5. Check tyre pressures.
- [ ] Job 6. Check front lights.
- [ ] Job 7. Check side repeater indicators.
- [ ] Job 8. Check rear lights and indicators.
- [ ] Job 9. Check number plate light.
- [ ] Job 10. Check interior light.
- [ ] Job 11. Check windscreen wipers.
- [ ] Job 12. Check screen washers.
- [ ] Job 14. Check horn.
- [ ] Job 15. Check tyre treads.
- [ ] Job 16. Check spare wheel.
- [ ] Job 17. Touch-up paintwork.
- [ ] Job 18. Valet interior.
- [ ] Job 19. Improve visibility.
- [ ] Job 26. Check wheel bolts.
- [ ] Job 27. Check handbrake adjustment.
- [ ] Job 28. Check windscreen.
- [ ] Job 29. Clean and lubricate aerial.

- [ ] Job 56. Check seat belts and mountings.
- [ ] Job 57. Check seat mountings.
- [ ] Job 58. Check fuel filler-cap seal.
- [ ] Job 59. Lubricate bonnet release.
- [ ] Job 60. Lubricate hinges, locks, check straps.
- [ ] Job 61. Check shock absorber action.
- [ ] Job 62. Check wheel alignment.

Every 6,000 Miles - Under the Car

First carry out all Jobs listed under earlier Service intervals as applicable.

- [ ] Job 30. Check exhaust system and mountings.
- [ ] Job 31. Check brake and fuel lines.
- [ ] Job 32. Check steering rack gaiters.
- [ ] Job 33. Check drive shaft gaiters.
- [ ] Job 34. Check underside of car for leaks.
- [ ] Job 35. Clean mud traps.

- [ ] Job 63. Check/renew front brake pads.
- [ ] Job 64. Check brake discs.
- [ ] Job 65. Check/adjust/renew rear brakes shoes.
- [ ] Job 66. Adjust rear brakes.
- [ ] Job 67. Check brake proportioning valve.
- [ ] Job 68. Check steering ball joints.

Every 6,000 Miles - Road Test

- [ ] Job 36. Clean controls.
- [ ] Job 37. Check instruments and controls.
- [ ] Job 38. Check throttle action.
- [ ] Job 39. Check clutch action.
- [ ] Job 40. Road test: brakes and steering.
- [ ] Job 41. Check C.V. joints for noise (part of road test).

EVERY 9,000 MILES - OR EVERY NINE MONTHS, WHICHEVER COMES FIRST

All the Jobs at this Service Interval have been carried forward from earlier Service Intervals and are to be repeated at this service.

Every 9,000 Miles - The Engine Bay

- [ ] Job 1. Engine oil level.
- [ ] Job 2. Check coolant level.
- [ ] Job 3. Brake fluid level.
- [ ] Job 4. Check windscreen wash level.
- [ ] Job 13. Check battery electrolyte level.
- [ ] Job 20. Check alternator drive belts.
- [ ] Job 21. Drain fuel filter.
- [ ] Job 22. **DIESEL ENGINES ONLY** Renew diesel engine oil.
- [ ] Job 23. **DIESEL ENGINES ONLY** Replace diesel oil filter.
- [ ] Job 24. Check brake and fuel lines.
- [ ] Job 25. Check air filter.

Date serviced:...

Carried out by: ....
Garage Stamp or signature:

Parts/Accessories purchased (date, parts, source) ....
....
....
....
....

Every 9,000 Miles - Around The Car

- ☐ Job 5. Check tyre pressures.
- ☐ Job 6. Check front lights.
- ☐ Job 7. Check side repeater indicators.
- ☐ Job 8. Check rear lights and indicators.
- ☐ Job 9. Check number plate light.
- ☐ Job 10. Check interior light.
- ☐ Job 11. Check windscreen wipers.
- ☐ Job 12. Check screen washers.
- ☐ Job 14. Check horn.
- ☐ Job 15. Check tyre treads.
- ☐ Job 16. Check spare wheel.
- ☐ Job 17. Touch-up paintwork.
- ☐ Job 18. Valet interior.
- ☐ Job 19. Improve visibility.
- ☐ Job 26. Check wheel bolts.
- ☐ Job 27. Check handbrake adjustment.
- ☐ Job 28. Check windscreen.
- ☐ Job 29. Clean and lubricate aerial.

Every 9,000 Miles - Under the Car

- ☐ Job 30. Check exhaust system and mountings.
- ☐ Job 31. Check brake and fuel lines.
- ☐ Job 32. Check steering rack gaiters.
- ☐ Job 33. Check drive shaft gaiters.
- ☐ Job 34. Check underside of car for leaks.
- ☐ Job 35. Clean mud traps.

Every 9,000 Miles - Road Test

- ☐ Job 36. Clean controls.
- ☐ Job 37. Check instruments and controls.
- ☐ Job 38. Check throttle action.
- ☐ Job 39. Check clutch action.
- ☐ Job 40. Road test: brakes and steering.
- ☐ Job 41. Check C.V. joints for noise (part of road test).

Date serviced:...

Carried out by: ....
Garage Stamp or signature:

Parts/Accessories purchased (date, parts, source) ....
....
....
....
....

EVERY 12,000 MILES - OR EVERY TWELVE MONTHS, WHICHEVER COMES FIRST

All the Service Jobs in the tinted area have been carried forward from earlier service intervals and are to be repeated at this service.

Every 12,000 Miles - The Engine Bay

First carry out all Jobs listed under earlier Service intervals as applicable.

- ☐ Job 4. Check windscreen wash level.
- ☐ Job 13. Check battery electrolyte level.
- ☐ Job 20. Check alternator drive belts.
- ☐ Job 21. Drain fuel filter.
- ☐ Job 22. **DIESEL ENGINES ONLY** Renew diesel engine oil.
- ☐ Job 23. **DIESEL ENGINES ONLY** Replace diesel oil filter.
- ☐ Job 24. Check brake and fuel lines.
- ☐ Job 42. Change engine oil and filter.
- ☐ Job 44. Clean and check ignition components.
- ☐ Job 46. Lubricate distributor.
- ☐ Job 47. Lubricate clutch cable.
- ☐ Job 48. Check gearbox oil.
- ☐ Job 50. Lubricate throttle linkage.
- ☐ Job 51. Lubricate carburettor linkages.
- ☐ Job 52. Adjust carburettor.
- ☐ Job 53. Check idle speed.
- ☐ Job 54. Check exhaust emission.
- ☐ Job 55. Check pipes and hoses.

- ☐ Job 69. Change air filter element.
- ☐ Job 70. Clean air filter housing.
- ☐ Job 71. Check/adjust valve clearances.
- ☐ Job 72. Renew contact breaker points.
- ☐ Job 73. Check ignition timing.
- ☐ Job 74. Check coolant.
- ☐ Job 75. Check vacuum hoses.
- ☐ Job 76. Check/renew crankcase ventilation hoses.
- ☐ Job 77. Clean oil filler cap.

- [ ] Job 78. Renew spark plugs.
- [ ] Job 79. Clean glow plugs.
- [ ] Job 80. Clean/protect battery terminals.
- [ ] Job 81. Check battery specific gravity.
- [ ] Job 82. Renew fuel filter.
- [ ] Job 83. **FUEL INJECTION CARS FROM 1989 ONLY** Read stored engine fault codes.

Every 12,000 Miles - Around the Car

First carry out all Jobs listed under earlier Service intervals as applicable.

- [ ] Job 5. Check tyre pressures.
- [ ] Job 6. Check front lights.
- [ ] Job 7. Check side repeater indicators.
- [ ] Job 8. Check rear lights and indicators.
- [ ] Job 9. Check number plate light.
- [ ] Job 10. Check interior light.
- [ ] Job 12. Check screen washers.
- [ ] Job 14. Check horn.
- [ ] Job 15. Check tyre treads.
- [ ] Job 16. Check spare wheel.
- [ ] Job 17. Touch-up paintwork.
- [ ] Job 18. Valet interior.
- [ ] Job 19. Improve visibility.
- [ ] Job 26. Check wheel bolts.
- [ ] Job 27. Check handbrake adjustment.
- [ ] Job 28. Check windscreen.
- [ ] Job 29. Clean and lubricate aerial.
- [ ] Job 56. Check seat belts and mountings.
- [ ] Job 57. Check seat mountings.
- [ ] Job 58. Check fuel filler-cap seal.
- [ ] Job 59. Lubricate bonnet release.
- [ ] Job 60. Lubricate hinges, locks, check straps.
- [ ] Job 61. Check shock absorber action.
- [ ] Job 62. Check wheel alignment.

- [ ] Job 84. Check toolkit and jack.
- [ ] Job 85. Check light seals.
- [ ] Job 86. Check door/tailgate seals.
- [ ] Job 87. Check headlight alignment.
- [ ] Job 88. Renew wiper blades and arms.

- [ ] Job 89. Check floors.
- [ ] Job 90. Renew batteries in car alarm sender.
- [ ] Job 91. Check wiring and terminals.
- [ ] Job 92. Clean radiator exterior.

Every 12,000 Miles - Under the Car

First carry out all Jobs listed under earlier Service intervals as applicable.

- [ ] Job 30. Check exhaust system and mountings.
- [ ] Job 31. Check brake and fuel lines.
- [ ] Job 32. Check steering rack gaiters.
- [ ] Job 33. Check drive shaft gaiters.
- [ ] Job 34. Check underside of car for leaks.
- [ ] Job 35. Clean mud traps.
- [ ] Job 63. Check/renew front brake pads.
- [ ] Job 64. Check brake discs.
- [ ] Job 65. Check/adjust/renew rear brakes shoes.
- [ ] Job 66. Adjust rear brakes.
- [ ] Job 67. Check brake proportioning valve.
- [ ] Job 68. Check steering ball joints.

- [ ] Job 93. Check wheel bearings.
- [ ] Job 94. Check steering and suspension.
- [ ] Job 95. Check steering rack mountings.
- [ ] Job 96. Check front suspension units.
- [ ] Job 97. Check front suspension bushes.
- [ ] Job 98. Check rear springs and shock absorbers.
- [ ] Job 99. Check rear suspension bushes.
- [ ] Job 100. Check engine and gearbox mountings.
- [ ] Job 101. Check/lubricate handbrake cable.
- [ ] Job 102. Check underside of body structure.
- [ ] Job 103. Clean drainage holes.
- [ ] Job 104. Renew brake fluid.

Every 12,000 Miles - Road Test

- [ ] Job 36. Clean controls.
- [ ] Job 37. Check instruments and controls.
- [ ] Job 38. Check throttle action.
- [ ] Job 39. Check clutch action.
- [ ] Job 40. Road test: brakes and steering.
- [ ] Job 41. Check C.V. joints for noise (part of road test).

Date serviced:..

Carried out by: ....
Garage Stamp or signature:

Parts/Accessories purchased (date, parts, source) ....
....
....
....
....

EVERY 15,000 MILES - OR EVERY FIFTEEN MONTHS, WHICHEVER COMES FIRST

All the Jobs at this Service Interval have been carried forward from earlier Service Intervals and are to be repeated at this service.

Every 15,000 Miles - The Engine Bay

- [ ] Job 1. Engine oil level.
- [ ] Job 2. Check coolant level.
- [ ] Job 3. Brake fluid level.
- [ ] Job 4. Check windscreen wash level.
- [ ] Job 13. Check battery electrolyte level.
- [ ] Job 20. Check alternator drive belts.
- [ ] Job 21. Drain fuel filter.
- [ ] Job 22. **DIESEL ENGINES ONLY** Renew diesel engine oil.
- [ ] Job 23. **DIESEL ENGINES ONLY** Replace diesel oil filter.
- [ ] Job 24. Check brake and fuel lines.
- [ ] Job 25. Check air filter.

Every 15,000 Miles - Around The Car

- [ ] Job 5. Check tyre pressures.
- [ ] Job 6. Check front lights.
- [ ] Job 7. Check side repeater indicators.
- [ ] Job 8. Check rear lights and indicators.
- [ ] Job 9. Check number plate light.
- [ ] Job 10. Check interior light.
- [ ] Job 11. Check windscreen wipers.
- [ ] Job 12. Check screen washers.
- [ ] Job 14. Check horn.
- [ ] Job 15. Check tyre treads.
- [ ] Job 16. Check spare wheel.
- [ ] Job 17. Touch-up paintwork.
- [ ] Job 18. Valet interior.
- [ ] Job 19. Improve visibility.
- [ ] Job 26. Check wheel bolts.
- [ ] Job 27. Check handbrake adjustment.
- [ ] Job 28. Check windscreen.
- [ ] Job 29. Clean and lubricate aerial.

Every 15,000 Miles - Under the Car

- [ ] Job 30. Check exhaust system and mountings.
- [ ] Job 31. Check brake and fuel lines.
- [ ] Job 32. Check steering rack gaiters.
- [ ] Job 33. Check drive shaft gaiters.
- [ ] Job 34. Check underside of car for leaks.
- [ ] Job 35. Clean mud traps.

Every 15,000 Miles - Road Test

- [ ] Job 36. Clean controls.
- [ ] Job 37. Check instruments and controls.
- [ ] Job 38. Check throttle action.
- [ ] Job 39. Check clutch action.
- [ ] Job 40. Road test: brakes and steering.
- [ ] Job 41. Check C.V. joints for noise (part of road test).

Date serviced:..

Carried out by: ....
Garage Stamp or signature:

Parts/Accessories purchased (date, parts, source) ....
....
....
....
....

EVERY 18,000 MILES - OR EVERY EIGHTEEN MONTHS, WHICHEVER COMES FIRST

All the Jobs at this Service Interval have been carried forward from earlier Service Intervals and are to be repeated at this service.

Every 18,000 Miles - The Engine Bay

- [ ] Job 2. Check coolant level.
- [ ] Job 3. Brake fluid level.
- [ ] Job 4. Check windscreen wash level.
- [ ] Job 13. Check battery electrolyte level.
- [ ] Job 20. Check alternator drive belts.
- [ ] Job 21. Drain fuel filter.
- [ ] Job 22. **DIESEL ENGINES ONLY** Renew diesel engine oil.
- [ ] Job 23. **DIESEL ENGINES ONLY** Replace diesel oil filter.
- [ ] Job 24. Check brake and fuel lines.
- [ ] Job 42. Change engine oil and filter.
- [ ] Job 43. Clean and check spark plugs.
- [ ] Job 44. Clean and check ignition components.
- [ ] Job 45. Check/adjust points dwell angle.
- [ ] Job 46. Lubricate distributor.
- [ ] Job 47. Lubricate clutch cable.
- [ ] Job 48. Check gearbox oil.
- [ ] Job 49. Check and turn air filter element.
- [ ] Job 50. Lubricate throttle linkage.
- [ ] Job 51. Lubricate carburettor linkages.
- [ ] Job 52. Adjust carburettor.
- [ ] Job 53. Check idle speed.
- [ ] Job 54. Check exhaust emission.
- [ ] Job 55. Check pipes and hoses.

Every 18,000 Miles - Around the Car

First carry out all Jobs listed under earlier Service intervals as applicable.

- [ ] Job 5. Check tyre pressures.
- [ ] Job 6. Check front lights.
- [ ] Job 7. Check side repeater indicators.
- [ ] Job 8. Check rear lights and indicators.
- [ ] Job 9. Check number plate light.
- [ ] Job 10. Check interior light.
- [ ] Job 12. Check screen washers.
- [ ] Job 14. Check horn.
- [ ] Job 15. Check tyre treads.
- [ ] Job 16. Check spare wheel.
- [ ] Job 17. Touch-up paintwork.
- [ ] Job 18. Valet interior.
- [ ] Job 19. Improve visibility.
- [ ] Job 26. Check wheel bolts.
- [ ] Job 27. Check handbrake adjustment.
- [ ] Job 28. Check windscreen.
- [ ] Job 29. Clean and lubricate aerial.
- [ ] Job 56. Check seat belts and mountings.
- [ ] Job 57. Check seat mountings.
- [ ] Job 58. Check fuel filler-cap seal.
- [ ] Job 59. Lubricate bonnet release.
- [ ] Job 60. Lubricate hinges, locks, check straps.
- [ ] Job 61. Check shock absorber action.
- [ ] Job 62. Check wheel alignment.

Every 18,000 Miles - Under the Car

First carry out all Jobs listed under earlier Service intervals as applicable.

- [ ] Job 30. Check exhaust system and mountings.
- [ ] Job 31. Check brake and fuel lines.
- [ ] Job 32. Check steering rack gaiters.
- [ ] Job 33. Check drive shaft gaiters.
- [ ] Job 34. Check underside of car for leaks.
- [ ] Job 35. Clean mud traps.
- [ ] Job 63. Check/renew front brake pads.
- [ ] Job 64. Check brake discs.
- [ ] Job 65. Check/adjust/renew rear brakes shoes.
- [ ] Job 66. Adjust rear brakes.
- [ ] Job 67. Check brake proportioning valve.
- [ ] Job 68. Check steering ball joints.

Every 18,000 Miles - Road Test

- [ ] Job 36. Clean controls.
- [ ] Job 37. Check instruments and controls.
- [ ] Job 38. Check throttle action.
- [ ] Job 39. Check clutch action.
- [ ] Job 40. Road test: brakes and steering.
- [ ] Job 41. Check C.V. joints for noise (part of road test).

Date serviced:..

Carried out by: ....
Garage Stamp or signature:

Parts/Accessories purchased (date, parts, source) ....
....
....
....
....

EVERY 21,000 MILES - OR EVERY TWENTY ONE MONTHS, WHICHEVER COMES FIRST

All the Jobs at this Service Interval have been carried forward from earlier Service Intervals and are to be repeated at this service.

Every 21,000 Miles - The Engine Bay

- [ ] Job 1. Engine oil level.
- [ ] Job 2. Check coolant level.
- [ ] Job 3. Brake fluid level.
- [ ] Job 4. Check windscreen wash level.
- [ ] Job 13. Check battery electrolyte level.
- [ ] Job 20. Check alternator drive belts.
- [ ] Job 21. Drain fuel filter.
- [ ] Job 22. **DIESEL ENGINES ONLY** Renew diesel engine oil.
- [ ] Job 23. **DIESEL ENGINES ONLY** Replace diesel oil filter.
- [ ] Job 24. Check brake and fuel lines.
- [ ] Job 25. Check air filter.

Every 21,000 Miles - Around the Car

- [ ] Job 5. Check tyre pressures.
- [ ] Job 6. Check front lights.
- [ ] Job 7. Check side repeater indicators.
- [ ] Job 8. Check rear lights and indicators.
- [ ] Job 9. Check number plate light.
- [ ] Job 10. Check interior light.
- [ ] Job 11. Check windscreen wipers.
- [ ] Job 12. Check screen washers.
- [ ] Job 14. Check horn.
- [ ] Job 15. Check tyre treads.
- [ ] Job 16. Check spare wheel.
- [ ] Job 17. Touch-up paintwork.
- [ ] Job 18. Valet interior.
- [ ] Job 19. Improve visibility.
- [ ] Job 26. Check wheel bolts.
- [ ] Job 27. Check handbrake adjustment.
- [ ] Job 28. Check windscreen.
- [ ] Job 29. Clean and lubricate aerial.

Every 21,000 Miles - Under the Car

- [ ] Job 30. Check exhaust system and mountings.
- [ ] Job 31. Check brake and fuel lines.
- [ ] Job 32. Check steering rack gaiters.
- [ ] Job 33. Check drive shaft gaiters.
- [ ] Job 34. Check underside of car for leaks.
- [ ] Job 35. Clean mud traps.

Every 21,000 Miles - Road Test

- [ ] Job 36. Clean controls.
- [ ] Job 37. Check instruments and controls.
- [ ] Job 38. Check throttle action.
- [ ] Job 39. Check clutch action.
- [ ] Job 40. Road test: brakes and steering.
- [ ] Job 41. Check C.V. joints for noise (part of road test).

Date serviced:..

Carried out by: ....
Garage Stamp or signature:

Parts/Accessories purchased (date, parts, source) ....
....
....
....
....

EVERY 24,000 MILES - OR EVERY TWO YEARS, WHICHEVER COMES FIRST

All the Service Jobs in the tinted area have been carried forward from earlier service intervals and are to be repeated at this service.

Every 24,000 Miles - The Engine Bay

First carry out all Jobs listed under earlier Service intervals as applicable.

- [ ] Job 4. Check windscreen wash level.
- [ ] Job 13. Check battery electrolyte level.
- [ ] Job 20. Check alternator drive belts.
- [ ] Job 21. Drain fuel filter.
- [ ] Job 22. DIESEL ENGINES ONLY Renew diesel engine oil.
- [ ] Job 23. DIESEL ENGINES ONLY Replace diesel oil filter.
- [ ] Job 24. Check brake and fuel lines.
- [ ] Job 42. Change engine oil and filter.
- [ ] Job 44. Clean and check ignition components.
- [ ] Job 46. Lubricate distributor.
- [ ] Job 47. Lubricate clutch cable.
- [ ] Job 48. Check gearbox oil.
- [ ] Job 50. Lubricate throttle linkage.
- [ ] Job 51. Lubricate carburettor linkages.
- [ ] Job 52. Adjust carburettor.
- [ ] Job 53. Check idle speed.
- [ ] Job 54. Check exhaust emission.
- [ ] Job 55. Check pipes and hoses.
- [ ] Job 69. Change air filter element.
- [ ] Job 70. Clean air filter housing.
- [ ] Job 71. Check/adjust valve clearances.
- [ ] Job 72. Renew contact breaker points.
- [ ] Job 73. Check ignition timing.
- [ ] Job 75. Check vacuum hoses.
- [ ] Job 76. Check/renew crankcase ventilation hoses.
- [ ] Job 77. Clean oil filler cap.
- [ ] Job 78. Renew spark plugs.
- [ ] Job 79. Clean glow plugs.

- [ ] Job 80. Clean/protect battery terminals.
- [ ] Job 81. Check battery specific gravity.
- [ ] Job 82. Renew fuel filter.
- [ ] Job 83. FUEL INJECTION CARS FROM 1989 ONLY Read stored engine fault codes.

- [ ] Job 105. Replace coolant and clean expansion tank.
- [ ] Job 106. Replace coolant expansion tank cap.

Every 24,000 Miles - Around the Car

- [ ] Job 5. Check tyre pressures.
- [ ] Job 6. Check front lights.
- [ ] Job 7. Check side repeater indicators.
- [ ] Job 8. Check rear lights and indicators.
- [ ] Job 9. Check number plate light.
- [ ] Job 10. Check interior light. Job 12. Check screen washers.
- [ ] Job 14. Check horn.
- [ ] Job 15. Check tyre treads.
- [ ] Job 16. Check spare wheel.
- [ ] Job 17. Touch-up paintwork.
- [ ] Job 18. Valet interior.
- [ ] Job 19. Improve visibility.
- [ ] Job 26. Check wheel bolts.
- [ ] Job 27. Check handbrake adjustment.
- [ ] Job 28. Check windscreen.
- [ ] Job 29. Clean and lubricate aerial.
- [ ] Job 56. Check seat belts and mountings.
- [ ] Job 57. Check seat mountings.
- [ ] Job 58. Check fuel filler-cap seal.
- [ ] Job 59. Lubricate bonnet release.
- [ ] Job 60. Lubricate hinges, locks, check straps.
- [ ] Job 61. Check shock absorber action.
- [ ] Job 62. Check wheel alignment.
- [ ] Job 84. Check toolkit and jack.
- [ ] Job 85. Check light seals.
- [ ] Job 86. Check door/tailgate seals.
- [ ] Job 87. Check headlight alignment.
- [ ] Job 88. Renew wiper blades and arms.

- [ ] Job 89. Check floors.
- [ ] Job 90. Renew batteries in car alarm sender.
- [ ] Job 91. Check wiring and terminals.
- [ ] Job 92. Clean radiator exterior.

Every 24,000 Miles - Under the Car

- [ ] Job 30. Check exhaust system and mountings.
- [ ] Job 31. Check brake and fuel lines.
- [ ] Job 32. Check steering rack gaiters.
- [ ] Job 33. Check drive shaft gaiters.
- [ ] Job 34. Check underside of car for leaks.
- [ ] Job 35. Clean mud traps.
- [ ] Job 63. Check/renew front brake pads.
- [ ] Job 64. Check brake discs.
- [ ] Job 65. Check/adjust/renew rear brakes shoes.
- [ ] Job 66. Adjust rear brakes.
- [ ] Job 67. Check brake proportioning valve.
- [ ] Job 68. Check steering ball joints.
- [ ] Job 93. Check wheel bearings.
- [ ] Job 94. Check steering and suspension.
- [ ] Job 95. Check steering rack mountings.
- [ ] Job 96. Check front suspension units.
- [ ] Job 97. Check front suspension bushes.
- [ ] Job 98. Check rear springs and shock absorbers.
- [ ] Job 99. Check rear suspension bushes.
- [ ] Job 100. Check engine and gearbox mountings.
- [ ] Job 101. Check/lubricate handbrake cable.
- [ ] Job 102. Check underside of body structure.
- [ ] Job 103. Clean drainage holes.
- [ ] Job 104. Renew brake fluid.

Every 24,000 Miles - Road Test

- [ ] Job 36. Clean controls.
- [ ] Job 37. Check instruments and controls.
- [ ] Job 38. Check throttle action.
- [ ] Job 39. Check clutch action.
- [ ] Job 40. Road test: brakes and steering.
- [ ] Job 41. Check C.V. joints for noise (part of road test).

EVERY 27,000 MILES - OR EVERY TWENTY SEVEN MONTHS, WHICHEVER COMES FIRST

All the Jobs at this Service Interval have been carried forward from earlier Service Intervals and are to be repeated at this service.

Every 27,000 Miles - The Engine Bay

- [ ] Job 1. Engine oil level.
- [ ] Job 2. Check coolant level.
- [ ] Job 3. Brake fluid level.
- [ ] Job 4. Check windscreen wash level.
- [ ] Job 13. Check battery electrolyte level.
- [ ] Job 20. Check alternator drive belts.
- [ ] Job 21. Drain fuel filter.
- [ ] Job 22. **DIESEL ENGINES ONLY** Renew diesel engine oil.
- [ ] Job 23. **DIESEL ENGINES ONLY** Replace diesel oil filter.
- [ ] Job 24. Check brake and fuel lines.
- [ ] Job 25. Check air filter.

Every 27,000 Miles - Around the Car

- [ ] Job 5. Check tyre pressures.
- [ ] Job 6. Check front lights.
- [ ] Job 7. Check side repeater indicators.
- [ ] Job 8. Check rear lights and indicators.
- [ ] Job 9. Check number plate light.
- [ ] Job 10. Check interior light.
- [ ] Job 11. Check windscreen wipers.
- [ ] Job 12. Check screen washers.
- [ ] Job 14. Check horn.
- [ ] Job 15. Check tyre treads.
- [ ] Job 16. Check spare wheel.
- [ ] Job 17. Touch-up paintwork.
- [ ] Job 18. Valet interior.
- [ ] Job 19. Improve visibility.
- [ ] Job 26. Check wheel bolts.
- [ ] Job 27. Check handbrake adjustment.
- [ ] Job 28. Check windscreen.
- [ ] Job 29. Clean and lubricate aerial.

Every 27,000 Miles - Under the Car

- [ ] Job 30. Check exhaust system and mountings.
- [ ] Job 31. Check brake and fuel lines.
- [ ] Job 32. Check steering rack gaiters.
- [ ] Job 33. Check drive shaft gaiters.
- [ ] Job 34. Check underside of car for leaks.
- [ ] Job 35. Clean mud traps.

Date serviced:..

Carried out by: ....
Garage Stamp or signature:

Parts/Accessories purchased (date, parts, source) ....

....

....

....

....

Every 27,000 Miles - Road Test

- [ ] Job 36. Clean controls.
- [ ] Job 37. Check instruments and controls.
- [ ] Job 38. Check throttle action.
- [ ] Job 39. Check clutch action.
- [ ] Job 40. Road test: brakes and steering.
- [ ] Job 41. Check C.V. joints for noise (part of road test).

Date serviced:..

Carried out by: ....
Garage Stamp or signature:

Parts/Accessories purchased (date, parts, source) ....

....

....

....

....

EVERY 30,000 MILES - OR EVERY THIRTY MONTHS, WHICHEVER COMES FIRST

All the Jobs at this Service Interval have been carried forward from earlier Service Intervals and are to be repeated at this service.

Every 30,000 Miles - The Engine Bay

- [ ] Job 2. Check coolant level.
- [ ] Job 3. Brake fluid level.
- [ ] Job 4. Check windscreen wash level.
- [ ] Job 13. Check battery electrolyte level.
- [ ] Job 20. Check alternator drive belts.
- [ ] Job 21. Drain fuel filter.
- [ ] Job 22. **DIESEL ENGINES ONLY** Renew diesel engine oil.
- [ ] Job 23. **DIESEL ENGINES ONLY** Replace diesel oil filter.
- [ ] Job 24. Check brake and fuel lines.
- [ ] Job 42. Change engine oil and filter.
- [ ] Job 43. Clean and check spark plugs.
- [ ] Job 44. Clean and check ignition components.
- [ ] Job 45. Check/adjust points dwell angle.
- [ ] Job 46. Lubricate distributor.
- [ ] Job 47. Lubricate clutch cable.
- [ ] Job 48. Check gearbox oil.
- [ ] Job 49. Check and turn air filter element.
- [ ] Job 50. Lubricate throttle linkage.
- [ ] Job 51. Lubricate carburettor linkages.
- [ ] Job 52. Adjust carburettor.
- [ ] Job 53. Check idle speed.
- [ ] Job 54. Check exhaust emission.
- [ ] Job 55. Check pipes and hoses.

Every 30,000 Miles - Around the Car

First carry out all Jobs listed under earlier Service intervals as applicable.

- [ ] Job 5. Check tyre pressures.
- [ ] Job 6. Check front lights.
- [ ] Job 7. Check side repeater indicators.
- [ ] Job 8. Check rear lights and indicators.
- [ ] Job 9. Check number plate light.
- [ ] Job 10. Check interior light.
- [ ] Job 12. Check screen washers.
- [ ] Job 14. Check horn.
- [ ] Job 15. Check tyre treads.
- [ ] Job 16. Check spare wheel.
- [ ] Job 17. Touch-up paintwork.
- [ ] Job 18. Valet interior.
- [ ] Job 19. Improve visibility.
- [ ] Job 26. Check wheel bolts.
- [ ] Job 27. Check handbrake adjustment.
- [ ] Job 28. Check windscreen.
- [ ] Job 29. Clean and lubricate aerial.
- [ ] Job 56. Check seat belts and mountings.
- [ ] Job 57. Check seat mountings.
- [ ] Job 58. Check fuel filler-cap seal.
- [ ] Job 59. Lubricate bonnet release.
- [ ] Job 60. Lubricate hinges, locks, check straps.
- [ ] Job 61. Check shock absorber action.
- [ ] Job 62. Check wheel alignment.

Every 30,000 Miles - Under the Car

First carry out all Jobs listed under earlier Service intervals as applicable.

- [ ] Job 30. Check exhaust system and mountings.
- [ ] Job 31. Check brake and fuel lines.
- [ ] Job 32. Check steering rack gaiters.
- [ ] Job 33. Check drive shaft gaiters.
- [ ] Job 34. Check underside of car for leaks.
- [ ] Job 35. Clean mud traps.
- [ ] Job 63. Check/renew front brake pads.
- [ ] Job 64. Check brake discs.
- [ ] Job 65. Check/adjust/renew rear brakes shoes.
- [ ] Job 66. Adjust rear brakes.
- [ ] Job 67. Check brake proportioning valve.
- [ ] Job 68. Check steering ball joints.

Every 30,000 Miles - Road Test

- [ ] Job 36. Clean controls.
- [ ] Job 37. Check instruments and controls.
- [ ] Job 38. Check throttle action.
- [ ] Job 39. Check clutch action.
- [ ] Job 40. Road test: brakes and steering.
- [ ] Job 41. Check C.V. joints for noise (part of road test).

Date serviced:..

Carried out by: ....
Garage Stamp or signature:

Parts/Accessories purchased (date, parts,
source) ....
....
....
....
....

EVERY 33,000 MILES - OR EVERY THIRTY THREE MONTHS, WHICHEVER COMES FIRST

All the Jobs at this Service Interval have been carried forward from earlier Service Intervals and are to be repeated at this service.

Every 33,000 Miles - The Engine Bay

- [ ] Job 1. Engine oil level.
- [ ] Job 2. Check coolant level.
- [ ] Job 3. Brake fluid level.
- [ ] Job 4. Check windscreen wash level.
- [ ] Job 13. Check battery electrolyte level.
- [ ] Job 20. Check alternator drive belts.
- [ ] Job 21. Drain fuel filter.
- [ ] Job 22. **DIESEL ENGINES ONLY** Renew diesel engine oil.
- [ ] Job 23. **DIESEL ENGINES ONLY** Replace diesel oil filter.
- [ ] Job 24. Check brake and fuel lines.
- [ ] Job 25. Check air filter.

Every 33,000 Miles - Around The Car

- [ ] Job 5. Check tyre pressures.
- [ ] Job 6. Check front lights.
- [ ] Job 7. Check side repeater indicators.
- [ ] Job 8. Check rear lights and indicators.
- [ ] Job 9. Check number plate light.
- [ ] Job 10. Check interior light.
- [ ] Job 11. Check windscreen wipers.
- [ ] Job 12. Check screen washers.
- [ ] Job 14. Check horn.
- [ ] Job 15. Check tyre treads.
- [ ] Job 16. Check spare wheel.
- [ ] Job 17. Touch-up paintwork.
- [ ] Job 18. Valet interior.
- [ ] Job 19. Improve visibility.
- [ ] Job 26. Check wheel bolts.
- [ ] Job 27. Check handbrake adjustment.
- [ ] Job 28. Check windscreen.
- [ ] Job 29. Clean and lubricate aerial.

Every 33,000 Miles - Under the Car

- [ ] Job 30. Check exhaust system and mountings.
- [ ] Job 31. Check brake and fuel lines.
- [ ] Job 32. Check steering rack gaiters.
- [ ] Job 33. Check drive shaft gaiters.
- [ ] Job 34. Check underside of car for leaks.
- [ ] Job 35. Clean mud traps.

SERVICE HISTORY

Every 33,000 Miles - Road Test

- [ ] Job 36. Clean controls.
- [ ] Job 37. Check instruments and controls.
- [ ] Job 38. Check throttle action.
- [ ] Job 39. Check clutch action.
- [ ] Job 40. Road test: brakes and steering.
- [ ] Job 41. Check C.V. joints for noise (part of road test).

Date serviced:...

Carried out by:...
Garage Stamp or signature:

Parts/Accessories purchased (date, parts, source) ....
....
....
....
....

EVERY 36,000 MILES - OR EVERY THREE YEARS, WHICHEVER COMES FIRST

All the Service Jobs in the tinted area have been carried forward from earlier service intervals and are to be repeated at this service.

Every 36,000 Miles - The Engine Bay

First carry out all Jobs listed under earlier Service intervals as applicable.

- [ ] Job 4. Check windscreen wash level.
- [ ] Job 13. Check battery electrolyte level.
- [ ] Job 20. Check alternator drive belts.
- [ ] Job 21. Drain fuel filter.
- [ ] Job 22. **DIESEL ENGINES ONLY** Renew diesel engine oil.
- [ ] Job 23. **DIESEL ENGINES ONLY** Replace diesel oil filter.
- [ ] Job 24. Check brake and fuel lines.
- [ ] Job 42. Change engine oil and filter.
- [ ] Job 44. Clean and check ignition components.
- [ ] Job 46. Lubricate distributor.
- [ ] Job 47. Lubricate clutch cable.
- [ ] Job 48. Check gearbox oil.
- [ ] Job 50. Lubricate throttle linkage.
- [ ] Job 51. Lubricate carburettor linkages.
- [ ] Job 52. Adjust carburettor.
- [ ] Job 53. Check idle speed.
- [ ] Job 54. Check exhaust emission.
- [ ] Job 55. Check pipes and hoses.
- [ ] Job 69. Change air filter element.
- [ ] Job 70. Clean air filter housing.
- [ ] Job 71. Check/adjust valve clearances.
- [ ] Job 72. Renew contact breaker points.
- [ ] Job 73. Check ignition timing.
- [ ] Job 75. Check vacuum hoses.
- [ ] Job 76. Check/renew crankcase ventilation hoses.
- [ ] Job 77. Clean oil filler cap.
- [ ] Job 78. Renew spark plugs.
- [ ] Job 79. Clean glow plugs.

- [ ] Job 80. Clean/protect battery terminals.
- [ ] Job 81. Check battery specific gravity.
- [ ] Job 82. Renew fuel filter.
- [ ] Job 83. **FUEL INJECTION CARS FROM 1989 ONLY** Read stored engine fault codes.

- [ ] Job 107. Renew drive belts.
- [ ] Job 108. Change gearbox oil.
- [ ] Job 109. Renew camshaft belt.

Every 36,000 Miles - Around the Car

- [ ] Job 5. Check tyre pressures.
- [ ] Job 6. Check front lights.
- [ ] Job 7. Check side repeater indicators.
- [ ] Job 8. Check rear lights and indicators.
- [ ] Job 9. Check number plate light.
- [ ] Job 10. Check interior light. Job 12. Check screen washers.
- [ ] Job 14. Check horn.
- [ ] Job 15. Check tyre treads.
- [ ] Job 16. Check spare wheel.
- [ ] Job 17. Touch-up paintwork.
- [ ] Job 18. Valet interior.
- [ ] Job 19. Improve visibility.
- [ ] Job 26. Check wheel bolts.
- [ ] Job 27. Check handbrake adjustment.
- [ ] Job 28. Check windscreen.
- [ ] Job 29. Clean and lubricate aerial.
- [ ] Job 56. Check seat belts and mountings.
- [ ] Job 57. Check seat mountings.
- [ ] Job 58. Check fuel filler-cap seal.
- [ ] Job 59. Lubricate bonnet release.
- [ ] Job 60. Lubricate hinges, locks, check straps.
- [ ] Job 61. Check shock absorber action.
- [ ] Job 62. Check wheel alignment.
- [ ] Job 84. Check toolkit and jack.
- [ ] Job 85. Check light seals.
- [ ] Job 86. Check door/tailgate seals.
- [ ] Job 87. Check headlight alignment.
- [ ] Job 88. Renew wiper blades and arms.

Job 89. Check floors.

Job 90. Renew batteries in car alarm sender.

Job 91. Check wiring and terminals.

Job 92. Clean radiator exterior.

Job 110. Top-up rustproofing.

Every 36,000 Miles - Under the Car

Job 30. Check exhaust system and mountings.

Job 31. Check brake and fuel lines.

Job 32. Check steering rack gaiters.

Job 33. Check drive shaft gaiters.

Job 34. Check underside of car for leaks.

Job 35. Clean mud traps.

Job 63. Check/renew front brake pads.

Job 64. Check brake discs.

Job 65. Check/adjust/renew rear brakes shoes.

Job 66. Adjust rear brakes.

Job 67. Check brake proportioning valve.

Job 68. Check steering ball joints.

Job 93. Check wheel bearings.

Job 94. Check steering and suspension.

Job 95. Check steering rack mountings.

Job 96. Check front suspension units.

Job 97. Check front suspension bushes.

Job 98. Check rear springs and shock absorbers.

Job 99. Check rear suspension bushes.

Job 100. Check engine and gearbox mountings.

Job 101. Check/lubricate handbrake cable.

Job 102. Check underside of body structure.

Job 103. Clean drainage holes.

Job 104. Renew brake fluid.

Every 36,000 Miles - Road Test

Job 36. Clean controls.

Job 37. Check instruments and controls.

Job 38. Check throttle action.

Job 39. Check clutch action.

Job 40. Road test: brakes and steering.

Job 41. Check C.V. joints for noise (part of road test).

LONGER TERM SERVICING

EVERY 48,000 MILES

Job 111. Renew HT leads, distributor cap and rotor arm.

EVERY 72,000 MILES

Job 112. Renew glow plugs.

Job 113. Check and renew fuel injectors.

SERVICE HISTORY

Date serviced:...

Carried out by: ....
Garage Stamp or signature:

Parts/Accessories purchased (date, parts, source) ....

Date serviced:...

Carried out by: ....
Garage Stamp or signature:

Parts/Accessories purchased (date, parts, source) ....

SERVICE HISTORY NOTES

NOTES

A

Accelerator linkages and cables ... 39, 49
Aerial, maintenance 35
Air cleaner 33, 34, 48, 61
Alarm sender unit 69
Alternator, drive belt 30, 31, 75
Antifreeze 22, 63, 73
Anti-roll bar 71, 72
Auto-Biography 1
Automatic transmission, fluid 40
Axle stands 16

B

Ball-joints, steering and suspension 59, 60, 70
Battery
   disconnecting 28
   electrolyte 27, 28
   safety 9
   specific gravity 66
   terminals 28, 64
Bellows, steering gear .... 36 to 38
Bodywork
   drain holes 72
   improvement 77, 78
   inspect underside 38, 72
   repair 79, 80
Bonnet release 51
Brakes
   ABS warning light 35
   adjustment .... 52 to 59
   calipers .... 53 to 55, 59, 99
   discs, front 56, 99
   discs, rear 59, 99
   drums 99
   excessive wear 99
   fluid 22, 23, 72
   fluid level warning light 23
   handbrake 34, 72, 94
   hoses 36
   lines 33, 36, 99
   pads .... 52 to 55, 58, 59
   proportioning valve 59
   safety 9
   shoes .... 56 to 58
Bulb renewal (see 'Lights')
Bushes
   anti-roll bar 71, 72
   suspension .... 70 to 72, 98
Buying
   cars 11, 12
   parts 13, 14
Buying Guide .... 11 to 14

C

Cables
   accelerator 49
   bonnet release 51
   choke 39
   clutch 39, 47
   handbrake 72
Caliper, brakes (see 'Brakes')
Camshaft belt 75, 76
Capacities and settings .... 101 to 104

C (cont.)

Carburettor
   adjust 49, 50
Car ramps 16
Catalytic converter, safety 7
Choke 39
Clutch adjustment 39, 47
Coil, ignition 46
Coil spring 71
Contant Velocity (C.V.) joints (see 'Driveshaft')
Contents 5
Convertible Soft-Top 69
Coolant
   check specific gravity 63
   drain and replace 73, 74
   hoses 73, 74
   radiator pressure cap 74
   top-up 22
Corrosion, MoT .... 92 to 95, 98 to 100
Crankcase ventilation system . 61, 63, 64

D

Damper, steering 71
Data .... 101 to 104
Disc, brakes (see 'Brakes')
Distributor 45, 46, 76
Door seals 68
Drain holes 72
Drivebelts
   air conditioning 31
   alternator 30, 31, 75
   brake vacuum pump (diesel models) ... 31
   camshaft 75, 76
   power steering 31
Driveshaft
   C.V. joints 40
   gaiter 37, 38
Drum, brakes (see 'Brakes')

E

Electricity, safety 8
Emergency starting 90
Emissions
   control equipment 75
   legal limits 100
   measuring 50
Engine mountings 72
Engine oil (see 'Oil')
Evaporative emissions control system 63
Exhaust
   system 35
   mountings 35
Expansion tank 22, 73, 74

F

Facts & Figures .... 101 to 104
Fast idle
   carburettor 49, 50
   fuel injection 50
Fault code readout 67, 68
Fault Finding
   diesel engines 89, 90
   petrol engines .... 87 to 89

F (cont.)

Filter
   air 33, 34, 48, 61
   fuel, petrol 32, 67
   fuel, diesel 32, 66, 67
   oil (see 'Oil filter')
Fire Extinguisher 8, 10
Floor, check 69
Fluoroelastomers, safety 10
Footbrake 94
Fuel Injection
   adjustment 50
   filter, replace, diesel 32
   injector overhaul 76
Fuel lines/pipes 33, 36
Fuel system 100
   filler cap 51, 98, 100
Fumes, safety 8
Fuses 26

G

Gaiter
   driveshaft joint 37, 38
   steering gear .... 36 to 38
Gearbox, oil
   automatic 20, 47
   manual 20, 48, 75
Gearbox, types 47
Generator drive belt (see 'Alternator, drive belt')
Glowplugs, diesel 64, 76

H

Hazard warning lights (see 'Lights')
Headlights (see 'Lights')
Horn
   location 28
   MoT 94
Hoses and clamps 63, 74
HT leads 45, 76

I

Idle speed adjustment (see 'Carburettor')
Ignition system
   safety 9
   clean 45
Ignition timing 62, 63
Instruments, check 39

J

Jacking
   wheelchange .... 17 to 19
   working on vehicle 16, 17
Jump leads 90

L

Lights
   adjustment 68, 95
   brake fluid level warning light (see 'Brakes')
   bulb replacement 24, 25
   driving lights 24
   hazard warning 92, 95
   headlights 24, 95
   indicators 24, 95
   interior 25

lens seals 24
light unit seals 68
MoT 92, 93, 95, 96
number plate 25, 96
rear foglight 25, 96
reflectors 96
reversing lights 25
sidelights 24
Locks and latches 51, 52
Lubricants and fluids 109

M

Mirrors 29, 93, 94
Mixture adjustment (see 'Carburettor')
Model years 101, 102
MoT, getting through .... 91 to 100
Mountings
engine/gearbox 72
shock absorbers 71

N

Number plates, MoT 94, 95

O

Oil change
disposal 4, 7
diesel engines 32
gearbox 75
petrol engines 7, 40, 41
safety 9
Oil filler cap 63
Oil filter
diesel 32
petrol 42, 43
Oil level
engine 21
gearbox 47, 48
topping up 21

P

Pads, brake (see 'Brakes')
Paintwork, touch up 29
Pipes and hoses 51, 63
Plastics, safety 10
Power steering
fluid 48
Production changes 101, 102

R

Radiator cap 7
Radiator, clean 70
Raising the car .... 16 to 19
Road test, brakes and steering 39, 40
Rotor arm 76
Rustproofing .... 76, 81 to 86

S

Safety First! .... 7 to 10
Seats 94
Seat belts 51, 95
Seat runners 51
Separator, diesel (see 'Filter, fuel, diesel')
Servicing Your Car .... 15 to 76
Shock absorbers 52, 71, 98, 99
Shoes, brake (see 'Brakes')

Sidelights (see 'Lights')
Spare·parts 13, 14
Spark plugs 44, 45, 64
Spark plug conditions 65
Steering
play 70
rack gaiters .... 36 to 38
rack mountings 70, 71
Steering wheel, free play 98
Switches 38

T

Throttle cable and pedal (see 'Accelerator linkage and cables')
Timing, ignition 62, 63
Timing belt 75, 76
Tools & Equipment .... 68, 105 to 108
Track rod ends 59, 60
Transmission fluid (see 'Gearbox oil')
Trolley jack, use of 16, 17
Tyre
checking .... 28, 29, 93, 96 to 98
pressures 23
spare 29

U

Upholstery, valeting 29, 78

V

Vacuum unit, distributor 63
Valve clearances 61, 62
Vehicle Identification Numbers (VIN) . 14
Visability, improve 29

W

Washer fluid reservoir 23
Water pump 47
Wheel alignment 52
Wheel bearings 70, 98
Wheel bolts 34
Wheel changing .... 17 to 19
Windscreen, damage 35, 93, 94
Windscreen washers
adjust 27
top-up 23
Windscreen wipers
MoT 93
replace 26, 69
Wiring and terminals 69